Writer and journalist Margaret Stenhouse lives in Italy, near the town of Frascati, where the memory of Henry Stuart as a loved and respected bishop is fondly preserved. Her passion for history led her to investigate the story of Henry IX, Bonnie Prince Charlie's little-known younger brother and the last direct heir of the Stuart dynasty, by consulting local books and documents that have not been translated from Italian into English. Her account of Henry's trials as he is forced to flee before Napoleon's invasion of Italy is based on the scanty recorded facts of his movements during this period.

To Jean, with thanks for all your support

Margaret Stenhouse

THE FLIGHT OF THE LAST STUART KING

Austin Macauley Publishers™

LONDON · CAMBRIDGE · NEW YORK · SHARJAH

Copyright © Margaret Stenhouse (2019)

The right of Margaret Stenhouse to be identified as author of this work has been asserted by her in accordance with section 77 and 78 of the Copyright, Designs and Patents Act 1988.

All rights reserved. No part of this publication may be reproduced, stored in a retrieval system, or transmitted in any form or by any means, electronic, mechanical, photocopying, recording, or otherwise, without the prior permission of the publishers.

Any person who commits any unauthorised act in relation to this publication may be liable to criminal prosecution and civil claims for damages.

A CIP catalogue record for this title is available from the British Library.

ISBN 9781528918275 (Paperback)
ISBN 9781528962247 (ePub e-book)

www.austinmacauley.com

First Published (2019)
Austin Macauley Publishers Ltd
25 Canada Square
Canary Wharf
London
E14 5LQ

Table of Contents

Preface	**9**
Part 1	**12**
Frascati	*12*
Velletri to Formia	*34*
Part 2	**55**
Naples	*55*
Caserta	*82*
The Battle of the Nile	*99*
Part 3	**107**
Sicily	*107*
Flight to Sicily	*115*
Messina to Palermo	*129*
Part 4	**144**
Corfu	*144*
The Siege of Corfu	*153*
Trieste – Padua	*168*
Part 5	**178**
Venice	*178*
The Venice Conclave	*198*

Part 6	**207**
Return to Frascati	*207*
Napoleon the Emperor	*219*
The Death of the Last Stuart King	*229*
Post Script	**234**
Main Sources	**237**
References	**240**
Author's Note	**241**

Preface

Henry Benedict Maria Clement Stuart, Duke of York and Cardinal Archbishop of Frascati, was the last direct heir to one of Europe's oldest royal dynasties which stretched back to the 14th century. After the death of his elder brother, Charles Edward, the legendary Bonnie Prince Charlie, who had tried unsuccessfully to regain the throne of his ancestors, the Cardinal, as the last Stuart heir, assumed the title of Henry IX, King of England, Scotland, Wales and France.

Henry was born in Rome, where the Stuarts had settled after the deposition of James II, Henry's grandfather. At the time of the prince's birth, hopes of a Stuart Restoration to the British throne, backed by both the Pope and the King of France, still ran high. The boys were brought up as royal princes, in anticipation of the day when the German House of Hanover would be ousted by the Stuart Jacobite supporters. However, after Charles' defeat at the Battle of Culloden in 1745, support from both France and the papacy dwindled and gradually fizzled out.

A couple of years after the Culloden debacle, Henry entered the Roman Catholic Church. This was a serious blow to the Stuart cause. By then, England was officially a Protestant country and Parliament was hostile to the idea of a Roman Catholic ruling family. Henry's father, James III and VIII, accepted his son's decision, but Charles was furious and resentful and the brothers were estranged for many years.

At the time, Henry was accused of opportunism, of opting out of involvement in what had become a lost cause, but there is no reason to believe that his vocation was not sincere. During his late teens, he gradually changed from a lad known for his charming ways and his love of music and dance, to become progressively withdrawn, serious and pious.

As Archbishop of his pleasant see of Frascati, in the hills above Rome, he enjoyed a peaceful and privileged life, respected by all and known for his many good works and acts of charity.

Henry's life, however, was turned upside down in 1798 when Napoleon's army invaded the Papal States and he was forced to abandon his home and flee south. It was the start of a journey fraught with dangers and unforeseen developments in a world full of uncertainties in the aftermath of the French Revolution and the Napoleonic conquests.

Henry was almost seventy-three when he was forced to leave his home and embark on a journey with an uncertain outcome. During two difficult and dangerous years, he faced a series of challenges with courage and fortitude. His journey is sketchily documented in the diaries kept by his secretary, Don Giovanni Landò. Landò, however, had stayed behind in Frascati and with much of continental Europe in a state of turmoil, communications were often interrupted. What little information Landò received of Henry Stuart's movements during that time is the foundation on which this novel is based.

Map Tracing Henry Stuart's Journey 1798–1800

Part 1
Frascati

February 9th, 1798

The household had been astir all night while the servants packed the travelling trunks and carried them downstairs to the carriages lined up in the palace forecourt. They had tried to be quiet, speaking with muffled voices and treading with soft feet, so that Cardinal Henry could enjoy a last night of peaceful sleep in his own bed.

Despite their efforts, he had not slept well. He had lain awake much of the night watching the stars dancing in the wind outside his windows. He hoped that the wind would forestall the threatened snowfall that would make their journey slow and difficult. It was cold in the palace, even though he had ordered that the fires be kept on in the rooms all night while his people busied with their preparations for his departure.

An hour before dawn, he finally stirred. At once his personal servant, the foundling Gigi-Moretto, who slept like a devoted guard dog on a pallet at the foot of his bed, was up and alert and at his side to help him rise. The Cardinal was approaching his seventy-third year and although he was still vigorous and hearty for his age, he was often stiff in the mornings. He needed Moretto to massage his calves and ankles to get the blood flowing freely through his limbs before he stood upright.

"Is everything ready?" he asked.

"Yes, sire," answered Moretto, opening the door and beckoning in the barber and his assistant carrying a bowl of warm water, while two footmen appeared with lit candelabras that filled the shadowy corners with wavering flickers of light.

Henry sighed. His eyes moved around the room, memorising all the familiar details. His gaze lingered on the portrait of his brother Charles Edward, painted when he was young and dashing, his father's darling and the toast of Europe. Next to it hung the painting of his saintly mother, the Polish princess, whom he barely remembered. She hung beside the portrait of his father, the melancholy

King James, who had lived and died in exile without ever putting his foot in his kingdom.

Even now, with the clergy under threat and danger at his door, Henry was glad that he had chosen a different destiny. His father and his brother had died unhappy men. Carletto (as his father called him) had wasted his last years in bitter recrimination and self-hate, bloated with claret and cognac, while he, Henry, had lived in peace and harmony, concentrating on his pastoral duties and transforming his see into a model community, complete with schools, a highly considered seminary and a hospital endowed with horse and carriage standing by to convey the sick and injured to and from their homes and fields. These things were a source of constant satisfaction to him and he could happily ignore the slanders spread by English spies and the machinations of the fading and frustrated Jacobite movement.

His ablutions finished, he summoned his valet, Eugenio Ridolfi, who removed his dressing gown. With the skill of long service, he helped his master into his shirt and waistcoat, his black velvet breeches, scarlet silk stockings and his black frock coat, while Libero, his wig-maker, fussed around his head, sleeking back the hair at the nape of his neck and tying it loosely with a black ribbon. When they had finished, he slipped his diamond cross over his head, hanging it round his neck. Usually, he wore it openly outside his cassock or his waistcoat, but today he concealed it under his shirt.

By then he was ready. The fears that had haunted the blackest hours of the night had gone. He waved the servants away and stepped alone into his private chapel to pray for the Blessed Virgin's protection during the hard and dangerous journey ahead.

Moretto was waiting for him in the next room, holding his morning cup of hot chocolate. Henry saw that the Boy's hands were trembling as he knelt down on one knee to hand it over. Henry smiled to himself. He still thought of Gigi as 'the Boy', though he had been in his household for over thirty years and the thick black curls that had given him the nickname Moretto, or Little Moor, were now grey and thinning. He sipped the chocolate slowly, looking around him. The antechamber, brightly illuminated with dozens of candles, always gave him a sense of satisfaction. He had personally chosen the theme of mythical figures and idyllic landscapes, bordered with grotesques in the Pompeiian style. The plump Polish artist he had hired had done a fine job, he reflected, of decorating La Rocca, as the Episcopal Palace was still called. It had been a grim fortress in the heart of the village of Frascati, when Henry, a newly appointed bishop, had taken it over all these years ago. Henry had spent a fortune restructuring and renovating the old castle in order to convert it into a suitable residence for a nobleman who was not only a Prince of the Church but also a prince of the blood.

His chaplain, Monsignor Angelo Cesarini, and his secretary, Don Giovanni Landò, stood waiting for him at the far end of the hall. Landò was holding the Cardinal's little dog in his arms. It was of an indeterminate breed, but it had attached itself to Henry one day when he was walking across St Peter's square, scampering round his heels and then sitting up and begging in such a pretty way that he had taken a fancy to it. "It has recognised I am a royal prince. It must be a King Charles spaniel," he had joked to Moretto, who was with him at the time. He had brought the dog home with him to Frascati and from then on it was known by the name of King Charles.

The little animal began to bark and struggle in Landò's arms as soon as it saw Henry but today he ignored it. He knew he could not take it with him on his hazardous journey and that it would have to remain in the charge of the few servants who were staying behind with Don Landò at La Rocca. Landò had chosen not to accompany them south. He suffered badly from gout that crippled him for days on end, and although he was ten years younger that Henry, he declared that he was too old to go adventuring. Henry had entrusted him with the palace keys, as well as the keys to the seminary and his precious library, with instructions that he was to give them up without argument if his life or the life of any of his servants should be threatened by the invaders.

Instead of holding back respectfully for Henry to beckon them over, Cesarini rushed forward, unable to control his agitation. His face was red and covered in sweat, and he mopped at it frantically with his lacy kerchief.

"My lord!" he said, forgetting in his excited state to address the Cardinal in the correct royal manner. When his brother Charles Edward died, he had assumed the title of Henry IX, King of England, Scotland, Ireland and France. His household had strict instructions to treat him with all the respect due to majesty or else incur his displeasure. His 'Family', as a Cardinal's household was called, complied, largely to please him rather than from a real conviction regarding his rights.

Henry was not a dreamer. He knew that it was an empty title and that the Stuarts would never again occupy the London throne. But he was convinced that by upholding the claims of his ancient

House, he was following the wishes of his late father, King James III, and honouring the memory of his brother Charles Edward, who had risked his life and reputation in the vain attempt to recapture the kingdom of their ancestors. Henry had never harboured doubts regarding his decision to be ordained as a Roman Catholic priest, despite the disappointment his choice had caused his father and the Stuart followers. But after Charles' only daughter, Charlotte, had died, a bare year after her father, a heavy weight of sadness and regret had settled on his shoulders. He had been stricken with keen awareness that he was a withered branch, the last of a royal dynasty that stretched back seven centuries and which would end with him.

"Bad news! Dreadful news!" His thoughts were interrupted by Don Angelo Cesarini, who was wringing his hands and crossing himself in succession – such was his state of agitation. "The French devils are at the gates of Rome! They will destroy everything – massacre us all! We must leave instantly. Without delay!"

Henry's long nose twitched and his nostrils contracted. It was a gesture that his Family knew well as a sure sign that he was displeased. However, when he spoke, his voice was calm.

"Be tranquil, Don Angelo, dear friend," he said. "The French are not the terrible *Lanzenicchi* of years ago! These terrors happened in the past, when armies behaved like savages. The French are a civilized nation. They have great thinkers and philosophers – Montesquieu, Voltaire, Rousseau. They are a Christian people, even if Napoleon has done his best to suppress our Mother Church. He did not succeed. The people fear God. They have remained true to the faith."

This only made Cesarini more agitated.

"My lord, do not delude yourself! These are not the stories we hear from the north. When the soldiers' pay is late in coming, the commanders give the men licence to plunder and take whatever they want…"

At that point, Landò intervened. He was a small man, usually timid and unassuming, but now he spoke in a firm voice, with a barely discernible undertone of contempt. "They will not find much plunder here! As you instructed, sire, everything of value has been removed from La Rocca and the Cathedral – all the chalices, the gold and silver, the holy reliquaries, the caskets of the saints, your own private treasures and paintings. All have been safely hidden where the French will never find them. Your parishioners are loyal. They will never betray you."

Cesarini waved his hands in exasperation. "If the rank and file find no spoils to appease their appetites, they will avenge themselves on the people. They may set La Rocca on fire. They may burn Frascati. They are capable of all kinds of outrages."

"Don Angelo!" Henry's voice was cold. "Stop this idle croaking! Once I am gone, there will be no danger. They are only interested in capturing me."

Although he kept up a calm appearance in order not to alarm his Family, Henry believed that his own life was in fact in danger. The horrors of the Reign of Terror in the aftermath of the French Revolution, when his own cousin king, Louis XVI of France, as well as many hundreds of aristocrats, had been mercilessly sent to their death, had burned a vivid and indelible memory in his brain. Scores of Rome's nobles and clergy shared his fears and were fleeing south. Like him, they would seek refuge in the Kingdom of Naples, which had allied with Austria, France's most powerful enemy, and had also the support of the British navy.

The Cardinal of the Organs

They became aware of a chant rising from the forecourt below. Before, it had been a soft murmur like the sound of waves advancing and retreating on a beach, but now it swelled and became louder and louder, in a growing crescendo: "*Cardinale degli Organi! Cardinale degli Organi!*"

Henry's features relaxed. He smiled, putting out his hand to fondle King Charles' drooping ears. The nickname that his people had given him always amused him. His hereditary title of Duke of York was impossible for the Frascati peasants to pronounce. The nearest they could manage was '*Eyorgani*', thus transforming him into 'the Cardinal of the Organs'. He had stopped trying to correct them years ago. He saw it as a mark of their affection for him when they hailed him from their workshops and market stalls as he walked around the streets. He believed that most of them were aware that the title they gave him was incorrect and that it even bordered on the absurd, but it had somehow remained and had gradually become a good-humoured joke among his servants at La Rocca.

He moved to the window and looked down at the waiting line of carriages and wagons, with their lanterns swaying in the wind. The unusual bustle had made the horses nervous. They were restless, shaking their heads and snorting as they stamped their hooves on the ground, cracking the thin spread of ice that lay, blackly glistening, over the paving stones.

Despite the hour and the bitter cold wind rattling around the roofs, a great crowd had gathered round the outer edge of the courtyard, waiting to salute him. He could just make them out – a bobbing, swaying host of black shadows, jostling each other as they inched slowly forward. The numbers continued to swell as more and more people emerged from the surrounding streets. They saw him at the window outlined by the light of the candles and fell silent, waiting like a sad company of ghosts.

Ridolfi appeared on cue to help Henry into his ankle-length fur-lined coat. With a swift and practised move, he placed the tricorn hat on his master's head while Henry was moving impatiently towards the stairs. The Cardinal walked down, casting a quick glance through the open door of his study, which had been completely emptied of all its contents. The sound of hammering broke out as the carpenters began to board up the windows.

"The French will find little to interest them here!" he remarked grimly to Moretto who was trotting behind him, carrying his ivory-topped cane

When he emerged from the palace portal, the waiting crowd set up a great roar. Many fell on their knees on the frosty pavements. Mothers held up their shawl-wrapped babies and fathers hoisted the smaller children onto their shoulders to get a better look. The entire company was wailing and tearfully imploring his blessing in a doleful chorus. They were afraid they would never see him again, due to his age and the dangers and difficulties of the journey ahead, which would try the strength and resistance of a much younger man.

As soon as he appeared, MacLaren jumped to attention and began to play a mournful old Scottish lament on his bagpipes. MacLaren had been one of Charles' retainers at Palazzo Muti Papazzurri, the Stuart's residence in Rome, and he was one of the few who had knelt before Henry after the Bonnie Prince's funeral and asked to be transferred to his service. Henry had been touched. Despite the passage of five decades, most of the old Scots chiefs in exile still regarded him as a traitor to their cause and he had understood their resentment. He had been aware that his decision to take holy orders after his brother's failed attempt to reconquer their father's throne had virtually shattered any hopes of a Stuart restoration. His decision had not been made lightly. He had been afraid that the blow would have been too much for his father to bear after all the anxiety he had suffered during Charlie's military campaign and the crushing disappointment of the defeat at Culloden. Charles had burned to make another attempt and begged the French king, who had initially promised support, to grant him ships and troops, but Louis XV was no longer willing to be drawn into a war against the British government and the Hanoverian House.

Duncan MacLaren, like many of the exiles who had followed the Stuarts to Rome, had a tragic history. Although a mere lad of eleven, he had been with his father and older brothers at the Battle of Culloden and he had seen them mown down by cannon fire before his eyes.

"My brother Hugh was hit in the leg and he couldn't walk," he had told the Cardinal. "I tried to drag him off the field where we could hide because I saw what the redcoats were doing to the wounded, but I wasn't quick enough. 'Run, Davie!' he said to me. 'Run off home – as fast as your legs can carry you – and don't look back!'

"I didn't obey him of course. Then this officer rode up on his horse. 'Finish that one off!' he told his men, pointing to my brother. I didn't know the English at that time, but his meaning was plain enough. Hugh was lying helpless on the ground and the devils began hacking at him with their bayonets until he was dead. They took me prisoner to Edinburgh Castle. I would have died of hunger and ill-treatment, shut in the dark and lying shackled in my own piss (begging your pardon, my Lord, but that was the truth of it!), but then my mother raised the money to buy my freedom and get me on a ship to France, away forever from that accursed land ruled by tyrants and heathens!"

As Cardinal York's servants began to pour out of the palace, a group of women and children detached themselves from the crowd and rushed forward to embrace their men. Henry allowed no women to stay in his residence, but many of his servants had wives and sweethearts living in the village. Men and women were weeping openly. No one knew when or if the Cardinal's followers would ever come home again. Henry sighed again. Most of his men had been in his service all their lives. They had grown old in his service. He had had many qualms about tearing them away from the lives they knew and exposing them to possible danger, but they had all clamoured to accompany him. He had not had the heart to leave them against their will, with all the risks they could run of suffering possible reprisals at the hands of the invading forces.

His eye ran over them – Garani his coachman, a grizzled giant of a man; his cook Giacinto Belisario, rough and ignorant as a mule, but able to produce a banquet that made his table the envy of Rome; Gigi 'Moretto', the foundling boy, now a man of middle years but who had retained his childish spirit and was always ready with a humorous quip; the venerable white-bearded Scotsman MacLaren, who had barely known the land of his birth and had almost forgotten his native tongue; the footman Giuseppe Zossi, whose constant wheezing sounded like wind forcing its way through a crack. The only young man among them was Eugenio Ridolfi, a beardless boy, who descended from three generations of valets that had served the Stuarts in exile.

Henry waited, allowing them a few more moments' grace to make their farewells before he signalled to Moretto to help him mount the steps into his carriage. Cesarini followed, carrying a large leather pouch with all the permits and passports the party would need to cross the border.

Annibale, the captain of his bodyguard, approached the carriage door and indicated that he wished to speak to him in private.

"Begging your pardon, Majesty," he spoke softly, not wanting to alarm the parishioners who were milling around the horses' heads, awaiting the Cardinal's farewell blessing, "I've just had news from the messenger over there," he pointed to a rider wrapped in a thick cloak with the hood drawn low down over his face, hovering on the edge of the courtyard on an exhausted horse that stood with hanging head and steaming sweat rising from its flanks.

"He brings us some bad news! He says that there are republican sympathisers in Albano and Marino. Some rogues have been filling the villagers' heads with these French notions of freedom and equality. He says he saw a few of them gathered in the market square with the Phrygian caps on their heads. They were saying they were off to plant a Tree of Liberty in front of St Barnabas."

"And do they have the support of the populace?" Henry asked.

"So far, it seems the people chased them off with insults but there is no telling how many may join their ranks!"

Cesarini broke in, his voice quivering with indignation. "These notions poison simple folks. They spread, sire, like creeping weeds and stir up violent thoughts, corrupting even in the minds of reasonable men!"

Annibale bent forward and his voice dropped almost to a whisper. "If you permit, Your Majesty, it would be well to avoid trouble. Do not pass that way!"

Henry thought quickly. He had worked out the plan of their flight several days before, but now it seemed he had to reconsider. He had sent out scouts who had confirmed that the Austrian General Baron Mack von Leiberich, who commanded the Neapolitan army, still held the Appian Way, which was the most direct route to Naples. However, in order to reach it, they would have to pass through the villages already mentioned. He decided that they would head instead up the Via Latina, the old Roman consular road that skirted the foot of the Tusculum hills, and then branch off to re-join the Appia by an alternative route.

It was not a choice he made gladly. He knew that the road was poorly maintained and that it was often impassable in winter. There was also the risk of running into brigands. Bands of outlaws were known to swoop down from the thickly wooded hills on either side of the track to rob and murder hapless travellers. Certainly, he reflected, they had a big enough escort of armed men to discourage possible ill-doers. He had enrolled a score of volunteer peasant lads to swell the ranks of his personal bodyguard. They had been eager for the adventure and to get away from the monotony of work in the fields, but they were inexperienced in the use of arms and would probably flee at the first sign of trouble. Their train was carrying a large quantity of valuables that he needed to defray expenses during a journey of uncertain length, but which he expected to last at least several weeks, until the Neapolitan army managed to drive the invaders out of the lands of the Church.

The previous evening, most of his silver plate had been stored under the carriage seats and concealed under thick woollen rugs, along with stacked strongboxes of gold and silver coins, precious jewels and ornaments. The operation had been carried out in great secrecy by a handful of his most trusted servants but he knew that, despite all possible precautions, indiscreet eyes could have seen the treasure they were carrying. Word could easily have spread and reached the ears of a band of desperate outlaws that might be waiting to waylay them on the lonely roads they were forced to pass.

Henry knew it was impossible that his train would pass unnoticed, even though he was travelling light by his standards. Normally, he was accompanied by a retinue of some seventy members of his household when he went on his lengthy pastoral visits to his other incumbencies north of the city of Rome, or to take the water cure at Pisa. His chest contracted with regret as he recalled these pleasant trips of the past, when he was received with every honour. He remembered how the good people came out to cheer as his procession filed through the villages and fields. He would hand one of his men a purse full of *baiocchi* to toss out of the carriage window. It always amused him to see the children scramble among the legs of the adults – they were so much quicker and more nimble! – to gather up the coins and run with them to their mothers.

This time, he was taking only a few of the aristocrats in his clerical staff. Most had powerful family connections and had been able to make their own arrangements. The dozen personal servants that he considered essential for his well-being, such as his valets, tailor, barber, cook, butcher, porters and so on, travelled in covered wagons or on horseback behind the carriages, alongside the heavy four-wheeled carts loaded with the household goods that the Cardinal never moved anywhere without, such as his bed, his writing desk and crates full of books. He had not harnessed his splendid team of six matched blacks to his carriage as he considered they were too high-bred and delicate to undertake the strain of such a hard journey. However, he was taking them along, led on the halter by the grooms. If they did go as far as Naples – and he hoped that would not be necessary, as he planned to stop at the frontier to await news of Mack's campaign – he was determined to arrive in the style of a royal prince, and not as a poor petitioner.

Ridolfi came up to the carriage door with warmed bricks that he carefully laid under the feet of the two prelates and wrapped rugs around their knees, while Moretto swung himself up on the seat beside Garani, the coachman, who was cursing under his breath about the choice of route. As he coaxed the horses forward, the townspeople moved towards them in a pincer-like movement, pressing around the Cardinal's carriage, while King Charles, yapping and barking furiously, leapt out of Landò's arms and ran whining and growling around the horses' hooves till Annibale rode up and chased him off.

Henry opened his window to give his blessing one last time. However, the crowds in the streets continued to block their advance. Garani threatened them, brandishing his whip, but Henry knocked sharply with his cane on the roof of the coach to show he forbade him to use it against them. It took a full half hour before they were able to reach the open countryside.

Even then, progress was slow. The way led uphill and the horses struggled and stumbled over ice-bound paving stones. It was bitingly cold and a flurry of sleet buffeted the carriage windows, slowly covering them with a silvery mosaic of crystals. The jolting of the carriage wheels over the many potholes was so severe that the occupants were almost thrown out of their seats. Ridolfi sat next to his master, trying to shield him from the worst of the knocks. Don Angelo opposite fared even worse, as his legs were short. With the seats raised to accommodate the hidden treasure underneath, his feet did not touch the floor. When the wheels hit the deepest ruts, he was flung forward and his hat and wig slid down over one ear. At first, he was annoyed and abashed, but it happened so often that soon he discarded his wig completely and covered his bald head with his lace kerchief. He glared at the Duke, daring him to laugh and Henry, out of respect for his old friend's discomfort, turned his head away and pretended not to notice.

The Fig Tree Inn

Henry closed his eyes and pretended to sleep. His brain was full of images and regrets. Yesterday had been a particularly sad and difficult day. He had gone, unaccompanied, for the last time to inspect the Herboracum Seminary, the college that he had founded and given the Latin name for York. He stood for a long time just inside the door, lost in thought. He considered this institution to be one of his greatest achievements and it was hard for him to abandon the building to its fate.

The students had all been sent home some days before and the rooms, which had always been bursting with life and activity, rang hollow with the sound of his footsteps as he began to patrol the corridors. He had ordered the maps, charts and the etchings illustrating scientific experiments removed from the walls. All the beds had been stripped of their linen. The refectory was bare except for the long wooden tables and benches. He had distributed all the tableware and utensils, as well as the kitchen equipment, among his parishioners.

Reluctantly, he had been forced to leave the billiard table, which was too heavy and bulky to be transferred elsewhere. When he was younger, he had sometimes joined the boys in a game. 'No doubt,' he thought, 'the French will make good use of it.' He prayed that officers would be billeted there – gentlemen who would not do too much damage to the place and who would appreciate all his modern improvements, like the water closets on all three floors and the hot and cold running water in the kitchen. He hoped they would not tear out the water pipes and melt down the lead for bullets.

He stood musing for a while in the Aula Magna, where the students and some of the servants got up performances for the court's amusement during the Carnival season. Last year, they had done a hilarious version of the adventures of 'Don Quixote', the mad knight, in which Moretto had excelled himself as the comical servant Sancho Panza. He remembered how amused they had all been at his antics. The Family had roared with laughter and even Don Angelo had managed a smile or two. As the college rector, Cesarini stood very much upon his dignity. He did not encourage frivolity, but Henry had over-ruled him, saying that sad boys do not study well, that they needed diversion to let off the natural high spirits of youth.

And he had been proved right. The college had a high reputation and was much respected. The local aristocracy begged to have their sons admitted, offering payment far beyond the required annual fees. Henry always refused these offers and forbade his teachers to accept gifts. He did not wish his students to be promoted thanks to bribes.

Henry prided himself on encouraging progress. He smiled briefly to himself, remembering the students' amazement and excitement when he invited the assistant of the famous Professor Beccaria from Turin University to demonstrate experiments with the mysterious physical force known as electricity. Some of his fellow prelates had disapproved. They warned him he was meddling with dark powers controlled by the devil. In order to avoid problems, he had turned his attention to setting up a printing workshop in the seminary precincts, with two presses and eight different sets of type, so that the students could learn to produce books in various characters, including Greek and Hebrew.

Putting his head round the door of the workshop, he was struck by the weight of the silence. Only a few days before, it had hummed with life and activity, but now the room was silent and deserted. The wooden trays of letters were stacked away on shelves. The printing presses sat huddled under sacking, like neglected and sulking creatures, obscure and unresponsive shapes in the gloom.

He locked the door of the seminary and walked briskly through the clipped rows of hedging and the pots of orange trees lining the garden path to his last stop. This was his favourite project, his beloved library, which he had opened latterly to the public. It was stacked with the twelve thousand volumes and the rare illuminated manuscripts that he had collected so lovingly over his lifetime. He knew the exact number, as he had instructed Monsignor Landò to record them all in the massive ledger that stood on the lectern by the door. Along with works of art, books had always been his passion. He had been acquiring both ever since he was a boy and his heart contracted in his chest at the thought of having to abandon them. His eye ran over the shelves of books on philosophy, geography, history, poetry, mathematics, physics and astronomy in various languages, lingering on Galileo and Newton, set side by side in both Italian and French translation.

It was very hard, he thought, to have to leave his home and his possessions, this world he had created and nurtured. It had been his consolation when the last of his family had died – first his father, then Charlie and last his niece Charlotte. Having to abandon his world was like tearing the skin from his body, leaving him raw and exposed to hostile forces and unknown elements. Until that moment, he had not felt his age. His health was still good and his memory had not begun to fail him, but now he wondered how much he would be able to adapt to the changes that lay ahead. The responsibility he felt to protect the men who were following him so blindly and so trustingly into the unknown weighed heavily. He did not know when – if ever – they would be able to return if the Neapolitan army failed to halt Napoleon, nor what they might find if they did come home again.

Finally, he straightened his shoulders. His ancestors had faced worse trials. Most had met violent deaths. Many had been cut off in their prime. The House of Stuart had known little peace during its history and it was now his duty, he thought, to play out the last act with the dignity due to his blood.

He turned back to his books and put up his hand to caress the gold-toothed spines of some of his favourites – the Greek tragedies and the Roman histories, Shakespeare and Cervantes. But he also enjoyed reading the more modern Italian and French writers, like Goldoni, Voltaire and Molière. High on a top shelf, away from prying eyes, he had placed Diderot and D'Alembert's monumental *L'Encyclopédie*, banned by Benedict XIV, the Pope who had christened him. The fact that he possessed a work listed in the *Index Librorum Prohibitorum* had never troubled his conscience. He had felt it was important for him to be informed concerning the new radical ideas that were transforming the traditional social order. It was common knowledge among the Vatican hierarchy that the Dominicans, who ran the Inquisition, had a copy in their library in Rome as well.

Skimming the lower shelves, where he kept recent acquisitions, he noticed one was missing. It described the adventures of a castaway seaman called Crusoe, based (he had been told) on the true tale of a Scots sailor by name of Alexander Selcraig, written by a popular London writer called Defoe.

'I wager that rascal Moretto has taken it!' he thought. 'Just the sort of far-fetched yarn he would like!' He had given his foundling the best schooling possible, alongside the sons of nobles and princes, but it did not seem to have had much effect. Moretto was not stupid and had a charming character, but he did not seem to have any aptitude for study. 'A pity!' Henry often thought. So unlike his contemporary Ercole Consalvi, the Cardinal's other protégé! The two had studied together at the Herboracum, but Consalvi, unlike Moretto, was a brilliant scholar. When Ercole had entered the priesthood, the Cardinal had done everything in his power to promote his career and now, in fact, he was regarded as one of the most distinguished diplomats at the papal court.

With a start, he brought his thoughts back to the present.

"I am anxious for Ercole," Henry remarked to Cesarini, who was visibly shivering. Lost in his own misery, Don Angelo merely shrugged.

"He chose to stay on in Rome to protect the Holy Father," Henry persisted. "It was noble of him. I hope he comes to no harm."

Cesarini merely grunted. Consalvi had been a difficult student when he was under his care at the Herboracum – a real smart-ass, always flaunting his aristocratic pedigree. He had not improved with age, his old teacher thought. He had become, if anything, more arrogant. He had wriggled his way into Pius VI's favour and now nobody could tell him what to do. He wondered how he would fare with Bonaparte, who was trying to stamp out the Roman Catholic Church altogether. His lack of humility would not go down well with the republican invaders. He would have to climb down if he wished to negotiate, he reflected.

Henry knew of Don Angelo's feelings of antagonism towards his protégé, but he preferred to ignore them. These sentiments, he believed, were unworthy of his friend, who was a fine scholar and a conscientious teacher, never neglecting any of his charges. But Angelo had a soft spot for Gigi-Moretto, who had often been the butt of Consalvi's scorn.

As if he had heard their conversation, Moretto leant down from his seat beside Garani and, suspended upside down, peered in at the window of the carriage, making gestures towards the road ahead, where they could just make out a glimmer of light through the thick curtain of fog that had descended over the valley.

The outriders spurred their horses and rode on ahead to investigate. They came back to report that it belonged to the Fig Tree Inn at the 13th mile, where groups of carters were gathered with their wagons, ready to set off for the Rome markets. Their hoarse, disembodied voices floated gruffly through the mist. A shadowy group clustered together in the courtyard, smoking long-stemmed pipes. The jugs of hot wine in their hands sent up thin streams of vapour. Their faces were dark and hidden, and the shadowy outlines of their tall conical hats gave them an unreal appearance, like strange animals with beaked heads, outlined against the light that streamed out from the open doorway of the inn.

A few were already perched high, balanced on top of the stacked wine barrels, the reins in their hands, ready to set out on their journey. As they cracked their whips and urged their mules forward, they blocked the road, forcing the Cardinal's train to come to a halt. Annibale rode forward, brandishing his sword, and angrily commanded them to make way for his master. They turned aside, but their movements were slow and insolent and they did not bother to call their dogs to order. The curs ran snapping and snarling around the horses' feet, so that the coachmen had trouble keeping them under control. The carters themselves watched silently as the retinue went by.

Henry's mouth turned down. He had a sour taste in his mouth. These were the same ignorant peasants who had so often knelt, kissed the hem of his cassock and presented him with their deformed children, begging him to cure them of the king's evil. In former times, they would have doffed their hats and fallen on their knees by the roadside as his carriage passed. Now they remained standing or sitting on their wagons, mute and sullen.

Only a few days ago, he reflected, it would have been inconceivable for them to watch his passage with eyes full of contempt. This, alas, was another sign of the changing mood of the times, when high-placed princes and prelates like himself could no longer be sure of the loyalty and respect of the peasantry. He felt his hands begin to shake and grasped the top of his cane firmly in order to regain his self-control. His Family depended on him for their safety and he knew he must not allow any show of weakness or apprehension to hinder their journey.

La Molara

Not long after that, they came to the bleak colony of La Molara, which had been a forgotten outpost of the Frascati diocese when he had visited it soon after his investiture. He had been told about that remote settlement of itinerant labourers, who lived like animals among the ruins of the ancient Molara castle and he had decided to go there at once and see it for himself. Although it was well over thirty years ago, he still remembered the day vividly – the bewilderment on the faces of these poor outcasts, the astonishment in their eyes, when he appeared unexpectedly at the head of the long procession of canons and attendants, whom he had instructed to appear in their best vestments. He had ridden solemnly behind the great jewelled crucifix on a milk white mare. He had worn a precious cope of heavily embroidered crimson silk, held with a diamond and emerald morse and a mitre of cloth of gold. The sacraments were bourne in a golden vessel under a canopy of cloth of gold, carried by four bearers, while two lines of the Cathedral altar boys swung the incense boats as they walked, chanting alongside.

He had told the canons, who were grumbling about the journey over the stoney, dust-covered tracks that even these poorest of parishioners were entitled to a vision of the glory of God and that their spiritual father, the Archbishop, should show them the same honour as he showed the aristocrats and wealthy merchants who packed into Frascati Cathedral on Sundays and Feast Days. There, among the hovels of the poorest village in his diocese, he had celebrated mass alongside scratching hens and rooting pigs, while the people knelt open-mouthed before him. He could see that they barely remembered even the most basic rites and he had resolved on the spot to build them a church and a school for the children.

He pulled back the curtain at the carriage window. Yes! There was the chapel, outlined against the first faint light of daybreak. He saw the houses he had built for the villagers. They no longer lived in clammy shacks with leaking roofs, wedged between the tumbled masonry of the old castle. He rapped at the roof, intimating to Garani that he wanted him to halt and Moretto at once leapt down from the driver's seat to help him alight.

His guards rode up immediately.

"Sire, you should not delay. We do not know what lies ahead!" Annibale was agitated. Cesarini's muttered laments and prayers filtered out from the coach interior. He looked around the anxious faces of his followers and nodded. Moretto still held on to his arm, his eyes cast down.

Henry wondered how much he remembered. He had only been a tiny child, half naked and as thin as a little fledgling bird, when the Cardinal had noticed him sitting apart in the dust and scratching figures with a stick. He had sent one of his men to enquire about the child and a woman had said he was an orphan, subsisting on scraps of food they put out for the pigs. Henry had taken him back to La

Rocca and brought him up like a son. He had been in his household, he reflected, for almost thirty years.

Henry shook himself out of his reverie. His men were right. His procrastinations were putting them all at risk. He would have liked to have paid a last visit to the chapel. He was also becoming tired of Don Angelo's endless prayers and complaints. He would have preferred to be travelling with the Boy Gigi, who usually drove his horses when he travelled to Rome on business and was always ready with a quip or a light-hearted remark.

A grey and watery glimmer of daylight etched the horizon as the Cardinal's retinue reached the desolate wasteland of the Latina Valley, spread out like a rush floor mat between two mountain ridges cloaked in thick, black forest. There were marshlands and expanses of shallow water on either side of the road. In happier times, his students used to come to this spot to hunt for wild duck and when he was younger, he would often accompany them. He had enjoyed the sport. At this very hour, as the mist was rising, he would crouch with Moretto and a couple of other boys in a punt concealed among the banks of bull-rushes. Sometimes, the birds were there in such great numbers that they seemed to cover the entire surface of the lakes. Henry would give Gigi, who was a skilled shot with a crossbow, the signal to fire and bring down the first bird of the day before the entire flock was alarmed by the blasting of the fowlers and rose out of the water in a great cloud of flapping and squawking. There was really not much sport to be had once the boys began firing away.

His thoughts drifted to the times when he and his brother Charles were young and went hunting together, riding tirelessly for miles and miles over the Roman countryside, giving their attendants the slip so that they could sleep out freely under the stars. But all their carefree comradeship had gone after the tragic Battle of Culloden. Charles had changed completely. The laughing boy with the cocky tilt of his head, the darling of the European courts, had disappeared. He was embittered by his defeat and the end of his hopes and he was furious when he learned of Henry's decision to enter the priesthood. He had gone off wandering for years, giving his father and brother no news of his doings or his whereabouts.

The old King James had grieved for him constantly. Whenever Henry came to visit, the first words that greeted him were always: "Have you heard from Carletto? Have you any news of your brother?"

Even after all these years, Henry's face would still grow hot when he remembered how he had noted the servants sniggering behind their hands. The English spies kept the whole of Rome informed of the Prince's affairs – his gambling, his debts, his mistresses and his escapades. Only the old King knew nothing of his elder son's misdeeds.

An owl floated past the carriage window, like an unquiet ghost, turning its pale baleful stare on them for a moment as it let out its mournful cry. It was hunting and he imagined its quarry crouched trembling in its hiding place, hoping to remain undetected. It seemed to Henry, in his dark mood, that there was little difference between his fate and that of the mice and rabbits and other wild creatures that were the owl's prey. Once he had been the feared pursuer, the merciless conqueror of the woods and hills, a king among the lesser beings of creation. But now an adverse destiny had reversed the roles, transforming him from the hunter to the hunted. It was not so difficult, he thought inwardly, with a smile of irony, for a man to be turned into a rabbit.

Across from him, Don Angelo was fervently reciting his rosary. Despite the cold, his face was beaded with sweat. Eugenio Ridolfi, who was seated beside him, was quietly weeping. He was one of the few young men in Henry's train – a fresh-faced youth whom the Cardinal had taken into his service when the boy's father had died. Ridolfi had had to leave behind the sweetheart whom he had been intending to marry the following month, before her belly had become too big to conceal.

Their progress had slowed to walking pace and Henry struggled to control his impatience. The outriders continued to ride on ahead with their torches held high so that the coachmen could pick out the track. Daylight had brought only limited visibility. A heavy mist lay over the road and the surrounding fields, so that they could only see a few yards around them. The mountains on either side were totally blanked out and the white curtain of vapour parted only to reveal black fragments of trees that floated in and out of their vision.

The road became rougher, littered with the boulders that had been scattered around by floodwaters. The horses stumbled frequently and the coachmen applied the brakes to the wheels and kept the reins tight but the carriages continued to teeter and sway violently from side to side. When the wheels stuck in the deeper ruts, Ridolfi and Moretto got down to help the guards push and heave the coaches free.

A steady stream of icy sleet sliced down and a harsh wind had their teeth rattling in their heads. A lace work of frost had settled over the windows, limiting visibility. Daylight had brought little change. A thick mist continued throughout to conceal the view of the road ahead. Henry began to shiver. The brick at his feet was rapidly losing heat and he realised it would be cold long before they reached their destination. He was determined not to stop till they reached the town of Velletri, which was the diocese of his old friend Cardinal Gianfrancesco Albani, who had stayed on in Rome to be near Pope Pius. Henry was anxious to have news of him.

Finally, they reached the brooding ruins of the Castle of Algida that guarded the pass leading down to the Sacco Valley. It was said to be haunted by unquiet spirits that lurked in the gloom and tormented travellers. The notion of an encounter with wraiths and fiends had Monsignor Cesarini reciting his rosary with more fervour than ever. Henry's lips closed tightly in disapproval. He deplored those ignorant peasant superstitions and thought it undignified for a man of Don Angelo's superior learning to give way to puerile fears. Demons, he thought, inhabited other regions concealed deep inside the souls of men, where they festered among illusionary aspirations, creeds and visions that falsely promised new and better worlds.

His worry was not ghosts, but bandits. The area was notorious for harbouring robber bands. The slopes on either side of the track were covered in thick woods that offered perfect concealment. Although he knew they had a good escort of armed men, he had heard of bands a hundred strong, like the army of desperate criminals commanded by *Fra Diavolo*, Michele Serra, the Devil Friar. Despite the recurrent massive manhunts carried out by the papal gendarmes, he had never been caught and brought to justice. The country people believed he was invincible. They held him up as a hero because he was said to protect them from tax collectors and avid landowners.

There were other, far worse, brigand chiefs in the south of Italy. The kingdom of Naples was known to harbour the outlaw Gaetano Mammone in its stony uplands and barren mountains – a monster who was more of a beast than a man, said to drink his captives' blood and to wear the skulls of his victims at his belt.

However, neither brigands nor phantasms materialised. Soon after, they turned off from the head of the pass without mishap and passed on to the postal route that wound downhill through the woods to Velletri. Henry heaved a sigh of relief and gave a silent prayer of thanks.

Their progress throughout the day had been so slow that the winter light had begun to fade as they entered the town of Velletri, the last outpost of order and civilization before the Old Appian Way entered the wastelands of the Pontine Plain. The lamps had been lit in the houses and the glow of cooking fires seeped through the chinks round the doorways and shutters.

As the horses and mules trotted along the beaten earthen road towards the Episcopal Palace, curious heads poked out of doorways. Almost at once, the Cardinal's coat of arms, with the royal crown and ecclesiastical insignia embossed on the doors of his carriage, was recognised and a shout went up: "*Il Cardinale Duca! E arrivato il Cardinale degli Organi!*" and the crowds came pouring out, clustering and jostling around the cavalcade and forcing it to a halt.

Henry was well known in the town, not only because of the frequent visits he paid to his friend, Albani, when he always distributed largesse among the inhabitants, but also because of the healing powers he was believed to possess as a true-born king, anointed by God. Country people flocked to Frascati from far and wide when he was distributing the silver touch pieces that cured the dreaded king's evil. How many countless times, he thought, had he comforted distraught mothers with misshapen children covered in unsightly nodules, gently stroking their poor swollen necks and handing them the blessed medallions with the image of St Michael the Archangel crushing the dragon of evil? He had his own profile stamped on the obverse with the inscription: 'Henry by the Grace of God, King of Great Britain, France and Ireland' as a gesture of defiance against Pope Pius VI, who had refused, unlike his predecessors, to acknowledge his ancestral Stuart claims.

Henry had actually consulted scientific books on the disease known as scrofula. No doctor knew what caused it or how it could be cured. He only knew that it was a sickness that tended to strike the poor rather than the rich, like a malediction adding to their other sufferings. He knew that there had been kings, like the saintly Louis of France, St Edward the Saxon and his own great-grandfather, Charles I, who had been able to lift the curse and cure the sufferers through a mysterious power that flowed through the veins of their pure royal blood,

His parishioners believed that he too had the gift. Crowds flooded the Cathedral after mass entreating him to give them the blessed medal that would make them whole. He had never turned anyone away, even when he had been almost too tired to stand upright, as he felt his strength ebb out of his legs after long sessions when he concentrated on gathering his power to send it surging into his fingertips. In the end, he could not cope with the demand and had been forced to limit the healing ceremonies to certain dates.

Fortunately, Don Angelo had anticipated the stir his arrival would cause in Velletri and had set aside a pouch of touch pieces, which Henry began to distribute through the carriage window, holding each one tightly in his palm before placing it, with his blessing, in the outstretched hand.

When the pouch was empty, Moretto, who had been riding postilion on the last stretch, when the horses were visibly flagging, beckoned to the servants on one of the supply carts to bring out supplies of loaves and cured sausages. They began to toss the food out among the crowds to draw them away from the Cardinal's carriage. At the same time, Annibale began to fling the handfuls of coins he carried for this purpose into the far corners of the square. As the mob, squabbling and fighting, scrambled to pick these up, the way ahead opened and Garani immediately cracked his whip and urged the horses forward.

The news of their arrival had already reached the Episcopal Palace. When they drew up in the forecourt, they were met by scores of anxious prelates, priests and seminarians on the run from Rome, who rushed to meet them.

Moretto leapt down to open the carriage door and help his lord descend. Henry was stiff and needed his support to climb the winding stairway that led up to the entrance, while his attendants followed at a respectful distance. Meanwhile, the palace grooms ran forward to conduct the carriages and carts into the stables and unharness the horses and mules under the coachmen's watchful eye. The Cardinal's prize team of horses needed special attention. Usually, Moretto looked after them personally, but since he was occupied with his master, Garani took over the task, ensuring that they were properly rubbed down, fed and watered and that fresh straw had been laid in their stalls.

Even in his absence, Gianfrancesco Albani kept a liberal table and although Henry, in the haste and flurry of their departure, had forgotten to send word ahead to advise his friend's household of his coming, a hearty meal appeared almost immediately. The mood of the men lifted as they filled their stomachs and settled down contentedly with Albani's servants in front of roaring fires lit at both ends of the Great Hall.

Henry, however, had no appetite. Despite reports to the contrary, he had hoped to find Albani in his house so that they could make plans for their next move. Velletri had seemed far enough from Rome to offer sanctuary, and he had hoped to be able to stay there for some time. He had not expected to find the palace full of refugees. Brooding and filled with foreboding, he retired to Albani's private rooms to rest for the night.

Velletri to Formia

January–February 1797

There was no news that night or the following day. Henry slept fitfully and spent most of the time either in prayer or pacing around Albani's vast garden. Meanwhile, more and more refugees arrived, all with tales of woe. The French had entered Rome. There had been no opposition. The Pope had initially ordered all the citizens to stay at home, with their doors and windows barred, but this had enraged the invading troops, who were eager to find plunder. The delegation sent by Napoleon's commander, General Berthier, had marched straight to the doors of the Pope's Palace on the Quirinale Hill. According to a papal attendant who said he had witnessed the incident, the general had arrogantly demanded to be admitted. The doors had not been barred, by the Pope's orders.

"The Holy Father was waiting calmly for them in his study," he told them, trembling with emotion and choking back his tears. "He offered no resistance whatsoever, but they continued to heap insults on his head. They pulled the ring of the fisherman off his finger and made him prisoner. No one knows where they have taken him, or what they will do with him, or if he will live or die."

Henry digested this news in silence. He walked to the window and stood looking out, his arms crossed tightly across his chest, fighting to keep control. His servants were crowding anxiously into the room and he did not want them to see how profoundly he was shocked. He had known that the new rulers of France had rejected the Church and had done everything in their power to stop the people worshipping, but he had never anticipated such an outrage.

"This is villainous!" Cesarini cried. "I would never have believed that the Corsican upstart would dare so much. There seems to be no limit to his treachery, his perfidy! He vowed he would respect the boundaries of the Holy See when he stripped Rome of so many of its treasures. He demanded great quantities of gold. He took cartloads of our works of art away to Paris. He made a bargain that he would not attack the city, do you remember?"

"Of course," said Henry, shaking his head in sad disbelief. "But he was back after less than a year with more threats. He wanted another 30 million francs that time."

He fell silent, remembering the anguish that had gripped the entire city. The Vatican did not have the money. The treasury had been virtually drained to satisfy Napoleon's previous demands and the Pope was unable to meet the sum. Aristocrats, merchants and humble tradesmen, terrified at the prospect of a French invasion, dipped into their purses to raise the ransom money. New taxes were levied, church plate was melted down and noble ladies donated their jewels to save Rome.

Henry had also rallied to the call. He had contributed a considerable portion of his income, as well as some precious family heirlooms, including the Great Ruby of Poland, the size of a pigeon egg, that he had inherited from his mother, and the golden shield of his maternal great-grandfather, John Sobiesky, the hero king of Poland, who had defeated the Ottoman army at the gates of Vienna and saved Christendom from an Islamic invasion. But it had all been in vain. Bonaparte had continued to break his word. His appetite was still not appeased and the city's sacrifices had only bought a short reprieve. Now he was back, pounding menacingly on the gates of the Papal State and even daring to kidnap the Holy Father himself.

Finally, Henry turned and asked about the Scots College, which was situated on the Quirinale Hill not far from the Papal palace. He was the college patron and had always taken a great interest in the formation of the young student priests who came from the land of his ancestors.

MacLaren stepped forward respectfully, leading a white-faced young novice.

"Your Majesty," he said. "This is my relative, the grandson of my sister in Scotland. He has been studying at the college these last two years, with great profit, if I may add!" and he clapped the young man vigorously on the back, sending him forward to fall on his knees.

"I was out on an errand for our rector," the young seminarian said in a trembling voice. "I saw the Holy Father carried away in a carriage. Then I rushed towards home but I found… I found…" Here his voice broke. "All the students had been turned out on the street with only the clothes they stood up in. The vines from our garden had all been uprooted and tossed out over the walls. The door of the college had been forced off its hinges. The soldiers were inside raiding. I heard much cursing and banging. I dared not stay. My uncle had sent me word that he was departing with you…"

The boy's voice tailed off and Henry asked no further questions about how he had arrived so quickly at Velletri. Someone must have let him have a horse, or perhaps he had stolen one. In these disastrous times, the world was upside down. It seemed totally out of place to worry about such niceties.

Henry and his train stayed another three days in Velletri, hoping that Albani would arrive. Meanwhile, the news brought by the swelling ranks of fugitives became gloomier and gloomier. The Basilica of St Peter's had been looted. The French agents had stripped it of all its gold and silver embellishments and treasures. These were destined to be melted down into coinage to pay the troops. A group of students from the English College also arrived. They recounted with horror that the soldiers had dug up the coffins from the crypt to melt down the lead to make bullets. The venerable bones of the martyrs, they said, had been treated without respect or regard – tossed out of their tombs, shattered and trampled underfoot, and the college church of St Thomas had been used as a stable for the officers' horses.

Almost all the Church hierarchy had left Rome. Many of those who had not escaped in time had been arrested, along with their families.

A constant flow of refugees continued to arrive. They recounted that the Tree of Liberty had been set up among the ruins of the Roman Forum while the conquerors proclaimed the Roman Republic, sister and ally of France, from the summit of the Capitol Hill. Bands paraded the streets, playing the *Marseillaise* while the French flag was raised above the battlements of Castel Sant'Angelo, the Vatican fortress. Amid the din of cannons booming and artillery blasting, the excited soldiers ran wild, bursting into houses, stripping everything of value they could lay their hands on and injuring or killing anyone who tried to resist them.

Finally, one of Albani's servants arrived, winded and dishevelled. Henry had him brought into his own bedchamber so that he could question him in private. The man fell on his knees and blurted out the news he had dreaded to hear. The French commander, Berthier, had sent out orders to capture the Cardinal, who was known for his outspoken stance against the French, and imprison him in Castel Sant'Angelo to await trial.

"My Lord Cardinal was alerted in time, God be thanked!" the servant said. "He sent me to tell you that he cannot return here to Velletri, as it would be too easy for the French to track him down. He has gone instead to the Cistercian Abbey of Casamari. It is in the mountains near the border of the Kingdom of Naples. He said he would wait there for as long as possible, hoping that the Neapolitan army will come as promised and drive out the invaders.

"Your Eminence, my lord urges all his friends to proceed to Naples without delay. He says that for the moment the situation is without hope, since the Holy Father has been made a prisoner and carried off into exile."

At that point, in fact, Henry became convinced that Velletri was no longer a safe refuge. The Cardinal's villa was a prize that Napoleon would be unable to resist. Albani was an avid collector of Roman antiquities and works of art. The outraged people of Rome had already witnessed the ruthless looting of churches and palaces. Helplessly, they had watched cartloads of the city's treasures being carried off in triumphal procession to adorn the Musèe Napoleon at the Louvre in Paris. The French army would not, as he had originally hoped, be content to confine their conquests to Rome. He knew too that when pay was not forthcoming (and his informers had told him that the French Directory was strapped for cash to finance Bonaparte's endless campaigns), the soldiers felt entitled to take whatever compensation they could find and that their commanders turned a blind eye.

He decided that it would be dangerous to stay any longer, but it was with a heavy heart and many misgivings that he imparted orders to be ready to start out in the morning for a journey that he knew would be full of dangers and uncertainty.

The Land of the Living Dead

Early the following morning, Henry IX's train joined the exodus south. They were no longer travelling alone. People of all rank and station were in flight – on foot, on horses or mules, in carriages and wagons. The poor walked with their few possessions wrapped in bundles balanced on their heads, their children in their arms. Men pushed loaded handcarts in front of them over the old Roman paving stones. The Old Appian Way became so crowded that the Cardinal's guards had to force a way through the rabble, pushing a number of cursing travellers into the ditches.

Henry had never travelled along this road before. The difficulties of the terrain were well known, and in normal circumstances he would have avoided it. The old Roman Queen of Roads, built over two thousand years earlier, ran inland, following the coastline between Rome and Capua before shifting direction east towards the Mediterranean port of Brindisi. It was the shortest route from Rome to Naples, but it had been allowed to deteriorate after the fall of the Roman Empire and the barbarian invasions. For many centuries, it had been virtually impassable as much of it led through a vast wasteland of shallow swamps, known as the notorious Pontine Marshes.

The rain-swollen torrents that flowed down from the Apennine mountains had no natural outlet. They were blocked from entering the sea by a long ridge of sand dunes, so that the water spread slowly over the flatlands of the coastal valley and stagnated, creating an evil-smelling alluvial plain, choked with weeds, alga, dead leaves and rotting debris that amassed around the ghostly stumps of stunted trees, where clumps of reeds and decomposing animal carcasses rose blackly out of the water. A thick sulphurous gas bubbled up from under the surface, creating shifting banks of yellowish vapour that gave off a nauseous stench. In summer, the effluence emanating from the marshes wafted as far as the gates of Rome.

From time to time, attempts had been made to restore the road. Fortunately, Henry remarked to Cesarini, Pius VI had carried out extensive repair works in recent years, opening it up sufficiently to allow passage, at least for the greater part of the year.

It was said that when weather conditions were good, a coach could cross the worst part of the marshes in around eight hours. However, it was now winter and it had rained heavily over the last month. He had consulted the maps with Annibale, and he knew the journey would tax the men, as well as the animals. They would have to stop and change horses at more than one post, which would most likely be some miserable inn offering little comfort. A couple of rivers had to be forded and very likely they would be in spate. There was little to be light-hearted about! If he could be thankful for one thing, it was that he was not crossing in summer, when he had been told thick swarms of black flies and biting mosquitoes tormented travellers and that there was a high risk of contacting the incurable marsh fever.

The Pontine Marshes were known, with good reason, as the Land of the Living Dead. The wretched herders and charcoal burners who lived there were virtually savages, often at war with the neighbouring hill dwellers over territorial rights. Sooner or later, they contracted the dreaded marsh sickness and wasted away. The fever slowly sucked all the blood out of the body till the sufferer's skin became transparent as an insect's wing. The area was notorious for other reasons. Bandits and criminals hid out in the marshes, where the gendarmes could not find them. They made a living robbing hapless travellers and holding them to ransom. Those with families who could not pay usually met a slow and miserable death, their mangled bodies left out in the open to be eaten by wild animals.

As the Cardinal had predicted, they soon ran up against their first obstacle. When they reached the ford at the Astura River, the horses had to be coaxed and flogged to enter the fast flowing current. The rain turned into hailstones that whipped up the surface of the water. The wheels sank continuously into ruts full of oozing mire and the carriages lurched and dipped alarmingly till his men ran forward to hold them upright with the weight of their bodies.

Soon afterwards, they arrived at Tres Tabernae, the fifth post. It was little more than a level clearing with a dirty, run-down tavern. The innkeeper, seeing a wealthy patron arriving at his door, rushed out to greet them, wiping his greasy hands on his apron. He fell on his knees in the mud as Henry stepped out, trying unsuccessfully to kiss the Cardinal's ring. Henry ignored him and gestured to Moretto to support his arm while he walked to and fro in order to get the circulation flowing once more in his legs. The cook, Giacinto Belisario, after a brief glance around the kitchen, refused to use it, so Don Angelo told him to distribute among the men some of the bread, cheese and cured meat they had brought with them, and to give them a swig of warmed wine.

Henry decided immediately that they would press on. The inn was already crowded with a noisy and petulant throng, the forecourt crammed with wagons and carts. Women clutching wailing babies huddled on the steps, with small children peeping fearfully out from under their trailing skirts and shawls. Old women came up, carrying rush baskets full of eggs, onions and dead fowl, pestering the Cardinal's men to buy. Recognising the carriage of a nobleman, the crowd began to gather around him, lamenting that they had lost everything. They cried that their homes had been sacked by the French, who had burned their barns and made off with their livestock and Henry gave orders to distribute alms as fairly as possible, starting with the women and children, till his purse was empty. The scene of chaos and desperation all around him filled him with a despair that caught at his throat. He felt angry and helpless. In Frascati, he was used to being able to alleviate the sufferings of the poor and sick, but here he was, powerless to offer anything more than crumbs of comfort. The knowledge of his uselessness weighed on his heart like a stone.

As soon as the horses had been changed, they went on their way, despite the innkeeper's protests. The man ran alongside the Cardinal's coach for several yards, extolling the merits of his wine: "blessed by the presence of the Holy Paul of Tarsus who stopped on this very spot on his way to Rome – many men of learning like yourself, Eminence, can attest to this truth."

But Henry ignored him and turned his head away.

They arrived at the most dreaded part of their journey. The marsh wastelands stretched before them, enveloped in an evil-smelling miasma drifting up from pools of brackish water. The men, who had been chatting among themselves to keep their spirits up, fell into a grim silence. Ridolfi's face took on a greenish tinge. Don Angelo continued to mop his wig-less head with his sodden kerchief.

MacLaren urged his horse forward to come level with the Cardinal's coach and rode close alongside, his grey beard dripping moisture and his eyes darting ferociously in all directions for any sign of an ambush. His right hand, half hidden by his plaid, lay ready on the hilt of his sword. Henry smiled grimly to himself. He doubted that the old warrior would actually be able to wield a weapon effectively, if the need should arise. In later years at La Rocca, the Scotsman had spent more of his time drinking with Belisario and his kitchen cronies than practising his swordplay. But this, he reflected, was true of all of them. They had lived in peace and prosperity for years, untroubled by events in the world around them. His household and friends had aged with him, placidly allowing themselves to drift through pleasant years of calm and everyday order that no one had thought would ever change.

'Habit is a treacherous master,' he thought. He had allowed his eyes to be closed. He had ignored the dispatches that came from the northern states of Italy, which Napoleon had conquered one by one, laughing as he progressed, sweeping aside the feeble little dukedoms, republics and fiefs – all fat chickens just sitting there waiting to be plucked. He, Henry, had sneered along with others when the Corsican had suddenly transformed himself from soldier to monarch, living with his concubine Josephine like a king and queen in the Palace of Mondello in Milan, where they held court, surrounded by fawning artists, scientists and *literati*. He, Henry, should have foreseen that a man like that would not be content with half of a whole, that he would have no regard for the sanctity of the Holy

Church or the sacred office of the Supreme Pontiff and that his boundless greed for conquest would overcome any obstacles in his path. And the obstacles had been so feeble! Rome had surrendered without a shot fired and now the price of their inertia, all the resulting suffering and chaos, was laid out before their eyes with no hope of a remedy.

At first, as the Cardinal's retinue cautiously advanced, there seemed to be no sign of life. In silence, they filed past a cluster of reed huts, set like the nests of water birds in the middle of a tangled pile of black stunted branches. But after half an hour or so, they heard a kind of sigh, almost like wind moving through leaves, and a few shadowy forms began to slink out of the undergrowth. Some of his men crossed themselves. These creatures were miserable wretches of skin and bone, with only rags and animal skins covering their bodies. They all had the spectral pallor of the marsh sickness. On their shoulders some were carrying little naked children with great, hollow eyes staring out of the shrunken faces of old men. The living dead stood there motionless. They did not whine or complain or ask for alms, but the air was thick with the force of their brooding and desperate hatred.

Only one man approached, holding two skinny and bloodless children by the hand. They gazed at the Cardinal's men without expression. Henry at once gestured to Cesarini to give them money but it was plain that Don Angelo was reluctant to touch them. Impatiently, the Cardinal snatched the pouch from him and emptied the contents out into the man's hand. But half of the coins fell on the ground and the man made no effort to pick them up. Too late, Henry thought that he would probably have preferred to receive food, but the guards had closed in around his coach and Annibale had urged the horses forward. At once, without a word or gesture, the man turned and vanished into the shadows.

They found no respite at the sixth post. The inn was little more than a shack with a sagging rush roof and it swarmed like an anthill with people. Henry had fallen asleep and his servants did not disturb him. They did not halt again till they reached the River Uffense. It was swollen with the floods and full of debris. The ferryman had to be persuaded with gold to undertake the crossing and he agreed only to take the Lord Cardinal and Don Cesarini. The others had to make do on foot, passing over a precarious boat bridge that swayed and lurched alarmingly. Meanwhile, the coaches and carts had to be loaded onto a raft that the boatman kept to transport heavier loads, while the mules were harnessed to long towropes.

Moretto went to get Henry's prized team of blacks, which were in a state of terror, eyeing the wild water with eyes that rotated in their sockets. As the Cardinal's personal coachman, he was the only person whom they trusted and who could handle them. He swung himself onto the back of Nero, the lead stallion, and coaxed him forward towards the fast-flowing current, while Henry watched anxiously from the opposite bank. The horse at first refused, shying and bucking, till lying low over the animal's neck and murmuring reassurances in his ear, Moretto managed to soothe him and persuade him to enter the water and swim across. Encouraged by their leader's example, the other five followed, led on a long rein that Moretto had fastened around his waist. They all emerged safely on the opposite side of the river, where they stood huddled together, heads drooping despondently and noses touching, as the grooms rushed to rub them down.

The carriages and wagons had to be manoeuvred onto the raft one by one, and the servants, cursing under their breath, formed chains to tow them across at the end of ropes. But the raft was too frail to bear the weight of some of the loads. The wagon containing Henry's large oak bed and all his bedding lurched to one side half way across the river and then slowly tipped over, emptying its contents into the flood with a violent crash of splintering wood. The spectators on the bank watched in helpless horror as the crimson bed drapes spread out over the current like a spill of blood, while the mules, tethered to the rear of the wagon, squealed and plunged in terror. Garani was the first to come to his senses. He threw himself waist deep into the fast-flowing current and cut the traces with his knife. The mules were saved but the bed was irretrievably lost. Henry told his men not to attempt to recover it.

"It is already ruined and useless," he said.

Soaked, cold and miserable, they hurried on. Fortunately, the next inn was more hospitable and less crowded. The innkeeper, seeing the state the travellers were in, hastened to build up the fire inside his tavern so that all the men could strip off their wet garments and hang them up to dry. The bodyguards and outriders clamoured for wine, while Giacinto got busy in the kitchen, roasting the meat he had brought with him, freshly butchered at Velletri. Soon the atmosphere in the inn changed from one of stoical gloom to raucous banter as the men ate and drank, recovering their good humour and spirits.

Henry did not eat and he found the wine undrinkable. He went instead to the stables to make sure that his horses were being taken good care of. They were valuable beasts that had cost him a princely sum of money, but he knew they had no match in the entire Roman court. He found Moretto with them, rubbing them down and talking to them.

"They've come to no harm?" he enquired.

Moretto laughed. "Not they, sire! They're soldiers. It would take more than a bit of water to damp their mettle. They're as fresh and ready as that time we beat the Princess Rezzonico. Remember how we raced her carriage and got first through the gates for Cardinal de Bernis' reception? She was so furious! I still remember the look on her face!"

Henry cut him off with a gesture of his hand. He had hoped the Boy had forgotten the incident. It had happened years before and although at the time he had enjoyed triumphing over the noble lady, who was an unpleasant and arrogant woman, very full of the fact that she was Clement XIII's niece, he had soon sobered up and realised his action had not befitted the dignity of his office. To make things worse, Moretto had cheated. He had thrown his torch into the faces of the princess' horses, making them swerve sharply. By a miracle, her carriage hadn't overturned. He had had to send her gifts and grovelling letters of apology afterwards and the Pope had never really forgiven him.

"I don't want to ever hear another mention of that episode!" Henry said, making his voice as stern and cold as he could, though it did not escape him that Moretto had turned away with a smile on his lips. "In any case, these are not the same horses. It was too long ago."

"Forgive me, Your Majesty," Moretto said, bowing low and attempting to look solemn. "I will, of course, obey you and cancel out all memories that displease you!"

Henry went out into the yard. "I ought to have that boy whipped for his impertinence!" he said to himself, knowing that it was an idle thought. He could never be angry with Gigi for long. In fact, he already felt a smile forming on his lips as he recalled the princess' indignation and the colourful insults she heaped on his head, more worthy of a Roman carter or fishmonger. Then, as now, he wondered where she had learned them!

The rain had stopped and a feeble sun was struggling to illuminate the pale horizon. He pulled himself together. It was imperative that they reach the garrison city of Terracina before curfew or they would not be allowed to pass. The fortress stood on the southern border of the Papal State, guarding the entrance to the Kingdom of

Naples and he wanted to get as near as possible to the frontier before nightfall.

He sent Annibale to rally the men, some of whom were already drunk. They obeyed, grumbling a little among themselves, and the convoy set off on what he hoped would be the last stage of their journey. He planned to cross into the territory of Naples and wait near the border for news. With the Neapolitans, the Austrians and the British navy united against the French occupation of Rome, he hoped that the invaders might be forced to withdraw.

In that case, he would be spared the necessity of travelling on to the Bourbon court to beg hospitality for himself and his retinue. He had never met the King and Queen of Naples, although they exchanged Christmas greetings and he had received the odd letter from Maria Carolina, Ferdinand IV's Austrian wife. He was uneasy about meeting this woman. He had heard strange stories about her. She was said to be bold and unfeminine – a shameless and immodest virago who ruled over her husband. According to all accounts, Ferdinand was a weak fool who only thought of amusing himself and preferred to mingle with low company, neglecting the affairs of state. It was his Queen who ruled the country, with the help of her English prime minister, who was (they said) her lover.

The prospect of having to deal with such a woman alarmed Henry. He had had very few dealings with women in the course of his life and they made him uneasy. Charles' widow, the Princess Louise of Stolberg-Gedern, had made a fool of him, weeping and pleading poverty, bombarding him with begging letters. He had felt it his duty to give her an allowance. Even when he had found out what all of Rome already knew – that she was living openly with her lover, Alfieri, the Italian poet, he had not found it in him to cut her off. He had also continued to support Clementina Walkinshaw, Charles' former mistress, even after the death of Charlotte, her daughter and Charles' only heir.

He would have been relieved if he were not required to meet the Queen of Naples at all – if he and his retinue could just simply turn around and go back home to his diocese at Frascati, with all its familiar comforts. But time never turns around, he told himself, pulling himself together. His pleasant little world of peaceful administration, study and contemplation was gone, as scattered and useless as old regrets. This new world, born out of blood and violence, would vanish too in time. These poor simpletons, the common folk, who cheered and exalted the new era, would soon see where these notions of equality, liberty and brotherhood would take them! Men, he thought, as he stroked his long nose, have never been equals and never would be. The French had destroyed the flowers of their country, only to make space for the weeds.

Terracina and St Andrew's Pass

The sun was sinking when the bulwark of the Terracino fortress, bristling with men and cannon, came into sight. Soldiers peered down at the party from the battlements, their helmets and bayonet blades flashing gold in the setting sun, and the door was heavily guarded. The foot of the walls were ringed with a straggling mass of tents and makeshift shelters where families clustered together around the little fires they had lit in an attempt to keep warm. Denied entrance, they waited in dread that the French army should arrive before they could obtain permits to cross the border.

To the Cardinal's annoyance, they had to submit to a long delay while the official in charge examined their safe conducts and passports and guardsmen went through all the contents of their baggage. Finally, he sent Annibale to the commander with his protests and the governor in person came rushing out soon afterwards, full of apologies.

"You must understand, Excellency," he said, breathing hard and wiping his forehead, "We have strict orders to control everyone who wishes to pass. We know that the French are advancing fast and may soon control the Appia before King Ferdinand has his army ready to confront them. We only have a small garrison here and will soon have to bar the gates to everyone who comes. Naturally, this does not include your august person and the servants who are travelling with you. You honour us with your presence, as a faithful servant of our Mother Church and an enemy of the godless and villainous Jacobins."

He carried on in this vein for some time until Henry signalled him to be silent.

"We do not intend to stay with you, Sir," he said. "We only wish to proceed these last few miles to the frontier of Naples and cross over before nightfall. We are expected at the Abbey of St Erasmus, which, as you know, is under the protection of the Duke of Gaeta. The journey has greatly fatigued our household and our servants need to rest."

Originally, Henry had intended to stop at Terracina to wait for news before taking the final step of crossing the border. But the reports brought from Rome by scouts sent to investigate the situation had made him decide to press on. Most of the country was now controlled by the enemy. The Holy City of Rome had been proclaimed a Republic and a French Protectorate. All titles and hereditary honours had been abolished. Everyone was now addressed simply as 'Citizen' – even the most respected and elevated members of the clergy and the papal court. It was a world in which he felt he had no longer any part.

Cowed by the Cardinal's haughty and unsmiling bearing, the commander dispensed with any further formalities and the party proceeded along the road that led through the Portello, the turreted gate that marked the limits of the Papal State. The men all heaved a sigh of relief as they rode through the narrow arch, where the guards, alerted by the governor, waved them through without further ceremony.

After that, they made quick progress. Although by now it was almost dark, the road through the Valley of Fondi was in good repair and the carriages and wagons rolled steadily along, to the immense relief of the bruised and battered passengers. The climate too had changed for the better. They had left winter behind, with its bitter winds and driving sleet. They found themselves instead in a wide and fertile plain, facing onto the sea and protected all along its length by a barrier wall of mountains. The air was soft and mild and scented with sea salt and lemon flowers.

"I would never have believed this!" MacLaren muttered to Moretto, who had climbed down from the coachman's seat and was now standing upright on the shafts. "I think we're bewitched. We've come to fairyland."

Moretto chuckled. "Well, they tell us the Queen of Naples is a witch. Maybe it's true."

Henry had arranged for his party to stay at the Monastery of St Erasmus at Castellona Moladi, some twenty miles further down the coast. Although darkness had fallen, there was a bright moon which illuminated the road and this last part of their journey passed smoothly.

The Appian Way continued to be in good condition as it wended through the valleys and mountain passes beyond the town of Fondi. It had been re-paved some twenty years earlier by the young King Ferdinand, in order to make a good impression on his Austrian bride, who was travelling from Vienna to Naples to meet him for the first time.

A few miles beyond the town, they entered the narrow Pass of St Andrew, which cut through a bleak and stony valley, compressed between steep and towering slopes. It seemed the ideal place for an ambush and the men fell silent, crossing themselves as they peered fearfully into the shadows. The moon rose, illuminating the road ahead with a feeble light. For a while the only sounds to be heard were the creaking of the carriage wheels and the sharp clang of shodden hooves against the old Roman paving stones.

Finally, to their relief, they reached an isolated fort that stood on the highest point of the pass. The commander came out to meet them, apologising that he had nothing to offer them except water from their well.

"We only have a small garrison here and we've already been attacked several times," he told Henry. "We're expecting reinforcements to arrive any time. The King is preparing a counter offensive to drive the rebels out of the lands of the Holy Mother Church."

Henry said he was glad to hear this. Privately, he thought that the Bourbons had hesitated long enough already. But everything that he had heard about Ferdinand had painted the image of a self-indulgent weakling, ruled by his courtiers and his wife, a third son who had not expected to occupy the throne and had little idea of the responsibilities required of a king.

Cesarini, who had overheard the commander's assurances, snorted. As if he read the Cardinal's thoughts, he remarked, "With such feeble defenders as these, we have small hopes of returning home soon!"

Henry ignored him. He felt it was unwise to sow further doubts in the minds of his men, who were visibly flagging after the strenuous journey. Most of them had already dismounted and were milling around the small forecourt, fraternising with the Neapolitan soldiers, who had come down from the walls, eager for company after long days of virtual isolation.

Although he was impatient to press on, he gave orders to share out some of the wine they were carrying and sat watching with satisfaction as the tension and fatigue faded from their faces. But just before their voices began to rise and they became drunk and querulous, he leant over and patted his old friend's hand. "We are priests, Don Angelo. Do your duty! I do not think these men have been inside a church for many weeks now."

Cesarini was a little startled, but he obeyed, rallying the men for prayers and confession, while the Cardinal imparted his blessing by the light of the moon that now hovered over their heads.

As they began the descent from the pass, they became aware of the softest sound, almost like the murmur of a faraway crowd or the rhythmic cooing of doves. To most of the men, this was mysterious, because they had always lived in their inland village and had never seen or heard the sea. It was a tranquil night and the sea lay quiet. The waves caressed the beach, tirelessly sucking in the shingle and breathing it out again. The moon shone on a sea as flat as a tabletop, under a cold and glittering sky of stars. A scattering of fishing boats were out, sitting motionless on the shining ebony water, the glow of their lanterns mirroring the firmament above, so that sea and sky seemed to blend together in a sparkling mesh of lights.

The whole party stopped to admire the spectacle. The farm boys especially were overawed and began to chatter excitedly with each other, but then MacLaren, who had been furtively imbibing from his silver flask throughout their descent, brusquely interrupted.

"Call that a sea!" he shouted, waving his arm vaguely towards the horizon. "This is a pond. It's a bathtub. You should see the sea in my country! It's like a mighty warrior – angry, never at peace. It roars like a bull. It battles with the rocks. It tries to destroy them. This sea is like a pussycat! It couldn't drown a fly!"

"That's where you are mistaken, old friend!" Henry broke in quietly, leaning out of the carriage window. "The Tirrenian Sea is a cunning sea. It can blow up storms when you least expect it! Many fishermen and sailors who set out on a clear morning have not come home in the evening. If you had paid more attention to the great poet Homer, you would have known this!"

His thoughts drifted. He had seen a furious sea. It was when he was still a boy and he had accompanied his brother to the English Channel, where he was preparing to embark on his campaign to re-conquer the Stuart throne. The French king had promised to send a supporting fleet but at the last moment he had gone back on his word. He remembered that Charles, ever the hothead, decided to go on alone as soon as the wind was favourable. He, Henry, had been desperate to accompany his brother but King James refused to allow it, saying that he did not wish to risk losing both his sons. Things might have gone so differently, if fate had helped their cause, he thought sadly.

Cesarini brought him back to the present. He came up, fingering his rosary beads, and leaned close to whisper in Henry's ear, "I hope, sire, that you do not for any reason plan to cross this sea. I have never been on water and I do not know if I would find the courage to follow you – even though the scriptures tell us that our Lord calmed storms and walked on water!"

Henry laughed. "Well, Angelo, our road leads overland to Naples, so it should not be necessary to put you to the test!"

The Weeping Madonnas

Privately, he wondered what would happen to them if Napoleon should invade the Kingdom of Naples, as he had invaded the lands of the Church. It seemed that nothing could stop the Corsican and that he was intent on becoming master of the entire continent. All the prayers, all the tears of blood shed by the Weeping Madonnas of Italy had not deterred him – not even the miraculous image of Our Lady in the Cathedral of Ancona. Bonaparte had seen her opening and closing her painted eyelids with his own eyes. His examining scientists could find no evidence of fraud. According to witnesses, Napoleon had turned pale when he witnessed the miracle and ordered the sacred icon to be covered up. But not even then had he stopped his campaign of conquest.

Henri's thoughts turned frequently to the Madonna of the Little Arch, which hung in the tiny Chapel of the *Archetto* at the back of the Stuart residence, Palazzo Muti. Two days after Pius VI had urged the people of Rome to pray for the intercession of the Blessed Virgin to halt the advance of Napoleon's Italian army, many people swore that they had seen the eyes of the ancient image move.

He had hurried to Rome as soon as the news of the miracle reached him. The chapel, where he often went for private prayer when he was staying in the palace, was packed with an excited crowd. Many more were on their knees in the street, weeping and chanting prayers and invocations. He had climbed up the ladder that had been propped up on the wall just under the image so that he could see for himself.

"Where does illusion end when the desire for the illusion to be authentic is so impelling?" he had asked himself. Did he, in fact, see the eyes move? At the time he had believed he had, but now he was unsure. In the dim light, with the flickering candles and the shifting shadows cast by the people pressing around him, it was so easy to be deceived. He tended now to think there had been no miracle. Even Pius VI had not been convinced and the investigations carried out by the Curia had not been conclusive. It was also to be regretted that despite all the sworn testimonies and sightings that went on for months all over the country, there had been no concrete sign of divine intervention interceding to save the Church from the greedy talons of the Corsican Devil.

The road followed the coastline for the last few miles till they finally reached their destination. The St Erasmus Abbey of the Olivetan Benedictines stood high on a hillside overlooking the sea. It was an austere-looking building. At that late hour, it was almost totally in darkness, with only one small light burning at the gate to guide them in. Annibale, whom he had sent ahead to warn the community of their imminent arrival, was waiting with the Guest-master, who dropped on his knees before Henry, kissing his ring and saying how honoured his House was to have such a distinguished guest. He apologised that the Abbot could not be there to welcome them in person but it was almost time for Matins and the community, according to the Olivetan rule, would be at prayer until Lauds. They had been expected a little sooner, he explained, but everything was ready for them and they would find food and all that they needed in the guesthouse.

Henry had originally planned to stay for only a few days at the Abbey, but he lingered there for almost two months, hesitating over travelling further south. He was reluctant to throw himself on the hospitality of the Bourbon monarchs, about whom he had heard such unfavourable reports. His men too were uneasy about going so far away. Spring was on the way and the farm boys were restless, anxious to get home to help with the ploughing and sowing.

The Olivetans followed a very strict rule that Henry admired, but his Family was less enthusiastic. The monastery offered none of the luxuries they had taken for granted at La Rocca, and few of the comforts. The Abbot had put the entire guesthouse at their disposal, but it was barely furnished, dark and perennially cold, despite the mild spring weather. Only Henry and Cesarini had individual cells, where there was room for little more than a bed. Their personal servants slept on straw pallets laid over the threshold of their doors. The rest of his retinue was accommodated in dormitories. Like the monks, they slept in their clothes, and water for washing had to be pumped up daily from the well in the forecourt.

The bells rang at all hours to call the community to prayer, from midnight Matins to Lauds, then through Prime, Terce, Sext, None and Vespers. This annoyed his men, who complained of interrupted sleep. Henry was kept busy attending all the functions, where he implored the intercession of the Holy Virgin and the Son of God to protect the captive Pope and spare the lands of the Church. Sometimes he took Moretto with him into the refectory while the monks were eating so that they could listen to the readings from the pulpit about the lives of the saints and martyrs, but Gigi soon objected. He complained it was gloomy stuff and spoiled his digestion.

His men grumbled about the frugality of the meals. Although they had their own kitchen and Giacinto prepared their food with the help of a couple of lay servants, there was little meat available and all supplies came out of the monks' own orchard and kitchen garden. The monks were forbidden wine and thus kept no wine cellar. This did not trouble Henry, who normally ate and drank very little, but his men were accustomed to enjoying the excesses of the groaning table he always provided for the many visitors who came to his door.

Henry's generosity was unlimited. No visitors were ever turned away. But while the guests were served with every honour and provided with silver tableware, enamelled finger bowls and linen towels, crystal glasses and cups of fine china, Henry himself used a stoneware salt cellar, rough pottery cups and earthenware porringers, similar to the unrefined monastery tableware. These shows of humility had often embarrassed and perplexed his guests at La Rocca, and the English spies, who came disguised as simple travellers, sneered behind his back, claiming that his simple preferences were nothing but affectation. Henry was unperturbed. He knew that they found it incomprehensible that a great prince should prefer to follow the habits of the poor and humble, rather than enjoy the comforts and gratifications his wealth entitled him to.

The men had very little contact with the monks, who observed the rule of silence and flitted around the cloister like spectres in their white habits and cowls, their faces hidden and their eyes cast down. Henry gave strict instructions that his followers should not disturb their quiet.

However, his servants soon found ways to escape the tedium. Moretto had nosed out a place in the wall that was easily scaled and when their master retired, groups would sneak out and go down to the village at the foot of the hill, where they could move around and speak freely. The local fisher folk, however, were wary of them, rebutting all attempts at conversation and keeping their women carefully out of sight.

Carnival and Lent

Carnival arrived, but they passed it in glum silence. Although they could hear the music and merrymaking in the town below, Henry forbade his men to join the revellers. He told them they were strangers and might not be welcomed by the local people, especially if they tried to dance or chat to the young girls. They could be harassed or robbed in the crowd. His men grudgingly obeyed, resigning themselves to long evenings playing cards in the kitchen after he had withdrawn and the monks had gone to bed.

Lent followed, imposing even stricter penitences on them all. Henry's eyes became inflamed and he could no longer read. The infirmarer and his assistants came daily to lay on his eyelids poultices of flaxseed and camomile while Moretto sat by his bed and read out loud from the history and scientific books he found in the monastery library.

Finally, after over a month's silence, a letter arrived from Cardinal Albani and Henry eagerly commanded Moretto to break the seal and read it out to him.

"Do not bother with the address and the formalities!" he urged. "Read me his news. How are things with him?"

"It would seem that all is well, sire," replied Moretto, quickly scanning the letter. "The Lord Cardinal says he is comfortably lodged with the good brothers in Casamari. The monks come from many parts. Many of them sought refuge in the community after the revolution in France and the purges of the refractory priests so he says he is glad of the opportunity to speak in different languages. He also praises the kindness of Father Simone Cardon, who guides the community, and also of a Friar Maturino Pitri, who was a soldier in the French army until he saw the light of God during a grave illness and was miraculously saved.

"He writes that all is tranquil but, my Lord, he ends by urging you to hasten south to the protection of Naples." Moretto's voice faltered just slightly. It had not escaped him that the final exhortation contrasted with the optimistic tone of the rest of the letter. Henry frowned.

"Does he say nothing else?" he urged.

"No, that is all," Moretto replied, smoothing the letter and placing it in his hands while Henry impatiently pulled the poultices from his eyes and squinted painfully at the page. That final warning made him uneasy. Was Albani as tranquil as he tried to appear? Had he news that he did not dare to set down in writing in case it fell into the wrong hands?

As Easter approached, his eyes healed, but he became more and more morose. He withdrew into himself and spent long hours pacing the cloister alone or in prayer in the chapel. No miracle had come to release him and his retainers from the heartache of exile. He believed that his home was lost, perhaps forever. Nonetheless, he continued to wait with as much patience as he could muster. He worried increasingly about the fate of his parishioners, left defenceless at the mercies of the invaders.

His agitation increased as more and more bad news slowly filtered through. Many cardinals and bishops had been arrested, their servants dismissed and their furniture and effects put up for public auction in the marketplace. The French troops had broken into La Rocca and they had also occupied the papal palace at Castelgandolfo, stripping both residences of all the furniture, which had been put up for sale to help pay the expenses of the invading army.

There had been an uprising in Rome when it was rumoured that the French were withdrawing and some daring Roman citizens had dislodged the Tree of Liberty, but the rebellion was quashed almost immediately. Ercole Consalvi, who had insisted on staying in Rome, was under house arrest and threatened with deportation. No further news came from his friend, Gianfrancesco Albani, hiding out at the Abbey of Casamari.

A messenger from Rome brought word that the Palazzo della Cancelleria, the Cardinal's official residence as Vice-Chancellor of the Holy See, had been searched by French officers who had made an inventory of all the furniture, paintings and other contents and requisitioned the horses from the stable. Fortunately, the servants left in charge had been alerted in time and had managed to transfer the state archives and documents to a safe hiding place.

In the end, after long hours of meditation and earnest consultations with Don Angelo, he finally decided that they would have to bow before the inevitable and he gave his servants orders to make ready for the next stage of the journey southwards to the city of Naples.

Initially, most of the men did not care for the idea. Naples was a foreign country, where they believed they would be regarded with suspicion. They were uneasy. They feared they would encounter difficulties and acts of hostility. They grumbled among themselves that the Neapolitans spoke another language that they would not be able to understand. They had heard that the people lived mostly on the streets and the city was full of charlatans, pickpockets and footpads, making it dangerous to walk around unescorted. The ploughboys whom he had enrolled at Frascati to swell his escort were particularly alarmed. They were totally unprepared for problems of this kind. There were no delinquents in the peaceful little village of Frascati, apart from the children who stole fruit from the orchards.

When they came to him to protest, Henry dismissed them impatiently. He told them the stories they heard were all nonsense. Naples was a great imperial city, a centre of learning and culture. In any case, he added, with a slight ironical smile, they would have no reason to go out at night. He would not expect them to run errands after dark.

As he expected, this news was not well received either. Many of his servants and guards were irked by the long period of seclusion and abstinence they had been submitted to during the weeks spent at St Erasmus and once they had resigned themselves to the move, they began to look forward to exploring the many after-dark delights a great city can offer. So they changed their tune. They said that, to tell the truth, they had also heard other reports about Naples. Far from being a hotbed of crime, they insisted that the capital was renowned as being a lively and merry city, full of festivals, amusements and music. They said that they expected the time would pass pleasantly enough until it was possible to go back home.

Henry said nothing, keeping his misgivings to himself. At the back of his mind, like a festering boil that gave him no peace, was his fear that Naples would not be the end of their journey, but only a temporary respite. He had received no news that gave him hope they would be able to go home in the near future. He feared it was more likely that they would be hounded onwards towards an ever more uncertain fate.

Part 2
Naples

April 17th – December 23rd, 1798

Henry IX, Cardinal Duke of York, alleged rightful heir to the thrones of England, Scotland and Ireland, entered the city of Naples in the style of a royal prince. MacLaren marched at the head of the procession, playing a rousing march on his bagpipes. He was followed by his guardsmen, riding two by two, their numbers swelled by the ploughboys he had enrolled in his retinue. His escort wore the royal livery of his House and carried lances with fluttering pennants bearing his insignia. The Cardinal's carriage had been thoroughly cleaned and polished, his coat of arms on the doors freshly touched up in scarlet, azure and gold. It was drawn by his prize team of blacks, trained to pace in unison, with scarlet plumes tossing and silver-bossed harnesses jingling. As was his custom, Henry himself was soberly dressed in black, with, as his only ornaments, his diamond cross dangling on his chest and the great sapphire of Scotland on the middle finger of his gloved hand.

Their entrance, however, did not cause too much of a stir. By now, the Neapolitans had grown accustomed to the arrival of eminent personages on the run from Napoleon and his troops. When they reached the market place, they were forced to a halt, their progress blocked by the press of carts, stalls, riders and hawkers that filled the entire square. The noise was deafening as men and women traded at the tops of their voices, haggling, screaming, singing and gesticulating. A flock of sheep, shaggy and brown with dust, scurried around the hooves of the horses and mules, bleating in fear and confusion while their shepherd laid about him with his stick as he tried to rally them and herd them forward. Accustomed to the quiet orderliness of daily business in Frascati, the Cardinal's men were disorientated. They gazed helplessly around, unable to decide how to go forward.

Beggars meanwhile had wormed their way up to the carriage window, shoving their dirty hands under the curtains, whining for alms. Annibale and the guards beat them off but more and more appeared till they were surrounded by a horde of ragged wretches banging on the doors with fists and crutches, waving withered arms and tearing back strips of clothing to reveal bleeding scars and suppurating sores. Normally, in similar circumstances, Henry would have given orders to throw out coins among the crowd, as he often did in the poorer areas of Rome or in the villages he passed through during his journeys to his incumbencies north of the city. This had always been enough to satisfy their demands for alms and, as soon as the monies had been gathered and distributed, the people usually dispersed quietly, saluting and bowing. But he had never come across anything resembling this surging, desperate mass and he was afraid that a similar gesture might provoke a riot, with unknown consequences.

MacLaren, who risked being submerged by the importuning throng, swung himself up onto the back of the lead horse, Nero, with a surprising show of agility for his age, his bagpipes tucked under one arm. With his other arm, he brandished the black knife he kept at his belt and roared an ancient battle cry of his people.

"Close your windows, sire!" Annibale shouted, laying around him with his whip and manoeuvring his horse between the carriage door and the clamorous mob. The guards closed in, drawing swords and pistols. In less than a moment, as if obeying some silent instructions, the beggars vanished. At the same time, a way opened up through the market, 'like the parting of the Red Sea', Cesarini described it afterwards, and the Cardinal's train passed through the middle of a mass of curious faces, suddenly unexpectedly silenced.

Moretto and Eugenio, perched together on the footboard, looked at each other in alarm. They were distressed and perplexed. They had heard many accounts of the splendour and gaiety of Naples and, once they had overcome their reluctance to venture into the unknown, they had begun to look forward to the experience of discovering a foreign metropolis, which was famed for its fine palaces and churches, its theatres and opera houses, its monuments and pleasure houses, all of which attracted hundreds of foreign aristocrats, like flies to a honeypot, as an essential part of their Grand Tour.

They had not been prepared to find a maze of squalid alleyways, where they could touch the buildings on either side with arms outstretched, or to see little naked children darting between dark doorways, ignoring the dangers of being knocked down by the passing stream of people, donkeys, horsemen and vehicles. There had been nothing like this in tranquil and orderly Frascati, or even in the poorest districts in Rome, where orchards, gardens and decorous religious houses alleviated the contours of streets lined with miserable tenements, open drains and rough workshops.

However, the variety of the merchandise displayed on the market stalls indicated that there was another face to the city. Naples possessed a vast social class that expected to be supplied with, and was able to pay for, refinements and luxuries. They drove past stalls heaped with the fruits, vegetables and foodstuffs from the Orient and the New World – purple-striped bean pods, glossy black aubergines, bulbous green peppers, strings of onions, garlands of tiny red chillies, sweet potatoes and tomatoes, 'the golden apples' once thought to be poisonous and now a regular part of the diet of the rich. The butchers' stalls displayed roast suckling pigs and sides of bloody meat and game, black and buzzing with voracious swarms of insects. On the fishmongers' slabs were spread the whole carcasses of swordfish and dolphins, alongside bowls of mussels and clams, piles of anchovies and sardines, mullet and mackerel, heaped octopus in a grey sprawl of tentacles, cuttlefish and squid and raw pink sides of tunny-fish. Set on the ground were barrels of writhing eels and buckets of crabs and lobsters with bound claws, struggling hopelessly to climb over each other.

Vendors approached offering delicacies such as shaved ice and fruit syrup drinks, honey cakes and sweetmeats. Groups of people stood chatting around the *maccherone* braziers, gathering up handfuls of noodles with their fingers and, heads tipped back, dropping the ribbons of food into their open mouths.

"They say that even King Ferdinand eats like that!" Moretto muttered softly to Eugenio. "So that curate told me – Father Biagio – the one that's really a spy. Do you remember him? He's been bringing our master news from Naples these past few months."

He lowered his voice to a near whisper. "He told us that the people love the King because he speaks their dialect and likes to consort with them in taverns, but there is no love lost between the King and Queen. She is a fine, proud princess of the House of Hapsburg, accustomed to refinements, and she does not tolerate his vulgarities and low behaviour. Once, he said, the Queen forced the King to go to the Opera House instead of the *Opera Buffa* where Giancola, the King's favourite comic actor, was performing. After the first act, and even before they had drawn the curtain, the King – in the royal box and in full view of everyone – started eating *maccheroni* with his hands, just like a man of the streets. The Queen was so angry that she jumped up and left the theatre. The courtiers were all thunderstruck. They didn't know what to do – whether they should follow the Queen or stay there with the King. The whole of Naples laughed for weeks!"

"So what did the King do?" asked an astonished Eugenio, who was usually kept busy attending the Cardinal and was thus excluded from the kitchen gossip.

"Well, Father Biagio said he just carried on eating. Down in the pit, the low fellows – they're known as *Lazzari* – were delighted. They started cheering: *Evviva Re Nasone!* – that's *Long Live King Beaky!* They call him that because he has a very prominent snout (much worse than our master's). He doesn't mind. It amuses him. But behind his back," and Gigi lowered his voice and spoke into Eugenio's ear, "they also call him *rrè de cuorne* – that means the king of cuckolds. They say the Queen has an English gentleman for a lover. She has made him her prime minister and they rule the kingdom together. The King doesn't interfere because he prefers hunting and fishing to the affairs of state.

"So the people love the King but they don't love the Queen. They call her the Austrian woman. They say she is cold and unfeeling and that she plots to overthrow France and unite the Austrians with the British, whom the people do not like or trust."

At that moment, Henry rapped sharply on the roof of the carriage with his cane and although they knew that he could not possibly have overheard any of their conversation, both servants started guiltily, knowing how he hated idle tales. However, he was simply drawing their attention to the sight of the volcano.

They had come out into a vast open square that led gently down to the bay, where the sea stretched tranquil, deep blue and sparkling, far off into the horizon. The whole company came to a halt to admire the vista opening up before them. A wide, paved road swept round the seashore, bordered with public gardens planted by King Ferdinand's father, Charles III of Spain. Behind them, the city climbed up steep hillsides crowned with the majestic Charterhouse of San Martino and the Sant'Elmo fortress. But all their attention was concentrated on the bayside where Vesuvius rose, almost at the city gates, cone-shaped and broken tipped, cobalt blue against the sky and lazily breathing out tiny plumes of white smoke.

"Look, Henry," Cesarini said, adopting the familiarity of old friends since they were alone together in the coach. "There's the sleeping monster. I heard that it erupts frequently. There was a great explosion only a few years ago! Lord Hamilton, the British ambassador, who has studied the phenomenon, estimated that it sent up a column of ash that rose over two miles into the air. At the time, many people were killed and many towns were destroyed."

Henry studied the volcano in silence. Even at this distance, he could see that the slopes were covered in vineyards. People had returned after the disaster. They had rebuilt their homes on the same spots as before.

As if reading his thoughts, Don Angelo remarked, "Many people think it strange that the people continue to live on the flank of a dangerous, unfriendly mountain, but the peasants here are very devout. They resign themselves to the will of God. They have a great faith in the protection of their patron saint, St Januarius – the people call him San Gennaro. His blood is kept in an ampoule in the Cathedral and liquefies every year as a sign that he will keep them safe."

"Let us hope then that he will look on us as well with favour," Henry remarked dryly.

Cesarini nodded, but without conviction. He was uncertain whether the Cardinal was being serious or whether he was poking fun at him. He knew that Henry tended to deride the simple religious rituals practised by his lowliest parishioners, saying these were linked to ancient pagan rites and superstitions and that they had nothing to do with the true faith. Henry fancied himself as a modern man, open to the new ideas of the Enlightenment that were sweeping Europe. Cesarini, however, crossed himself, thinking it better to be on the safe side. It was not wise to mock the saints.

During the second half of the 18th century, a series of disasters, including a drought and a famine, an eruption of Vesuvius and outbreaks of cholera, had driven masses of starving peasants to abandon the impoverished countryside for the Neapolitan capital. At the time of Henry's arrival, Naples' population had swelled to some three to four hundred thousand, making it the largest city in the Italian peninsula and the third biggest city in Europe, after London and Paris. The immigrant masses were crammed into overcrowded slums in the city centre and sprawling shanty towns climbing up the surrounding hillsides. They lived in conditions of bare survival, exploited by unscrupulous middlemen and landlords.

But this was only one face of the city. Reigning over the misery of the warren-like streets was the richest, most glittering and most cultured court of continental Europe. The ruling House of Bourbon of the Kingdom of Naples and Sicily lived in a state of splendour that rivalled Vienna and pre-revolutionary Versailles. The city was full of palaces, monumental churches and works of art. It boasted the oldest public lay university in the world, a botanical garden, prestigious libraries and scientific institutions, as well as four renowned music conservatories that attracted students from all over Europe. There were three opera houses, including the sumptuous San Carlo, built by the Bourbons adjoining the royal palace, but open to the general public.

Entertainment abounded to suit all tastes, ranging from refined recitals in the private salons of noble palaces, to improvised street performances and raunchy comedies centred round *Pulcinello,* a traditional masque personifying a plebeian good-for-nothing that the *Lazzari* identified as an alter ego. Contrary to many other countries of the period, women sang and acted alongside men in the popular *Commedia dell'Arte* theatres. The *Opera Buffo* specialized in comedy performances where masters and servants were on an equal footing, reflecting the new trends of the Enlightenment and the genre was copied all over Europe.

Charles Bourbon, the son of Philip V of Spain, had inherited the kingdom after the Spanish conquered Naples and Sicily in 1735. He immediately launched an ambitious building programme which his son Ferdinand IV had continued. During a half century of expansion and reconstruction, elegant new residential quarters were built outside the cramped city walls and streets were widened and paved with brick. Several new royal palaces were constructed to add more lustre to the monarchy, including the vast hunting reserve at Portici and the royal residence of Capodimonte, built as a show place for the prestigious Farnese collection of antiquities that Charles Bourbon had inherited from his mother, Elisabetta Farnese. The most splendid of them all was the vast summer palace of Caserta with its magnificent gardens and fountains.

No young aristocrat from Northern Europe would have dreamt of giving Naples a miss on his Grand Tour. Archaeological excavations, funded by Charles, had begun at the buried city of Herculaneum in 1738, to be followed a decade later at Pompeii. By the mid-1750s, both sites were opened to the public. Tourists looked forward to the thrill of climbing up Vesuvius and picking their way around the fumaroles of the fiery fields in the Phlegraean Plain. They wandered among the ruins of the ancient Roman cities and marvelled at the rare works of Greek and Roman art in the Capodimonte Palace.

Henry had rented a spacious mansion house on the fashionable Via Toledo, near the Royal Palace, where he settled down with his household to await events. He found himself in good company.

Many other high-ranking clerics had taken up residence nearby and in no time his house became the focus of streams of visitors, some imploring help, others simply begging for news.

A couple of days after his arrival, a servant in court livery arrived with an invitation from the First Minister, Lord Acton, begging the honour to invite His Royal Highness the Cardinal Duke of York to luncheon on the morrow. At first, Henry was somewhat piqued to receive an invitation from the minister, rather than the King and Queen, but he felt that as he was a guest in this country it would be churlish to refuse. He was also curious to meet this Englishman, known to be the Queen's right hand and the true power behind the throne.

Any reservations he might have had were immediately overcome by the honour that Acton accorded him. A richly accoutred palanquin, with an escort in royal livery, was sent to fetch him, even though the minister's house was situated not more than two or three hundred yards away from the Cardinal's residence. The English lord met him personally on the doorstep, bowing deeply to kiss his ring and bidding him welcome.

John Acton was a tall man in his sixties, sparely built and with a long, thin face. He had the high colouring of his race with the characteristic blotches of red on his cheekbones, which he disdained to conceal under powder. He wore no wig and his thinning grey hair was simply combed back and tied with a black ribbon at the nape of his neck. His most noticeable feature was his eyes, light coloured and half hidden under heavily drooping lids, but gleaming reflected light and in constant restless movement. He was plainly dressed and if Henry had not known the power that he wielded at the Neapolitan court, he might have mistaken him for a steward or doorman.

Acton's manners were restrained but impeccable as he guided his guest through his mansion house towards the dining room. He conveyed the apologies of the King and Queen, who had been unable to receive him immediately, as they would have wished, 'due to incumbent and impellent commitments that had arisen connected with present particular difficulties.' He enquired after their journey from Rome and hoped he and his entourage would find their sojourn in Naples pleasant, albeit enforced by circumstances. He said it was a pleasure for him to be able to converse in his native language – "The only people who speak it here are the English soldiers sent to defend our ports so I have little opportunity to discourse on serious subjects with persons of superior standing such as yourself."

During the meal, however, Acton skilfully avoided touching on any subject that might have been described as 'serious'. This did not surprise Henry. It was the mark of a skilled diplomat, whose every move was ruled by caution. Henry knew that his presence in Naples could be an embarrassment to the minister, who was committed to maintaining good relationships with the British crown. The London Parliament, he suspected, had already been informed of his arrival and although, contrary to his brother Charles Edward, he had never posed a direct threat to the Hanoverian establishment, the mere mention of the name of Stuart still resounded darkly in many quarters.

He therefore took his cue from the minister and kept the conversation light. He complimented him on the quality of his champagne, which, Acton explained, could still be obtained from the best French cellars, smuggled into port by seamen in the French navy, under the very noses of their officers. "The officers turn a blind eye, of course. Naturally, they have their reasons," and he gave a thin smile, raising his eyebrow in a knowing gesture.

The meal was lavish, but both men ate sparingly, waving aside the silver platters of oysters, octopus, sardines and fried cod, the roast turkey and veal, the pheasant baked with figs, the rice sartù and the *maccheroni,* served with a sauce made from tomatoes, which Acton said were now successfully cultivated on local soil.

"At first, people were afraid to eat them. They believed they were poisonous. But now they are considered a great delicacy and our cooks have learned to use them in many dishes," the minister explained as he captured a few strings of noodles daintily with his fork and lifted them to his mouth.

Henry obliged by taking a few mouthfuls of the many unfamiliar culinary concoctions placed before him, as well as the numerous rich desserts, but he was relieved when at last the ice cold lemon sorbet arrived and the bowls of peaches, cherries and apricots were set on the table alongside the dried fruits and nuts, indicating that the meal was over.

John Acton conversed pleasantly throughout. He said that Henry must visit the buried city that had been excavated by the father of the present king, with Roman houses full of treasures, sculptures and painted walls, buried under layers of volcanic ash deposited during the great eruption described many centuries before by Pliny.

"If you are interested in antiquities, Your Excellency, the British Envoy, Lord Hamilton, has a notable collection that I am sure he will be glad to show you once you make his acquaintance. He also collects works by our most eminent artists that you may enjoy viewing. I believe that he has well over three hundred paintings. Our city has much to offer to the discriminating visitor."

When he took his leave, Henry inquired politely after the health of the King and Queen as a tactful reminder of the awaited invitation. Acton, understanding him perfectly, replied with equal tact that they were well, and that Her Majesty in particular was anxious to meet him, but she was much troubled by recent events and fearful for the safety of her family. She occupied a great deal of her time studying the progress of the war on her borders, receiving dispatches and consulting her ministers and generals.

Henry was surprised to hear no mention of the King in this context and Acton, seeming to read his thoughts, momentarily let slip his habitual courtier's mask of caution and spoke confidentially:

"King Ferdinand is a lighter spirit. He does not enjoy listening to talk of war. He has other interests. But I am sure, if you remain here in our city for some time, you will hear many tales about our monarchs. Do not, I pray you, pay too much attention. Much of it is slander and a man of sense and experience like yourself will be able, I am sure, to distinguish between idle gossip and what may be true."

He looked directly at Henry with his steady grey eyes. His voice dropped low, becoming almost a murmur, so that Henry had to strain his ears to catch what he was saying. "Our Queen is not loved because she is the daughter of Maria Teresa, the Austrian empress. Her ways are very different from the ways of the people of the south and are often misunderstood. I, myself," and here he gave a little cough, "as a northerner, have often encountered similar difficulties. She comes from a cultured court, more open – may I say – to modern and progressive ideas. She has tried to do good. You shall no doubt be invited to Caserta for the summer as it gets too hot here for comfort. You should visit the Royal Silk factory there. You will see many things that will surprise you."

The minister hesitated again and then resumed in a firmer tone. "If I may presume to offer you a word of advice, do not use the French language when you are in her company. She has refused to speak it ever since she heard of the savage execution of her sister, Marie Antoniette, whom she loved dearly. She will not suffer to hear any reference to France. Many illustrious visitors have made this mistake and she has always brought the interview abruptly to an end. Speak to her in Italian – or in German, if you know the language. You will also find that she speaks English fairly well."

During the next few days, Henry waited with some impatience for the royal invitation to arrive. He had expected a warmer welcome from what he considered his cousin kings, due to his rank and ecclesiastical standing, but time passed and no summons came. He filled in the long hours by getting to know the city. He visited the great churches, which astonished him with their magnificence, surpassing even those of Rome in splendour and riches, and climbed up the Vomero hill to the celebrated Charterhouse of San Martino to contemplate the sweeping view of the bay and the city far below.

He hired an open landau for drives along the sea front in the evenings when it was cool, taking only Moretto as his driver. Sometimes he ordered the Boy to harness up his team of blacks, which were getting fat and heavy through lack of exercise. The horses, however, were not content to adapt to the sedate progress imposed by the ritualistic evening promenade. They tossed their heads and stamped their feet impatiently and Moretto had to struggle sometimes to keep them reined in. He told his master that they were longing for the wild, free gallops through the Roman countryside which the Lord Cardinal indulged in when he had urgent business in the city.

These leisurely excursions, however, raised Henry's spirits as he liked to observe the common people out strolling. Men and women walked arm in arm, chatting animatedly and handing each other posies. Little groups would suddenly burst into song and dance, accompanied by the music of mandolins and tambourines, and spectators would form a ring around them, applauding and cheering. He envied the fact that they seemed able to forget the toils and trials of the day so easily, throwing themselves into simple pleasures and untroubled companionship. as if they were unaware that tomorrow might bring no work and therefore no food on the table, as if there were no savage wars raging in Europe, as if the Holy Father, pinnacle of the Church, had not been abducted and the very structure of their faith threatened by atheist philosophers and law-makers. By contrast, when he visited his fellow prelates, he found the palaces and mansions of the rich draped in an atmosphere of gloom, with pale and worried faces flitting along the corridors, and where both servants and masters spoke hurriedly in muted voices, glancing furtively over their shoulders.

The sense of peace that he had found was abruptly shattered early one morning, when Cesarini unexpectedly came into his room to tell him that Giuseppe Zossi, a footman who had been in his service for over forty years, had died through the night.

Henry rose at once, calling for Eugenio and Moretto to dress him. They came in, befuddled and half asleep, no doubt, Henry thought in annoyance, after a night of drinking and carousing at a tavern, and they were so slow that he became impatient and simply had them pull on his dressing gown. He hurried downstairs to the kitchen, where he found the corpse of the old servant laid out on the marble table used for cutting meat. His anger became a rage and he railed at his men, who were huddled close to the walls, visibly frightened.

"How did this happen? Why I was not called?" he shouted at them.

When no one replied, he became even angrier. "Is it possible that none of you were here with him? That he died alone without comfort?"

Don Angelo stepped forward, attempting to calm him. "I confessed him at Mass only yesterday and absolved him. He was an old man, a good and dutiful servant. Rest assured, he died in a state of grace."

But Henry would not be comforted. He remembered how he had noted Zossi's laboured breathing even before they left Frascati, but the old man never complained and he had subsequently forgotten to enquire about his state of health. He blamed himself bitterly for taking him along and submitting him to the rigours of their journey, which had obviously proved too much for his frail and ailing body. Numbly, he composed the dead man's features and traced the sign of the cross on his cold forehead. As his sense of shock abated, grief flowed through him. Until now, he had managed to hold his Family together, preserving them from dangers. But now he had lost his first battle to conduct them all safe back home again when the right time came and Napoleon was defeated. There was no remedy for death, no second chance. Behind his back, he became aware of his men shuffling their feet and muttering. The farm boys clustered together with terrified faces. He knew they were ignorant and superstitious. They would interpret Zossi's death as a curse laid over the whole company. He was tempted to dismiss them immediately and send them home but then he reflected that they would be lost. They were like sheep without a leader. He could not consign them blindly to the French who were now occupying their homes, eating their corn and stealing their livestock.

So he called for calm. He said they had to organise a worthy burial for an old companion, who had reached the end of his allotted days and been recalled to God the Father. He conducted the funeral mass personally, in the private chapel of their residence, with his whole Family present and Zossi was laid to rest in the crypt of the nearly church of St Nicholas the Charitable.

The Queen of Naples

Finally, the long-awaited invitation to the Palace arrived, written in Queen Maria Carolina's own hand and sealed with her seal. She said she was anxious to meet her dear Brother King informally, in private audience.

Unfamiliar with Naples court etiquette, he hesitated about appearing in his Cardinal's robes. He told Eugenio to dress him in his purple coat and gold brocade waistcoat, with black velvet breeches and his red-heeled shoes. He had his team of black horses harnessed to his carriage with its royal insignia, and took a small escort of men-at-arms in dress livery, with MacLaren marching at their head playing his pipes. As they made their way slowly down Via Toledo towards the Royal Palace, curious crowds gathered. Small children ran alongside their procession, pointing at their mouths to indicate they were hungry. This time, however, he did not give the signal to throw out coins to them as he usually did. The street was so packed that he was afraid the little ones would be crushed in the rush to pick up the money.

Since the meeting was to be informal, he allowed only Don Angelo and his servant Moretto to accompany him inside, while the rest of his men waited in the forecourt, complaining of the overwhelming stench of rotten fish, refuse and excrements wafting up from the nearby harbour.

"You can tell these great folk don't have much sense," Annibale muttered. "Even my mother, who was as ignorant as a sheep, God bless her, would have known not to build right next to the port. Just look at it – all this grand palace and they didn't even know to face it towards the morning sun."

"Well, they can't open their windows, that's for sure," said Eugenio, with his kerchief pressed over his nose.

"Great folk never have any sense!" MacLaren re-joined. "They are too occupied with boosting their own grandeur."

"Our lord is sensible enough!" Eugenio retorted in a reproachful voice.

"Well, he's an exception!" MacLaren replied. "Look at Albani, hanging on at his villa because of his plants and ornaments. Much good it did him! And the others are just as bad. All arriving here in haste and disorder. I wonder the city can contain them all!"

Despite the presumed unsuitability of its site, the royal palace had been built to impress. It was a monument to the glory of the Spanish Bourbon house, with a massive 550ft-long facade that ran along one side of a vast open space, used each day for military drills. Inside the palace, no expense had been spared. Precious crystal chandeliers hung from the lavishly frescoed ceilings, the floors gleamed with rare coloured marbles, set in geometric patterns, and the tall windows were draped in curtains of sumptuous silk brocade and velvet.

John Acton was waiting to greet Henry at the foot of the great marble Stairway of Honour, flanked by two footmen and followed by a dwarf. The little man was elaborately dressed in a long silk coat and a waistcoat embroidered with flowers in gold and silver thread. He had gold tassels dangling from the knees of his breeches and a fashionable cocked hat topped with ostrich feathers on his head. He carried an ivory-topped cane that was a whole head taller than himself and wore pointed silk shoes with such high heels that he advanced with the swaying gait of a wader bird.

Acton bent his knee to kiss the Cardinal's ring, and then moved to stand on one side while the dwarf hobbled forward, doffing his hat and bowing so deeply that his ostrich feathers swept the floor.

"Welcome, Your Majesty," he said in a high piping voice. "I am sent personally by her gracious Majesty Queen Maria Carolina to welcome you and guide you to the chamber where she awaits you. Allow me to present myself. I am Don Rodrigo Constantino Ferdinando Giovanni Severino Raffaelo Bellego della Torre. As you can see, my name compensates my height!"

He straightened and looked up with a sideways glance. Henry stood motionless for a moment, taken by surprise. He had not expected to be met by the court dwarf and he wondered fleetingly if he was the victim of one of King Ferdinand's jokes. Only the presence of John Acton, who stood unsmiling and apparently unperturbed, stopped him from turning on his heel and walking back the way they had come. The little man looked up at him grinning, a gleam of malice in his narrow green eyes, and Henry realised that he had guessed what he was thinking and that he was enjoying the Cardinal's discomfort.

He studied the little man coolly for a moment and decided that, although he was a midget, Don Rodrigo was not simply a Queen's pet, but a person who counted at court. His clothes were costly and impeccably cut to suit his small and short-legged build. A miniature sword with a jewelled-eyed panther carved on the hilt hung on a scarlet sash that crossed his shoulder and chest. He wore a ridiculous wig that resembled a piece of confectionary, elaborately styled to end in a tall, sweeping cone, freshly curled over his ears and powdered to a snowy white. At first glance, he was the epitome of the court jester, kept for amusement, like a dog or a cat, a harmless ornament to be flaunted before foreign visitors such as himself.

Henry ran his eyes over the upturned visage. The dwarf's face was set in an expression of guileless deference but he noticed that the eyes that briefly met his own were sharp and astute. Henry had met that kind of look many times, ever since he was a boy, and he had learned to recognise the veiled cunning glance of an informer. So the Queen, his 'dear sister', as she called herself, had not trusted him but she had sent her spy to weigh him up.

He became aware that Cesarini was red in the face with embarrassment and that Moretto was struggling not to laugh. He understood that his two followers believed that this small and unorthodox welcome committee was an insult and expected him to turn and leave. However, his curiosity was aroused and it over-ruled any misgivings he had with regard to propriety or due respect for his rank.

With an imperious gesture, he signalled them to wait where they were, while he went on alone. The silent John Acton fell in respectfully a few paces behind him while the little man led them slowly up the Stairway of Honour and through a succession of vast high-ceilinged rooms decorated with riotous and exuberant scenes of historical and mythological episodes, representing scenes of Bourbon conquests, ancestral deeds of glory, gods and heroes, angels and nymphs, virgins, saints and martyrs, all posing, gesturing and cavorting inside elaborate stuccoed and gilded cornices.

As they walked through room after room filled with sculptures and works of art positioned among precious cabinets, tables, armchairs and vetrinettes, all intricately inlaid with designs in slivers of coloured marble, gem stones and sea shells, the dwarf, who plainly wished to impress the cardinal from Rome, pointed out paintings by celebrated Neapolitan and foreign masters, precious tapestries, made, he said proudly, not in France, but at the Royal Bourbon workshop, set up by the King with the looms he had transferred from the Grand Duchy of Florence. The magnificent brocade drapes, embroidered in gold and silver thread, were also produced in Naples, he said, at the royal Manufacturer of San Leucio, which was Her Majesty's special project. The rooms were a succession of showpieces of ancient Greek and Roman sculptures from various inherited royal collections, set among alabaster urns, gold candelabras, jewelled clocks, porcelain statuettes and other *objets d'art*.

Henry paused to admire many things. He was intrigued by a skilfully designed London clock with a carillon and moving figures, as well as the displays of porcelain figurines of fishermen, hawkers, milkmaids, shoemakers, smiths and other street characters, created at the royal workshop of Capodimonte. He had never seen anything like them before. In Rome, they would have been considered inappropriate in the reception rooms of noble houses.

"Our King likes to honour the common people," remarked Don Rodrigo, with just a hint of a sneer in his voice, as he turned his head away and busied himself with his gold snuffbox. "Our Queen is of another nature!"

The fact that the King of Naples preferred low company to that of highborn courtiers was well known, even to Henry, who heard more gossip than he would care to admit, and he also knew that the King's preferences were a constant source of irritation to his refined Austrian wife. Ferdinand was also known to love childish practical jokes, and York, in fact, had personally witnessed one of his pranks. One morning, looking down from his window onto Via Toledo, he had seen the King with his own eyes, alone and driving his pony and trap along the crowded street while he threw handfuls of sugar almonds to the passers-by. However, a few of these sweets turned out to be sugar-coated pebbles that the unwary bit into, breaking their teeth. Henry had watched in disapproval as these unfortunates ran off howling and cursing among a chorus of jeers and hilarity.

They were moving through another vast hall when Henry's attention was caught by a life-size painting of the royal family, posed in an idealised bucolic setting. The King stood at ease, with his gun propped casually at his side and his dogs at his feet, while the Queen sat solemnly among her children. Don Rodrigo stopped at once and pointed with his cane.

"I see this interests Your Majesty," he said. "It is a work by the famous lady artist Angelika Kauffmann. I have been told that you are a great patron of the arts and that you frequented her studio in Rome."

Acton glanced at Henry to see if he had taken offense, but he was too absorbed examining the portrait to wonder how the dwarf could have got hold of this information. His friend Madame Kauffmann had painted with her usual delicacy and skill. The group was charming, a depiction of an ideal family and the image that rulers of the enlightened age would wish to project.

"You see there our gracious King Ferdinand, with his dogs – his great passion is hunting, as you no doubt have heard!" the dwarf intoned, as if reciting in a theatre. "That is our Queen Maria Carolina – a true beauty, you will agree. And these are the royal children. There is the Princess Maria Teresa with her harp and that is Prince Francis, the eldest, growing up to be a fine little king! Princess Maria Cristina – we call her Mimi – is the one standing beside her mother and that is the little Prince Januarius – named in honour of our blessed saint, the protector of our city of Naples. These other two children are Princess Maria Luisa, holding in her lap her small sister, Princess Maria Amelia – she was only two years old at the time this was painted. You will agree that this is a splendid representation of our noble king and his family."

The Cardinal, lost in his own thoughts and memories, seemed oblivious to the confidential tone that Don Rodrigo had assumed and which normally he would have considered bordering on insolence, simply nodded. He reflected that it would be difficult to find a more delightful portrayal of a family in peace and harmony. From what he had heard of the Bourbons, he knew that the reality was quite different, but he found it entirely understandable that they desired to leave a pleasing vision of themselves for posterity.

As if he had read his mind, the dwarf's voice dropped and he continued in a more sombre tone:

"Alas! There is also a sad tragedy in this painting. Observe the baby carriage behind Princess Maria Luisa. That should have contained the baby prince Joseph, but he died just before the portrait was finished. The child is still there, lying on these pillows, but Madame Kauffmann painted a veil over his face. You can see it if you look carefully."

He looked briefly up into Henry's face, his thick lips pushed out in an expression of regret. "Our Queen has favoured the realm with many children, but half of them have died. Luckily, she is of sturdy Austrian stock and recovers every time."

Henry had stopped listening. His thoughts were elsewhere. Turning away, he murmured absently to himself: "Madame Zucchi, my dear Angelica. How have you fared? I heard you were still in Rome when the French arrived. I pray you have come to no harm."

"You need not grieve, my Lord Cardinal," Don Rodrigo purred like a cat. "I have it on good authority that the lady was able to put her talents to good use."

At this sly remark, Henry's face darkened. He had been vaguely aware of the subtle tone of confidence that the diminutive courtier had assumed as they strolled together through the rooms, but he had ignored it. He considered it beneath his dignity to be provoked by a being who was inferior to himself in rank. But now he felt that the dwarf had gone too far. It was plain what he was insinuating. Angelika Kauffmann, the famous and respected artist, had been a good friend of his. The studio that she kept with her husband, Antonio Zucchi, had been a gathering place for artists, writers and poets and he had enjoyed long afternoons there conversing with Antonio Canova, the sculptor, the German poet Goethe and Pompeo Batoni, the artist who had painted the portrait of himself that he had commissioned as a gift for his brother Charles.

Seeing him frown, the little man immediately changed his tune.

"I speak of her talents as an artist, of course," he said, all innocence. "She has found a protector in the French General Augustin de Lespinasse, who is deeply in favour with the Corsican. She has painted his portrait and continues to hold her admired salon where the highest of society clamour to be admitted. They say her collection of paintings is equal to none, and that the Holy Father himself sighs to possess her St Jerome by the great Leonardo da Vinci."

Henry frowned even deeper. He was unaccustomed to being addressed with such familiarity by a servant and he was both surprised and offended. The dwarf must indeed enjoy great favour with the Queen if he could permit himself such liberties, he thought. However, he suppressed his mounting feelings of irritation and merely turned away without replying, If Don Rodrigo – or whoever his true masters were – had been hoping to extract some sort of information out of the Cardinal, he had not succeeded and Henry noted with satisfaction the grimace of disappointment that flitted for an instance across the little man's face.

Nothing more was said while they walked the rest of the way to the Throne Room, where two bowing footmen stood waiting to open the gilded doors. The throne, at the far end of the vast hall, stood empty under its canopy of cloth of gold, the sign that this was not, in fact, to be a formal audience. Other footmen came to lead them to a small side room, where Maria Carolina sat waiting with an embroidery frame on her lap, while two of her ladies sat near her sewing. Behind her chair stood a black slave moving a fan gently and rhythmically up and down behind her head. John Acton kissed her hand and then withdrew discreetly to the other side of the room, while the dwarf, bent over and walking backwards, his ostrich feather trailing on the ground, left them. There was no sign of her husband, the King.

Henry had to suppress a pang of regret when he saw the Neapolitan queen. She had once been renowned as a great beauty, with a skin of milk and roses, large blue eyes and a slim and graceful figure, as, in fact, she had appeared in the portrait he had just seen. But the years had gone by and she was now well into middle age. Her many pregnancies had left her stout, with heavy jowls under her chin. Her bosom was carefully powdered and pushed up high by her stays but the lacy flounces around her collar only partially concealed the flaccid and puckering skin. Her blue eyes had narrowed, weighed down by drooping lids and the rosy colouring of her cheeks was artificially applied. She was sumptuously dressed in a heavy brocade gown with such enormous panniers flowing out over the arms of her chair that Henry doubted she would be able to rise without the help of her ladies. She wore earrings of matching pearl droplets and an elaborate white wig, decorated with jewels and flowers.

She looked up from her work and studied him for a moment, and then she invited him to come nearer, offering him her cheek to kiss. "Dear brother," she said in Italian. "The King and I are very happy to finally make your acquaintance. My husband is not here and I apologise for his absence, but, as you probably know – as everyone in Naples knows – he is always busy with harmless pursuits that do little for the good of his country, especially in these times of danger with a tyrant threatening our borders."

This unexpected greeting took Henry aback and he did not know how to reply.

The Queen looked at him with the hint of a malicious glint in her eye. She indicated he should take the chair next to her, which one of her ladies-in-waiting hastily vacated.

"I see I have disconcerted you, my Lord Cardinal. You need not be so prim. We are cousins, are we not – brothers in royalty. We should understand each other better."

She paused thoughtfully and fingered a corner of her embroidery.

"My husband is rarely here, as I am sure you have been told. I wish to God that he were more diligent. I would have preferred him to do everything by himself, but his life of distractions makes it impossible for him to attend to his duties!"

Before he could find anything to say, she went on tell him that she regretted she had been unable to receive him earlier but his arrival in Naples had coincided with that of many other fugitives, including (and here she made the sign of the cross) the late King of France's two elderly aunts who had required every assistance.

"You cannot imagine the trouble I was put to for these two pitiable old maids! They came with a suite of eighty courtiers and servants. I did not know where to put them. We are already crowded out in Naples. I had to move many of my own people out of our Palace of Caserta to free up the rooms. It was all extremely tiresome!"

Henry murmured a polite reply. He was at a loss how to proceed with the conversation. From the other end of the room, Lord Acton caught his eye and gave a small shrug.

The door opened quietly and a servant came in bearing a tray with glasses and a Venetian decanter that he set down on a small table at Henry's side, while one of the ladies rose and came forward ready to pour. Henry tried to refuse, saying he did not drink in the morning, but the Queen waved away his protests.

"I hope you will not offend my country by refusing to taste the sweet wine of Vesuvius. I can assure you that it is excellent and it soothes my nerves more readily than the opium my doctor prescribes for me. Come Acton," she called, raising a hand. "You will do us the honour of joining us, I hope!"

Lord Acton bowed and came forward to take the small glass of wine that had been prepared for him. He offered a toast to Her Majesty that Henry felt obliged to second. The Queen, however, took only a few sips before she handed her glass back to her maid. Her mood had changed. She sighed and launched into the usual conventions, enquiring about his health and how he had stood up to the journey. She said she had felt very sorry to hear of all his trials and hoped his stay in Naples would not prove too tedious. In reply, he expressed his profound gratitude for the safe haven that she and the King had given him and thanked Their Majesties for their hospitality and kindness.

Towards the end of this exchange, Maria Carolina began to move restlessly in her chair, showing signs of impatience. Believing he had overstayed his welcome, the Cardinal began to rise, but she put out a hand to detain him. Leaning towards him, she fixed him with a keen stare so that he was forced to look straight back into her hooded blue eyes.

She said, "I have heard much of your poor brother, the Prince, and how he attempted to regain his kingdom. When I was a young girl in my home in Vienna, he was my hero! My sisters and I often talked of him and how he hid in the hills from his enemies and commanded so much love that no one betrayed him, not even the poorest clansman, despite the great price set upon his head. He must have been a man of exceptional charm and ability."

Henry bowed in acknowledgement. The mention of his brother's name always saddened him, but he was gratified to hear him praised. The Queen sat silently for another long moment, playing with the rings on her fingers.

Finally, she said, "I heard of the death of your brave brother Charles. They tell me the circumstances were unfortunate."

"He had been ill for some time, Madame. Our Lord in his mercy thought fit to release him from his suffering."

A strange glint came into the Queen's eyes, which seemed to deepen and change from blue to grey.

"We were told his desperation stemmed from the conduct of his wife," she said.

Henry was caught off guard. He flushed red and began to cough.

"Indeed, his marriage ended in very unfortunate circumstances," he replied after a pause while he regained his composure.

Maria Carolina kept her gaze fixed steadily on him. "Certainly, for her to run off with that Italian poet was a great insult to his honour," she remarked.

Henry did not reply, but he was deeply offended. He raised his head and looked at her coldly. Lord Acton, who had stayed nearby, bent down and whispered a few words in her ear. The Queen waved him away impatiently but she changed her tone.

"But we of the royal blood are indeed unfortunate," she said after a moment. "We have so little choice over our destinies. Would you not agree, my dear brother?"

The Cardinal coughed again, passing his kerchief over his mouth.

"We are all in the hands of God," he said finally.

"Said like a true priest, Your Grace!" she said. Her maids put their hands under her elbows to help her to rise and distribute the folds of her dress while Lord Acton offered her his arm.

The interview was at an end. The Cardinal was dismissed and made his way thankfully to the door, where Don Rodrigo was waiting, with a sly smile on his face, to conduct him back through the rooms to the Stairway of Honour.

Emma Hamilton's 'Attitudes'

Although Henry would have preferred to mix as little as possible with the court and Neapolitan society, he felt obliged to attend events whenever he received a personal invitation from the Queen or from Lord Acton. He therefore decided that he could not refuse to present himself at a reception in Villa Sessa, the home of the British Envoy, Sir William Hamilton, who was known to be an intimate friend of the royal family's.

Henry knew that Lord Hamilton was an avid collector of antiquities and works of art. He was known to be a respected scholar, as well as a Fellow of the prestigious Royal Academy of London, with interests in many branches of the sciences. He looked forward to the opportunity of viewing Sir William's celebrated collection of Etruscan, Greek and Roman vases and discussing, if the occasion presented itself, his observations on Vesuvius and Etna and the bubbling caldera of Puteoli.

He also knew that Lord Hamilton had a young wife, Emma, who was a close companion of the Queen's. He had heard that she was very beautiful. The scandalmongers of the court said that she had been a whore before she had bewitched the aged lord and inveigled him into marrying her. Henry, however, despised gossips and talebearers and dismissed the stories as the typical malicious tattle of idle courtiers and sycophants.

Cesarini, who tended instead to lend an ear to servants' talk, was less conciliatory.

"Henry," he said, when the servants were out of hearing. "I do not think it wise that you, a Prince of our Holy Mother Church, should attend revels in the house of a foreigner we know little about. These Englishmen have different customs from us. What they consider acceptable may not be so by our moral code."

He lowered his voice and cupped his hand around his mouth, glancing furtively around in case the rascal Moretto, or even the prim Eugenio, was listening behind the door. "I have heard that the Lady Hamilton is of very low extraction – the daughter of a blacksmith. She has even changed her name. She was born Amy Lyon but she changed it to Emma Hart to appear more refined. This alone shows that she was bent on following the most ignoble and degenerate trade of women. Before poor Lord Hamilton, bereaved by the loss of his dear wife of twenty years and no doubt failing in the judgement and acumen of his younger years, was seduced by this siren…"

But at this point, Henry abruptly cut him off. "You are not obliged to come with me, Angelo, if meeting a siren is against your finest principles. I, however, would not insult Lord Hamilton by refusing his invitation, especially as we are guests here, dependent on the goodwill of our hosts," he concluded briskly.

In actual fact, his curiosity was piqued. Many of the Cardinals in the papal court had concubines – this was well known and accepted as a fact of life. 'The flesh is weak and many men are unable to live alone,' he thought. It had never been a cause of much scandal, as long as they were discreet. But he was intrigued by the fact that a great lord, descended from an ancient noble Scottish House, could have compromised his reputation by making a woman of ill repute his lawful wedded wife.

With much grumbling, Cesarini accompanied him, frowning disapprovingly when he saw that the Cardinal was not dressed in his scarlet-trimmed black soutane and his *zucchetto*, but was wearing a black velvet coat and breeches, scarlet silk stockings, his red-heeled shoes and a fashionable tricorn hat over his curled and powdered wig. His bottom lip protruding in protest, Don Angelo took his seat in the carriage opposite Henry and pointedly studied his book of daily devotionals during the entire ride up the Pizzofalcone Hill to the ambassador's residence. Henry contemplated him calmly, his hands folded over his diamond cross.

With a smile, he said in mild tones, "Angelo, dear friend, we are not going into the Gates of Hell. I will tell you a secret that should reassure you. We are actually going up the Mount of God – this is the true name of this hill."

Moretto, who was driving the carriage, emitted a snort which he immediately suppressed by turning it into a cough. Eugenio, on the footboard, looked studiously in another direction. Cesarini clapped his book shut and sat huffily, staring straight ahead.

Every room of the Hamilton's villa was blazing with lights and lanterns hung from the branches of the trees in the garden. Music from harpsichord and violin streamed out of the open windows. Footmen in formal livery lined the path leading up to the door, where the butler waited to welcome each arrival and announce their names. Lord and Lady Hamilton stood just inside the vast salon greeting the line of guests. Henry noted that Sir William was a tall man, slightly stooped but with an elegant deportment. His face was thin, with a high forehead and deep-set eyes under a straight line of thick black eyebrows. He wore a small wig, close fitted to his head, and full court dress, with a scarlet velvet jacket covered with the gold embroidered oak-leaves of his office.

Henry's eyes moved to his wife, who stood at his side. She was small, barely reaching her husband's shoulder, and slight. She did not wear a wig and as she curtseyed deeply before him, displaying the top of her head, he was struck with admiration at the mass of shining chestnut hair, skilfully dressed into a Grecian knot and decorated with a garland of white roses.

As she rose, she looked him candidly in the eyes, without coquetry or false modesty. Her skin was smooth as ivory and her cheeks were lightly touched with a soft pink bloom. Her small lips parted slightly to reveal a row of perfect teeth and she bid him welcome in Italian. Even Don Angelo, who was following him with a sullen expression on his face, was unable to resist her charm. His mouth twitching in an effort to suppress the smile that had appeared spontaneously on his lips when she addressed him, he hurriedly withdrew to a corner of the room behind some pillars, clutching his crucifix tightly to his chest.

Henry ignored him. Instead, he sat down on one of the gilded and tasselled armchairs arrayed around the centre of the floor, so that he could study the other guests. He noted with some amusement that many of the Roman Cardinals, who, among themselves had called Emma Hart a witch and a harlot, had been unable to resist the temptation of attending the Hamilton's soiree.

The evening wore on with dancing and music. Servants circulated constantly with plates of delicacies and crystal glasses of wine and port. Henry, who was at the best of times a poor eater, declined all the dishes, taking only a lemon ice to refresh his throat, which had become dry with the hot, sweat-laden air in the room. He watched with wonder and admiration as Lady Emma circulated in her role of graceful hostess, perfectly at ease. Amy Lyon, the blacksmith's daughter, seemed to fit effortlessly into the shoes of great lady. Anyone who did not know her history would have taken her for a baronet's daughter, raised in society and presented at court. He noted too how her elderly husband's eye followed her dotingly everywhere she went.

At a certain point, Sir William, who was a known to be a competent musician, took up his violin and entertained his guests with pieces from contemporary composers such as Haydn and Piccinni. He then moved onto a selection of melodious Neapolitan folk songs, which Emma sang in a sweet and vibrant voice, her hands crossed over her breast. The performance ended with thunderous applause and loud cheers from a group of young English officers, plainly inebriated and swaying on their feet.

Cesarini came out of his corner and sat down near him. He was red in the face and sweating heavily, moping his brow and cheeks with his lace kerchief. He looked enquiringly at Henry but the Cardinal seemed to have no intention of leaving just yet. With a sigh, Don Angelo sat back in his chair and resigned himself to a tedious wait.

Sir William went on to play some popular airs from the *opera buffo* repertoire, with one of the ladies accompanying him on the harpsichord, and Henry, who was fond of all music, sat tapping his cane softly in time. Finally, when the applause had died down, the Ambassador gave a sign. His servants moved to extinguish most of the candles, leaving the room dimly lit. Unnoticed by the guests, who had been absorbed in listening to the recital, a large dais, with a curtain around it, had been wheeled in and placed in front of an alcove at one side of the hall.

A signal was given to the musicians, who began to play softly while the curtain was drawn aside. The whole room gasped. Standing motionless on a dais, clad in a short tunic and with a bow and arrow in her hands, stood Emma Hamilton, impersonating the Roman goddess Diana. The ring of candles, hung suspended over her head, illuminated her face and her round white arm with the diffused light of morning sunshine seen through mist. After a long moment, she turned, graceful and lithe as a panther, to face her audience, pulled back the bow-string and released her arrow to land at the feet of the same group of noisy young officers, who scrambled and jostled each other to retrieve it. But before the winner could carry it back to the goddess, the curtain softly closed.

Henry and Don Angelo looked at each other. Angelo spread his hands out at his sides with a worried expression.

"This must be one of her famous 'Attitudes'," he said, with an apologetic cough. "I heard about them from… from…" his voice faltered. He did not want Henry to think he had been fraternising with his inferiors in the public squares, where, in fact, he had overheard passing groups commenting on 'the English lady and her scandalous ways'.

The curtain opened again, saving him from further embarrassment. This time Emma was posing as the Greek Princess Andromeda chained to her rock, where she writhed voluptuously in her bonds when a monster with a gigantic papier-mâché head and a gaping mouth emerged from a cavern under her feet, threatening her horribly. Then, at a signal, the masked Perseus, carrying his magic shield, leapt out from behind a pillar and pierced the monster with his lance, to the loud cheers of all the young gentlemen present. Andromeda, freed from her chains, descended from her dais and danced barefoot with her liberator, swirling her muslin veils around her head and body.

When she had finished, she sank down on the floor at her husband's feet. He was flushed and his protruding eyes were fixed on her in open adoration. The whole room burst into cheers and applause as he raised her up solicitously and led her out of the room on his arm.

Henry cast a sideways glance at Angelo who was gazing fixedly at the floor, muttering to himself:

"If this is not a house of sin, I don't know what is!" he whispered, trembling with indignation. "The very mistress of the house, with the compliance of her husband, exhibiting herself like a... like a..."

"A hetaera," said Henry, adopting the firm tones he used when he would brook no argument. "A hetaera – a much respected performer in Ancient Greece."

Although the performance had perturbed him, he did not find it in him to condemn it as licentious or even in poor taste. Of course, it would not have been tolerated in Rome, he thought, but then – what did he know? It was some years since he had frequented the theatres or the receptions of Roman society. And in Naples customs were obviously more liberal than they were under the shadow of the cupola of St Peter's.

Just as he was about to tell one of the footmen to call his carriage, Lord Hamilton's butler appeared to his side, bowing deeply.

"Your Grace," he said. "Lord Hamilton asks whether you would be interested in joining a small company to view some of the best pieces in his collection."

Henry immediately accepted. He knew that the Ambassador owned some of the most exquisite antiquities in the kingdom of Naples and he was eager to see them. Ignoring Don Angelo, who was scowling and shuffling his feet with impatience, he followed the butler through a series of small rooms and corridors to a small study. Hamilton was there with a group of six or seven *cognoscenti* who were admiring the decorated terracotta bowls and vases that he was taking out one by one from a series of inlaid ivory and ebony vetrinettes. "These objects once graced the house of some man of substance," the Ambassador was saying. "To think that they have lain buried and forgotten for many centuries! They survived the terrors and destruction of that great eruption described so vividly by Pliny while their owners were reduced to cinders. But we can see, by the great skill involved in making these objects, how well those people must have lived!"

"And this is the jewel of my collection," he said finally, as, with infinite care, he lifted out a splendid volute-krater in dark red and black, with exquisite figures of warriors and priestesses revolving around a white sepulchre containing the statue of a horseman. Hamilton caressed the sides, as he would have stroked the head of a beloved dog, gently tracing the outlines of the designs with his finger, and Henry recognised the possessive passion of the true collector, the lover of beautiful objects for their own sake alone. Not for the first time in his life, he had to struggle against the deadly sin of covetousness. There was nothing in his own collection to compare with the ancient vases extracted from the buried cities of the Kingdom of Naples.

"A god-like race of hero-men, who were called demi-gods, the race before our own, throughout the boundless earth," Hamilton murmured in reverent tones as he turned the vase slowly around in his hands.

"But," Henry said, picking up the quotation, "grim war and dread battle destroyed a part of them, some in the land of Cadmus at seven-gated Thebes…"

For the first time, Hamilton turned to look at him with frank interest. "I did not think, Your Grace, that Hesiod was part of the instructions of the Roman Church. However, you will remember the *seguito:* 'Only Hope remained there in an unbreakable home within the rim of the great jar and did not fly out of the door…'" and he ran his finger lightly around the rim of the krater in his hands before putting it carefully back on its shelf and closing the cabinet with a key that he put in his coat pocket.

Henry bowed his head with a smile. "You are right, of course, my Lord. Hope must always be cherished, even in these times of grim war and dread battle."

As he prepared to leave, Lord Hamilton grasped his hand with genuine warmth, urging him to visit Villa Sessa any time he wished and Emma Hamilton, who had joined them to bid the guests farewell, curtseyed deeply, echoing her husband's words. Henry thanked them for their splendid hospitality, but privately he thought that his friend Cesarini had been right: the Hamilton household was a place of temptation, if not perdition. It was not a fitting venue for a prince of the Church to frequent.

This opinion was reinforced when he got to his carriage and found that his men had strange smirks on their faces. He at once suspected that they had been able to witness Emma's performance through some peep-hole or concealed window in the servant's stair that overlooked the ballroom. Eugenio's face was flushed and MacLaren was obviously drunk, humming and swinging his legs in an undignified manner from his perch on the boot.

Henry settled back against the red velvet cushions with the uneasy feeling that he had been lax in his supervision since they came to Naples. He had been too preoccupied with the news of the war to pay attention to where his men went or what they did when he did not require their services. He imagined that they had just spent an unedifying evening in the kitchen, gossiping with the cooks and under-servants, imbibing rough wine and enquiring about the local whorehouses.

Caserta

June–August 1798

As the weather grew hotter, the stench from the harbour came drifting up as far as the Spanish Quarter. It wrapped itself, like an obnoxious presence, round the houses and palaces on Via Toledo, where the windows were left open at nights to allow in the cooler air of the evening. Candles were burned on the windowsills to discourage the flies and stinging insects, which had multiplied as the weeks progressed. The Cardinal could not sleep. His breath had become laboured and he suffered from an uncomfortable tightness in his chest. Moretto sat by his bed, fanning him in an attempt to bring him some relief.

The word finally arrived that the royal family would be moving to their country residence in Caserta, some twenty miles from Naples, where the air was more salubrious. It was a signal for all the illustrious refugees to move with the court out of the city. Henry gave his men orders to prepare for the exodus while Don Angelo went to find them lodgings at a monastic house near San Leucio.

A few days after their arrival, Acton sent a letter to say that the Queen invited His Majesty her brother to walk in the royal park at Caserta whenever he wished. In a footnote, with many apologies, Acton explained that this was a rare privilege, accorded to few guests because Her Majesty desired to live very quietly when she was in the country, away from the formalities of the court. She preferred to spend time with her younger children and seldom accorded audiences or saw people outside her intimate circle.

He, Acton, regretted that he could not offer the Cardinal his company, as he would be travelling back and forward to Naples to look after the affairs of state, but he was sure that His Majesty would find relaxation and relief from care in the magnificent park that their Majesties had created, which was said to rival Versailles, the pleasure ground of the Sun King as well as the Queen's late sister, the unfortunate Queen Marie Antoinette, may the Lord have mercy on her soul.

Henry took full advantage of this invitation, driving to the palace every morning in his carriage, accompanied only by Moretto, who was overawed at the sight of the grand facade, the four internal courtyards and the great marble Stairway of Honour. Work on the palace was still on-going and they passed swarms of Moorish slaves labouring on an unfinished wing, splitting stones with sledgehammers and climbing up and down wooden scaffolding with loads on their backs, under the watchful eyes of Neapolitan overseers.

One morning, they came across the master architect, Carlo Vanvitelli, his draft sheets spread on a trestle table in front of him, and Henry stopped to speak to him. He complimented him on his father's magnificent project and the improvements that he, Carlo, and his brother Pietro, had brought to the original project.

Vanvitelli bowed low, acknowledging the compliments with a certain complacency, but when Henry enquired about the workforce, his mouth turned down and he shrugged. Looking around to ensure that no courtiers were listening he spoke in the forbidden French language.

"Your Grace, we could not have brought this work forward without these –" he gestured towards the black labourers. "They're all prisoners, captured at sea by the Neapolitan navy. Fishermen mostly, but also pirates, merchants and thieves. Some of them get redeemed if they can pay ransoms. Otherwise –" he shrugged again. "They stay here. There are too many of them, to tell the truth. It gets unmanageable, but their Majesties want the work finished in a hurry. We can't be indulgent. Later maybe they'll be released or they'll be exchanged for Christian captives kept as slaves in their countries. It isn't my affair."

Henry saluted him and told Moretto to drive on, taking the long road that ran right up the hillside along the side of the fishponds to the highest point of the park. He liked to stop there where he could admire the fountain of Diana and the huntsman Actaeon, who had been condemned to death because he was indiscreet and a meddler, and he always made a point of teasing Moretto regarding his incurable habit of putting his nose into affairs that did not concern him and he wanted to warn him of the dangers of spying and tale bearing. This tendency, he repeatedly told him, would get him into bad trouble one day. But straight talk did not seem to do any good, so he resorted to describing the horrible fate of the hunter who spied on the goddess and her nymphs while they were bathing in a forest pool. It was difficult, in fact, to look at the sculptor's masterly rendering of the legend without shuddering, as it depicted the exact moment when the outraged Diana transformed the unfortunate man into a stag about to be savaged by his dogs. Moretto was tired of listening to the tale. He would stand, gloomily staring into the fountain basin, at a loss as to why the Cardinal was so attached to pagan fables.

Henry liked to sit whole hours there, refreshed by the tumultuous motion of the cascade that plunged down into the bowl behind the sculpture group while he admired the vista of green lawns and long pools that unfolded below him, sweeping gently downhill towards the palace in the distance.

One day, the Queen approached, accompanied by her bosom companion, Lady Hamilton, and two of the young princesses. They were followed by her black slave-girl, carrying her parasol, a few footmen with chairs and baskets and a pageboy with a birdcage.

Emma did not wear a wig, but had bound up her shining mass of chestnut hair in the style of an ancient Greek goddess. She was dressed in a flowing white dress gathered below the breast with a golden band, the revolutionary new dress style adopted by Josephine, Napoleon's wife, rapidly being copied throughout the courts of Italy. It flattered her slim, graceful figure, but when she curtseyed deeply and sank down to kiss his ring, Henry was shocked. He noted with disapproval that the lack of petticoats revealed the movement of her legs in a way that would have been considered scandalous in Rome.

Maria Carolina, on the other hand, had refused to follow the fashion since it had come from France and she would have nothing to do with anything French. However, she dressed more simply when she was in the country, with fewer petticoats and flounces. She wore only a small wig on her head adorned with a single crimson camellia, plucked from the English Garden she had created in a corner of the park.

Henry rose immediately, making the customary three ceremonial bows, but the Queen impatiently motioned for him to be seated. Like a well-trained servant, Moretto at once retreated a discreet distance away while the footmen set down chairs near the Cardinal's seat. Maria Carolina and Lady Emma sat down and they all remained in silence for a while, contemplating the view.

"So, my Lord," said the Queen at last. "How do you find your exile in our realm? Is it not a splendid cage of gold?"

"Golden indeed, Madame," Henry replied courteously. "Though the bird would always choose to return to its forest nest."

"Yes, that is so!" she remarked. She sighed and sat in silence for another long moment, her blue eyes fixed on some unseen point in the far distance.

"The destiny of birds is to be free," she said at last. "But many birds fall victim to hawks and buzzards. Others are trapped by huntsmen or shot for sport. Not all birds can rest easy in their nests and at any moment their tranquillity can be destroyed."

"Yes, that is so," he replied in agreeable tones. His expression, however, betrayed a certain wariness, as he was unsure where these remarks were heading.

The Queen gestured to her pageboy to bring her the cage he was carrying. It contained a little bird with brightly coloured plumage giving endless voice to a stream of trills and notes.

She sat gazing at the bird for some minutes then she said as if to herself, "The bird does not sing for happiness, as we believe. He sings out of rage because he is a captive. If he were free, his song would be to challenge the other birds and assert his supremacy. That is the way of this world."

Emma laid her delicate white hand on her friend's arm.

There was another long pause, then the Queen enquired, in an altered tone, "Have you found the time, my Lord, to visit my silk manufactory at San Leucio?"

He confessed that he had not, having been completely occupied with enjoying peace and finding consolation in the beauty of the Royal Park to venture further afield.

"I have heard you are a cultured man and that your see in Frascati was a model of good government," she said. "Oh, do not look so surprised. I have informers everywhere that keep me in touch with the world outside my gilded cage. It is the duty of all wise monarchs to know what is happening around them. There is much evil in the world, many people who show me every honour but secretly hate me and plot to bring me down. Therefore I know that you have brought very much good to your people. You built a hospital for the sick and injured, where the poor are treated free, and schools for poor boys and girls where they can learn an honest trade.

"I also know –" he had been about to speak but she gestured him to be silent. "I know your seminary is a respected school of learning. I heard of the scientific experiments with the magnetism they call electricity that links the earth to the sky. These are things that interest me. When I came from Vienna, I was a young girl. My head was full of poetry and love. I had read the philosophers. I was open to the great changes in the society of our age, as taught by the enlightened masters I shall not nominate since they belong, alas, to that accursed nation of France."

She reached up her hand and pulled the camellia out of her hair, twisting it distractedly in her fingers. A few strands of the wig came loose, fluttering on the top of her head. Emma made a move to smooth them down, but Maria Carolina brushed her away.

"I wished to be a great and benign ruler like my brothers, respected by their subjects in peaceful states," she went on in the same low tone of voice. "It was with these ideals in mind that I persuaded my husband to set up a perfect society modelled on equality and justice. The Royal Colony of San Leucio is a small world where peace and harmony reign. I had houses built for the workers and a school for the children. We are not too different, as you can see. But I went a step further. I made women equal to men, with the same wages and duties. I decreed that girls should not have their husbands chosen for them, but that young men and women should freely decide who they were to marry, so that they, at least, would be spared the fate of those of higher rank."

She began to twist her fingers together in a compulsive movement. Her voice rose.

"San Leucio was to be only the beginning. It was an experiment I planned to extend to our entire realm. Naturally, this proved impractical. I was grossly deceived. It is not possible to create a better world. The human race cannot be redeemed. Men are savages and will remain so."

She stared wildly around her and swayed in her seat. Emma Hamilton tightened her grip on her arm. Henry was alarmed, fearing she was about to fall into a fit. Her wild talk had repulsed him, but his expression remained calm and he looked at her with pity.

"Madame," he said. "Do not believe that I do not understand your despair and your grief for the fate of the King and Queen of France. But you have allowed these feelings to corrupt your mind and imperil your immortal soul –"

He leant towards her, about to say more, but she signalled him to be silent. With a brusque gesture, she rejected Lady Hamilton's consoling hand. Her eyes glittered and her jaw was set in a long, hard line.

"Do not give me your priest's claptrap, my Lord Cardinal, about the grace of God and the love of our Lord Jesus Christ. It did nothing to protect my poor sister, who was the sweetest and most innocent lamb upon this earth. Even her little children are kept captive by cruel gaolers. And the streets of France run with the blood of innocents, slain by ruffians and thieves."

Lady Hamilton intervened at this point. She spoke in Italian, in a low, sweet voice.

"Do not despair, dearest," she said. "These events will be avenged. Lord Hamilton tells me that our valiant commander, Lord Horatio Nelson, is already at the coast of Egypt and hard on the Corsican's tracks. Our royal navy will find him soon and give him the lesson he deserves."

This was the first time that Henry had heard this news, though he had noticed the increased presence of English seamen in Naples during the month before his departure for Caserta. The Queen's attention was diverted. She began to talk animatedly with Emma in German and the Cardinal rose to take his leave, beckoning Moretto to bring him his cane.

But before he could move, Emma Hamilton moved swiftly to his side. Ostentatiously, she approached to pick up her silk shawl, which she had left draped over the back of her chair. As Maria Carolina walked away, Emma looked up into his face with an earnest expression.

"Sire, dear lord," she said in a low tone. "I would entreat you not to judge Her Majesty too harshly. She has suffered a great deal and now she is afraid for herself and her children. There are dangers all around her. Her husband, His Majesty the King…" Here she paused, blushing, and bit her lip, glancing up once more into his face. "The King is very occupied with his own affairs – his own interests. He leaves her too much alone."

Henry stiffened. He felt his face flush red. He did not wish to be drawn into confidences that he believed to be more appropriate to the confessional and he was about to say something of the sort when Emma, divining his thoughts, straightened up, her shawl folded over her arm, and said calmly, "I have taken this liberty, sire, because I know you to be a man of experience and sense, as well as a priest, and it is my hope that you may be of some spiritual support to our Queen in this difficult time."

Curtseying again, she turned and followed the royal party into the secluded English garden, which was Maria Carolina's special retreat. Henry watched them disappear among the trees and ornamental flowering shrubs.

Church Versus State

The Cardinal made his way back downhill to the palace in silence. Moretto knew better than to interrupt his master when he was deep in thought. Henry, however, had already forgotten Emma's furtive plea. His mind was on other things. The previous day he had received a visit that had troubled him deeply. A messenger had brought him a letter from his secretary, Monsignor Landò, who had remained at La Rocca. Henry opened it with a sense of foreboding and, in fact, his worst fears were confirmed. Landò wrote that Frascati had been proclaimed a sister Republic of France and the Tree of Liberty had been raised in front of the Cathedral.

Worse still, one of Henry's protégés, Canon Gian Battista Arini, a lecturer of theology at the Herboracum College, had been won over to the revolutionary cause.

"He inflamed the crowds in the public square. He filled their simple minds with his talk of freedom and equality!" Landò wrote. "I would never have believed that I would have seen and heard such talk in our peaceful diocese! Arini was rallying them with cries like, 'Restore mankind's primary rights that despots have trampled on!' and 'Cast off the chains of the long era of slavery!' He had them all stirred up into a frenzy!"

Henry controlled the anger rising in his throat. He kept his tone light as he turned to Don Angelo. "I did not realise when I employed Arini that he had such fine gifts of oratory!"

Cesarini took the letter from his hand and scanned it rapidly.

"Well, you may joke, Stuart, but the results have been serious," he said in a reproachful tone. "Just listen to the rest."

"The rabble stormed the Cathedral and they have stripped it of everything of value that was not removed before you left. Now, the French have put their own administrators in all the positions of command and imposed their laws. Some of the small towns and villages in your diocese tried to resist but all attempts at rebellion were brutally crushed... Many poor working men, armed only with hoes and spades and hunting guns, were slaughtered without mercy."

Cesarini threw the letter down on the floor and gave vent to his rage. "That upstart Arini! That traitor! That snake whom you advanced and heaped with favours! All these years, we've had a snake in our household! May he rot in hell!" he spluttered, spitting in his rage.

Normally, Henry did not tolerate oaths and blasphemy coming from the mouths of members of his Family, but this time he did not even seem to hear his friend's imprecations. His anger lay cold as a lump of ice in his chest. He would not forgive Arini his treachery, nor for the fact that he had led other members of the Frascati congregation astray, but he knew this was not the moment to give way to violent threats and remonstrances. He realised that in the present circumstances, he was powerless to inflict any kind of punishment on the faithless canon. Revenge would have to wait until the natural order of society was restored, as he was sure, by the grace of God, that it must be, sooner or later.

Instead, he put his hand on Cesarini's arm to silence him.

"Take care! Do not let the household hear this kind of talk. They look up to us as their pillars of strength and support. If we falter, they are lost."

Cesarini sighed and drew himself upright. "You are right, of course. It is best that they know nothing of all these disturbances or they will clamour to be released so that they can go home – and who knows what they will find there? Surely, only heartbreak and danger. We must wait till King Ferdinand rallies his army and marches on Rome to cast out the usurpers! But sometimes, my friend, it is indeed hard to bow before the will of God!"

Gradually, Henry became calm and began to reason. He knew that at the present time they were outcasts from their homes and virtually helpless. The French were hostile towards the Holy Mother Church. The French Directoire had been trying for years to suppress the Roman Catholic religion. Ten years previously, the newly created French Constitutional Assembly had appropriated all Church property and most of France's 40,000 churches had been closed. The buildings were subsequently destroyed or converted into warehouses, factories or barns and by 1794, only a handful of churches were able to hold the Easter services. Meanwhile, all members of the clergy, including high-ranking bishops and cardinals, had been ordered to renounce the authority of the Pope and swear an oath of loyalty to the new state instead. From then on, they too were to be addressed, like the rest of the population, as simple *citoyens.* They were forbidden to wear their habits or carry Christian symbols like crucifixes or rosaries. New patriotic icons took their place, like the tricolour cockade and the red liberty cap.

Obviously, the Church of Rome had viewed these developments in the Gallican Church with considerable alarm. Pope Pius VI had denounced the French constitution in 1791 and many French priests refused to submit to the new order. These non-juring or refractory priests, as they were called, took great risks in defying the state and many of them were killed. There were incidents of horrific reprisals, like the so-called September Massacres, where over two hundred priests and three bishops were lynched by blood-crazed mobs. Parish priests who persisted in ministering to their congregations were imprisoned. The clergy fled the country in their thousands.

Henry had attended endless meetings with the College of Cardinals to discuss the situation but all attempts to intercede with the French government had been in vain. In fact, they had appeared only to make the situation worse. The Directoire seemed to be prepared to go to any lengths to stamp out all the power and influence of the Church of Rome in France, even to the point of inventing a new calendar. The years no longer were to be dated from the birth of Christ, but from the foundation of the French Republic. The week was transformed from seven days to ten, in order to eliminate Sunday as the day of worship. Festivals celebrating revolutionary heroes substituted the traditional saints' days and holy days.

The Pope had taken ill when he had heard that the French republicans had decided to eliminate Christianity and substitute it with a new 'Cult of Reason', introduced with due pomp and ceremony in Notre Dame Cathedral in November 1793, a little over a year after the monarchy had been abolished. The population, however, remained sceptical and refused to participate in the unfamiliar rites. Seven months later, Maximilien de Robespierre, one of the instigators of the Reign of Terror, tried again. This time he launched a religion of the 'Supreme Being', which was intended to take the place of God and the Holy Trinity. Again, this cult was ignored. The faithful continued to gather around their parish priests, who secretly celebrated the illegal masses, baptisms, marriages and funerals in stables, barns and private houses.

Finally, the Directoire made a last attempt. Hoping to finally woo the stubborn population away from popery, it concocted a creed closer to Christian doctrine and the spirit of charity, giving it the high-sounding name of Theophilanthropy. This was no more successful than the previous attempts and the new places of worship remained empty. Two years later, in 1795, the revolutionary government officially admitted failure. Church and State were formally separated. Those churches that had survived were re-opened. The centuries-old Christian rites were restored and priests were allowed to preach as before. There was, however, one fundamental difference. All Church property remained in the hands of the State.

As Henry and Moretto approached the palace, their path was crossed by the dwarf, Don Rodrigo, who was heading with all speed up the hillside. He was seated in a little cart drawn by a dog, and he raised his whip in a salute as he passed them, throwing the Cardinal his sly, sideways glance.

"He's got some urgent news for his mistress, no doubt!" Moretto ventured to comment, but Henry did not reply. The chance meeting with the Queen's spy, however, put other thoughts in his mind and he decided to act immediately. He had allowed the leisurely days at Caserta to lull him into a false sense of peace, as if the affairs of war and the perils menacing the world as he knew it did not concern him. He realised he had lost track of what was happening outside this gilded haven. He knew nothing of recent battles or how far Bonaparte had advanced. Emma Hamilton's remark about the arrival of Admiral Nelson must mean that the British believed the Kingdom of Naples was under threat and unable alone to defend itself.

As they turned into the forecourt of their lodgings, they found some of their men lounging under the shade of a tree with a pack of cards and a flask of wine.

'They too have become lax,' Henry thought. 'I have left them too much in idleness.'

Then, before he had even descended from the carriage, he called his captain of the guard, "Annibale, I have an urgent errand for you!"

Beckoning the man to follow him, Henry strode into the refectory, which was deserted at that hour.

"Take horses and go into Naples. Find out all you can about the Corsican's latest moves. I believe the British are making ready to launch a decisive attack. You need to go among the soldiers and officers stationed here. You'll find them in the taverns, no doubt. Take Moretto with you – he is familiar with these places, I believe. And take McLaren as well. He speaks the English language."

He was about to take the stairs to his room when he paused as another thought occurred to him. "You may need something to help loosen tongues," he called to Annibale. "Go to Monsignor Cesarini and tell him I authorise him to give you whatever money you need."

The three men jumped to obey. They had become bored with the seclusion and tranquillity of the Caserta countryside and welcomed the excuse to visit the city, especially with a pouch of the Cardinal's silver to spend at their discretion. They conferred together as they stuffed some provisions in their packs and saddled their horses.

"We'd best not stick together," said Annibale. "It could arouse suspicion. They might take us for spies. We'll fix a meeting place so that we can compare the information we've been able to winkle out and then we'll come back here separately."

"I won't have any trouble," MacLaren retorted. "They know me in every inn and tavern round Spaccanapoli. I'm everyone's friend – especially when I'm the one that's paying. I must say I'll be thankful to get a decent drink after that dog's piss the holy fathers around here call wine!"

Annibale frowned. "Take care!" he said. "Your tongue can be loosened along with theirs. If our master is sending us on a secret mission, there must be a good reason."

"Naples is full of spies!" the old Scotsman answered. "One more, one less! These *Lazzaroni* couldn't care less. All they care about is getting food in their bellies. I don't believe they care if it's the Frenchies or the Bourbons at the top. It's all one to them."

"That's careless talk!" Annibale said curtly. "If the gendarmes hear you, you'll find yourself in Castel Sant'Elmo quicker than you can say snap. And I wouldn't count on our master coming to save you. You're enough of a problem for him as it is. He might just decide to leave you there!"

MacLaren's chest puffed out. His face became a deep red and his hand strayed towards the knife he carried in his boot, but Annibale merely shrugged and swung himself up into the saddle.

"Don't say I didn't warn you!" he called as he set off at a gallop.

"Take no notice. He merely wants to needle you," Moretto commented. He was fond of the old warrior and tolerated his rages, but he knew that in this case, Annibale was right. Their master must be desperate indeed to risk sending MacLaren to mingle with the hated English. He would have gone with him to keep him out of trouble but he had his own contact to see, one he was sure could give him reliable information. This was an Austrian courtier, who had come to Naples as a pageboy in the train of Maria Carolina when she arrived as a bride some thirty years earlier.

He had met Heinrich one afternoon in Naples when his master was asleep and he was free to go out alone to the seafront to watch the fishermen repairing their nets. It amused him to listen to the fishwives accosting cooks and servants with their shrill singing voices, praising their fine catch of the day. He had noticed this tall, fair foreigner, dressed in the Queen's livery, sitting on the sea wall prising open the shells of tiny clams with his knife and sucking out the contents with obvious enjoyment. Heinrich had learned to speak the

Neapolitan language and converse with the people, so he was a wealth of information about what was going on. When he learned that Moretto was a newcomer to the city, he laughed. He claimed he knew the best taverns and the cleanest whorehouses and offered to introduce him to the capital's secret pleasures. But Moretto had refused, because of a secret vow he had made the day before they had set off in flight from Frascati, when he had knelt before the altar of the Madonna della Molara and sworn to remain chaste until he could bring his master back home safely again.

At first, the Austrian was somewhat perplexed and eyed him curiously. Then, thinking he had guessed the reason for Moretto's reluctance, he said he knew where they could find young boys, if that was what he preferred. He laughed when this suggestion was also turned down and said, "I did not take you for a priest. But I see you are, even if you do not wear the habit and I must say you are the first priest I have met in this city that practises abstinence. The strumpets are getting rich on these old men arrived from Rome, with or without their *zucchetti* on their heads!"

Moretto did not enlighten him further and he did not insist. They became good companions and thanks to Heinrich he learned a great deal about what was happening at court. To his surprise, Heinrich was loyal to Maria Carolina. He said she was much maligned and that before her sister Marie Antoinette was murdered by the French, she had been quite different. But now she lived in fear. She feared that the people, like the French, would turn against the monarchy, He said she trusted foreigners more than the Neapolitans, whom she considered cunning and inconstant.

"Of course, her husband is a weakling," he said, with a lift of his shoulders. "That's why the ignorant *Lazzaroni* love him. He's as ignorant as they are and he's indolent. He underestimates the threat of the Corsican. It is thanks to her that the English are in Naples to defend the kingdom, since the Austrian army seems incapable of checking the upstart's advance."

The moment he reached the city, Moretto sent his friend a message to meet him, as soon as he was free of his duties, in a tavern at the seafront. As usual, Heinrich was well informed.

"There's something big hatching," he said. "Naples is full of English seamen. But it appears that this is not Napoleon's objective. Now that he's brought most of Italy under his control and hedged in the Austrians, he's got his sights set on blocking the British trade routes to India and the Orient. The French have occupied Malta, and that's a big worry for His Majesty in London since it makes an ideal base for them to intercept his merchant ships in the Mediterranean. Bonaparte's no fool. He knows that if he can scupper the British economy, he'll win the day in the end!

"You wonder how I know all this?" he went on, almost teasingly. "Remember I'm well introduced at court. The Queen keeps close council. She's closeted in for days with Acton and Hamilton but things get out. Servants have more than two ears! Anyway, since you ask, over a year ago we began getting reports that the port of Toulon was bustling with an unusual amount of activity – just as if the French were building up for a major attack. But no one knew where. They kept it pretty close – probably even the commanders hadn't been informed. Nelson tried to block the port, but he was unlucky. A storm blew up and Boney slipped through out into the open sea. They're still looking for him. Nelson is prowling all over the Mediterranean like a furious beast."

"What's this Nelson like?" Moretto asked, pouring out another couple of glasses of red wine for himself and his companion.

Heinrich considered for a moment before replying.

"I only know what I've heard. He was here five years ago to pledge British support against the Corsican. I only saw him from a distance. He was mainly with the King's entourage. Even then he was known to be an exceptional commander. You wouldn't really take him for a hero if you saw him. He's quite short and pasty-faced. But I could see he wasn't like other men. He had an air of determination you don't often see. I wouldn't like to get on his wrong side. Did you hear about the Battle of Tenerife?"

Moretto shook his head and Heinrich sighed.

"You men of the cloth! Do you look beyond the mass table? It was a couple of years ago. Nelson stormed the Spanish town of Santa Cruz, but it went badly. He lost a lot of men as well as his right arm. His government wanted to pension him off but he wouldn't give in. The man is made of iron. He pestered and pestered the British Admiralty to give him another command and in the end he got his ship. He's just itching to get his hands – well, he only has one hand, but you get my meaning! – on Bonaparte, but the Corsican's more cunning than the devil. Next, we've heard, he's headed for Egypt. By now he'll have landed his army at Alexandria and he'll be marching on Cairo, with nothing in his way."

Moretto was stunned. He had not envisioned a war beyond the boundaries of Europe.

"Do you think Nelson will be able to stop him?" he asked.

Heinrich shrugged. "I would say he's the only one that could do it. They say he's set on it and he fears nothing. He's lost an eye, you know, as well as an arm. His men worship him. Tenerife was his only failure and he's out for revenge. Boney should look out for himself, I'd say!"

Henry listened attentively to Moretto's report, tapping his fingers impatiently on the table. In the end, he said simply, "It seems we must await events. Instruct all the Family to pray for Lord Nelson and victory."

Moretto was quite disappointed. He had expected a more incisive reaction, as well as some praise for his ability and astuteness. Of the three, he was the only one to bring back useful information. Annibale had got into a quarrel with some *Lazzaroni* and had had to take to his heels in order to save his life. MacLaren had got into a gambling game with a group of English seamen in one of the taverns.

"Thought they'd let things slip while they were busy playing," he said sheepishly. "But all they spoke was nonsense. They talked about things like 'Chicory Day' and 'Pig Day' and the months of 'Thermidor' and 'Messidor' and so on and then they started laughing and poking each other in the ribs and talking poetry nonsense like Drippy, Nippy, Showery, Flowery and so on. I couldn't make head or tail of it."

Cesarini, who had been sitting in a corner with his hands folded, now came forward. He was quite excited.

"You're a fool, MacLaren!" he said. "That's the new French calendar. They've got different names for the months and all the days of the year. The Directory wanted to toady to the peasants with homely names linked to farming instead of the Blessed Saints, may our Lord Jesus Christ forgive them! The sailors you heard were poking fun at these absurd names."

Henry drummed his fingers thoughtfully.

"Maybe that was their way of concealing information from the *Lazzaroni*. Try to remember their exact words."

But MacLaren shook his head sadly. He was sorry to disappoint his master, but he couldn't recall any more. He had taken the conversation among the players for meaningless banter and he hadn't paid a great deal of attention. He omitted to confess that at the time his head was already in a fog after a lengthy drinking contest, which he had won, but at great cost to lucidity.

However, as Henry soon discovered, rumours of an impending showdown between Nelson and Napoleon had spread through the court. Although it was July and the summer heat had not abated, the Bourbon court decided to move back to the capital to await events, and the colony of high-ranking refugees followed them.

Back in his palace in Via Toledo, Henry held almost daily discussions with the other prelates who had fled to Naples. His house was converted into a kind of general quarters where the exiled cardinals met up to exchange information. The month of July ended and August began. The city was oddly quiet, as if all the inhabitants were holding their breath, awaiting the news that would determine their future.

Finally, a messenger arrived at Henry's door, but the news was not about the impending battle. The letter communicated the death of Pope Pius VI at Valence, a prisoner of the French and exiled from Rome. The news was not entirely unexpected. The Pope was an old man of eighty-two and the shock of his captivity and deportation had crushed his will and stripped away his courage. But the College of Cardinals had hoped against hope that the French Directoire might have relented and allowed him to pass what little was left of his life in the Holy City of Rome, surrounded by his friends and comforted by the devotion of his subjects.

Henry was sincerely grieved, despite the many slights he had received from Pius VI, who, unlike his predecessor, Clement XIV, had refused to acknowledge the Stuart claims to the British throne. He had forbidden Henry to give his brother Charles Edward the funeral rites due to a king, like those that had been held for their father, James, and he had even commanded him to remove the royal escutcheon he had placed above the door of Palazzo Muti.

The other cardinals in Naples gathered in anxious haste to debate what should be done. On his deathbed, Pius VI had left instructions to reunite the Sacred College in conclave without delay to elect his successor. However, this was obviously impossible in the present circumstances. The cardinals were dispersed. Some were in prison. Rome, where the papal elections were traditionally held, was occupied by Napoleon's troops. And it was not easy to find an alternative venue where the scattered cardinals would be able to assemble.

Despite Henry's efforts to keep to the business on hand, these meetings tended to lapse into laments, recriminations and nostalgia for the world they had lost.

Many of them had suffered arrest and imprisonment when the French had invaded the Papal States. Cardinal Giuseppe Maria

Doria Pamphilj, the Vatican Secretary of State, trembled with emotion when he recalled how he had begged to be allowed to accompany the late Pope on his forced journey into exile, but had been turned back at Genoa.

"The Holy Father had the mark of death on him," he said. "It was obvious to the French doctors as well, who were there looking after him. But the governor was inflexible – a man of stone, without faith or compassion. If the French dictators would not concede this small thing – the comfort of a lifetime friend at the end of an earthly life – they will do everything in their power to prevent the election of a new head of the Church."

Cardinal Francesco Maria Pignatelli was equally gloomy. He talked about the privations and indignities he had suffered when he was the papal legate in Ferrara and Bonaparte had held him hostage for many months to discourage uprisings in the Holy See territories in Northern Italy. He too did not believe that Napoleon would permit a conclave to be held in any of his conquered territories.

Cardinal Romualdo Braschi-Onesti, who was the late Pope's nephew, was louder in his protests than all of them. He raged at length about the cruel and unjust fate suffered by his venerable uncle, carried forcible off to France, with no consideration whatever shown, either for his sacred office or for his great age.

"The French killed him, as surely as if they had cut his head off at the guillotine," he said with a dark look around the room. "And now our Mother Church has become a rudderless ship at the mercy of the winds."

As he talked on at length in this vein, with his eyes fixed in the distance and his fingers travelling with absent-minded restlessness along the beads of his rosary, Henry observed him thoughtfully.

"That's a man with his sights fixed on winning the Throne of Peter," he reflected. "As if our situation is not difficult enough without a war between aspiring candidates."

Henry had already attended enough conclaves in his lifetime to have no illusions regarding the ambitions of individual participants. Conclaves could be battlefields, fought out against a background of bitter undercurrents, secret alliances, betrayals, promises and exchanges of favours, all aimed at influencing the voting procedure. His own candidacy had been blocked several times because of his name. Great Britain, although officially Protestant, would not have looked with favour on a Stuart pope and the major European powers feared upsetting the Continent's delicate political balance. This was true now, more than ever, he thought, with Austria flagging in the war against France and Britain a valued ally of the Kingdom of Naples and Sicily.

The Battle of the Nile

August 1ˢᵗ, 1798

The Battle of the Nile at Aboukir Bay took place on the 1ˢᵗ August, 1798, but the news of Nelson's victory did not reach Naples for a couple of weeks.

Henry was one of the first to receive the glad tidings. He was out driving when he met Sir William Hamilton. Recognising the Cardinal's royal insignia on the side of his coach, he drew level with the window, reining in his horse.

"I beg pardon of your Eminence for stopping your carriage, but I am sure you will be glad to hear the good news which I have to communicate."

Henry had not met the Ambassador for over two months. He had not returned to Palazzo Sessa since the time of the reception when he had seen Emma perform her *Attitudes* and he had not been back to court since the royal family had come back from Caserta.

Hamilton was visibly struggling to maintain his normal grave and dignified manner. He was flushed with excitement and, despite his efforts, his face broke into a wide and complacent smile when he spoke.

"Our Royal Navy has utterly defeated Bonaparte off the coast of Alexandria. Admiral Nelson conducted a brilliant operation. Most of the French ships have been destroyed or captured, while our fleet has suffered hardly any damage. Napoleon is now blocked in Egypt. He has no ships to take him home and his supply routes have been cut off. His army will soon be starving. He'll be forced to surrender."

Henry leaned out of the carriage. "Please, Sir, I beg you to tell your countrymen that no man rejoices more sincerely than I do in the success and glory of the British navy!"

They drove on and Cardinal Stuart leaned back in his seat, smiling wryly to himself. Hamilton was a good man, well meaning, cultured and ingenuous, like many rich men's sons who had never come up against any serious forms of adversity in life. The irony underlying Henry's message would have totally escaped him. Some, however, would understand: those who drank to the 'King over the Water' and sang in chorus 'O, Come all Ye Faithful' on certain days of the year. He thought of the endless bitter scenes years back in Palazzo Muti, when Henry had struggled to comfort his brother Charles during his attacks of grief and recrimination. That was now all in the past. Charles was dead and the dreams of restoration with him, while a German king continued to sit on the Stuart throne. But a few minutes earlier, the last Stuart heir, albeit in veiled and cryptic language, had reminded the British Ambassador of his House's rightful claim.

When the news of the victory spread, Naples went mad with joy. Day and night, the streets were full of jubilant crowds, acclaiming Nelson, the Saviour of Italy. Ferdinand gave orders that the entire city be illuminated for three nights in celebration.

Nelson himself did not arrive until the twenty-second of September, over a month later. As soon as a fleet of battleships flying British colours was spotted on the horizon, hundreds of little Neapolitan fishing boats took to the water and rowed out to meet the victors. They carried bands of musicians with mandolins, guitars and tambourines, playing a jaunty version of the British national anthem. At the same time, the cannons of Castel Sant'Elmo boomed out a continuous earth-shaking salute. The entire population converged on the waterfront, cheering and waving. Ferdinand hurriedly arrived and boarded the royal launch. He wanted to be there to greet the Admiral personally when Nelson's flagship entered the harbour.

As the ship drew near, Henry was able to scrutinize the hero through a spyglass he had obtained from Acton. Nelson stood motionless on the quarterdeck, with his seamen standing to attention in line behind him. The Cardinal noted that he was, as he had been told, short of stature and pallid of complexion and that he wore a patch over the eye he had lost some years previously in Corsica. The empty coat sleeve of his missing right arm was tucked neatly into the front of his coat. As he walked down the gangway onto the harbour, Henry saw that his face was further deformed by an ugly scar that swept across his forehead, starting at his hairline and reaching almost to his ear.

Suddenly, a great commotion came from somewhere at the back of the crowd. Lady Hamilton had pushed her way forward to greet Nelson, but she had fainted when she saw his injuries. Moretto, who had been separated from his master in the crush, saw her being carried away by her maids. He was trying to reach the Cardinal when he ran into his friend Heinrich, who poked him in the ribs and gestured with a grin in the direction of Emma's enforced retreat.

"The lady there hasn't seen the Admiral for five years. That was when he first came to Naples to pledge the support of the British government against Napoleon. At that time, he was still young and comely and a whole man. But now, even though he holds himself proudly enough, he seems more half of a man. It is evident that Lady Emma was not prepared to see the price her hero has had to pay for his heroic deeds!"

The festivities in Nelson's honour went on for days. At night, Villa Sessa was illuminated with three thousand lamps arranged to spell out 'Viva Nelson'. A gala evening was held at the San Carlo Opera House where all the ladies of the court wore the words 'Viva Nelson' sewn on blue armbands, and Emma wore a blue shawl embroidered with golden anchors round her white shoulders. The celebrations culminated on Nelson's fortieth birthday, when Emma organised a party at the residence for eighteen-hundred guests. In the course of the evening, she performed another of her famous *Attitudes* starring herself as Penelope, welcoming back her long absent hero Ulysses from the war in Troy.

In Naples, Nelson was showered with gifts and honours. Ferdinand nominated him Duke of Bronte in the Kingdom of Sicily and granted him a large estate at the foot of Mt Etna. Other tributes and awards came from the Tsar of Russia and the Sultan of the Ottoman Empire. However, the hero was bitterly disappointed when the British government nominated him a baronet. He had expected a viscountcy at the very least as a reward for his clamorous success at Aboukir Bay. He complained his country had treating him shabbily and spent long hours brooding. Fortunately, he did not have to wait long to find consolation.

The Hamiltons had invited him to stay at Villa Sessa as their guest and he accepted very willingly. Very soon, the beautiful Lady Hamilton could be seen accompanying the Hero of the Nile everywhere he went, with the excuse that she was acting as his interpreter, and the entire court was whispering behind fluttering fans that the two had become lovers. Servants reported they had seen them locked in each other's arms in the moonlight garden of the Villa, while the elderly cuckold of a husband was in his observatory above, absorbed in studying the stars.

During the first few days of the fleet's arrival, hundreds of British seamen, bent on pleasure, descended on Naples. The already chaotic city was transformed into an ungovernable maelstrom, full of taverns and wine cellars packed with men intent on drinking themselves into oblivion. Long queues of men who had spent months at sea formed in front of the brothels. Fights broke out in the streets. By nightfall, the alleyways around the harbour were heaped with slumped figures that had fallen asleep where they dropped.

Meanwhile, Heinrich and Moretto moved around the city, listening to accounts of the epic sea battle as recounted by drunken seamen, who tended to brag about their alleged individual acts of heroism. Heinrich had picked up English, thanks, he said, to a brief but intense romance with a young English widow, in Naples with her son on a prolonged Grand Tour, and he was able to communicate with the sailors they met in the taverns.

They learned of the gruelling, nerve-wracking weeks spent combing the Mediterranean ports between Greece and Sicily, searching in vain for the French fleet that had slipped out of Toulon under their noses. Finally, in the middle of June, Nelson learned that Napoleon had captured the Island of Malta. This was the clue he needed to divine the Corsican's objective, which must either be Sicily or – more likely – the Egyptian port of Alexandria.

They got a full story from an old gunner who had just come off duty and was still sober.

"We set sail at once for Alexandria," he recounted in return for the offer of a drink. "But blow me, we didn't find a single warship in the harbour there! Our Commander, bless him, was sick with rage. But here's the joke! We wor too early. Boney hadn't arrived yet. Of course, we didn't know that at the time. Off we set again – back and forth, back and forth all along the Levant. We didn't realise then that we had missed the devil and he was set for Alexandria all the time!"

"Well, we wor into the month of July and reports started coming in that the French had beaten the Ottoman army and they were already marching on Cairo. We headed back hot foot, as it were, to Alexandria, but we only found transports anchored there – no warships at all. We wor all downcast. We'd been sharpening up for an engagement, you see. I was on the *Orion* with Captain Saumarez and you never saw a man so down. But then our luck changed. The officer of the watch got a signal that the enemy was moored in Aboukir Bay just twenty miles along the coast."

"You're too slow, old man!" broke in a young seaman, who had taken a seat nearby to follow the conversation. "Get on with the real stuff! The Battle! It's that they want to hear about."

He moved in closer, leaning over the table and prodding Heinrich's arm. "We found the French all ready for us, set up in battle formation. It were a fine sight, I tell you – thirteen ships of the line spread across the bay, with the *Orient* – De Brueys' flagship – the French commander – right in the centre, bristling with her 120 guns all pointed towards us. He thought he'd made a barrier we couldn't penetrate. The bay was full of shoals, you see, and he reckoned we wouldn't have charts."

"In fact, the *Culloden* came to grief right away!" the old gunner interrupted. He was flushed and becoming more and more excited. "Troubridge wor so eager to be first into the battle that he got 'imself grounded! But that didn't discourage our brave boys! It wor getting dark but Nelson signalled to continue the attack. The French didn't expect that. They thought we'd wait till morning, but Nelson would have none of it. We all bore down on them bravely. Then the *Goliath* – Captain Foley commands her – spotted a gap at the end of the French line and she slipped through sweet as you like, with the *Orion*, the *Theseus*, the *Zealous* and the *Audacious* right behind her. We knew we had 'em then! De Brueys had reckoned we wouldn't get between him and the shore, you see. He had all his guns lined up on the van so his rear was undefended. So then we had fun! With Nelson and his other ships attacking front on, we got them in a crossfire – a pummelling on all sides that they hadn't been expecting."

His companion took up the tale, dipping his hand into his tankard and sketching the battle formation on the tabletop with his wet finger. "Even when darkness fell, we didn't let up. Nelson ordered we hoist lamps on our mizzenmasts so we wouldn't be firing on each other. The *Orient* caught fire around 10, I believe it was, and the fire spread fast. She had a lot of inflammable stuff stacked on deck. We knew at once that she was doomed! She would go up when the fire reached the gunpowder magazines. Her crew threw themselves into the sea and tried to swim away as fast as they could, poor devils, while all the ships that were around – French and British – cut their anchors and moved away smart as they could!"

He was quiet for a moment while Heinrich ordered another round of drinks. Wiping his mouth with the back of his hand, he resumed his tale, "She blew up with a crash that would've deafened the angels. They even heard it in Alexandria. If you never seen anything like that, you can't imagine the devastation – the sea bucked and churned like an earthquake. Bits of burning timber and clouds of sparks flying high up into the air. Lord Nelson had signalled to pick up the survivors but the explosion killed over a thousand of 'em. Only seventy were saved. We had damage as well. The *Swiftsure* and my ship, the *Alexander*, as well as their *Franklin*, were all set alight by bits of debris, but we all managed to put out the flames before they could catch on."

As Moretto and Heinrich sat, gripped with horror at the scene unfolding inside their heads, the older man gestured towards a young boy who was sitting alone in a corner near them, slumped over the table top, and he shrugged.

"That lad there's new to action. He hasn't got the stomach for it. He wor on the *Alexander* with me as well when we closed in on the *Orient*. We were placed aft, where we could fire shot through her stern. I saw Admiral de Brueys hit right in the belly – nearly cut him in half. Then De Casabianca, the second in command, took a bad hit as well."

He moved across to the boy and gave him a clap on the back. "Cheer up, son! It's over now. Time for celebration, not for brooding."

The boy looked up. His face was pale and glistening with sweat, his eyes staring and vacant. "I saw him," he said in a faint voice. "He was standing on the deck right opposite me and I saw him clearly. He was my same age, I swear, and I saw him standing there in the middle of the flames."

The younger seaman sneezed, sending a shower of powdered brown tobacco all over the table.

"Well, what did you expect, lad? War's not all glory, you know. While you're in action, you're all fired up. But afterwards, well, it can be another story – comes the morn and you see the bay covered with dead bodies, mangled, scorched, legs and arms, in pieces. I admit it's not a pretty sight. That was De Casabianca's young son you saw, serving on board with him. A lad of twelve. He refused to leave his father and save himself, though we were all urging him to jump off before she went up. This lad here saw him and it's put him out."

"That's truthfully said," his companion nodded. "But we 'ad a great victory, no way you can deny that. As for this lad here," he rose to go, jerking his thumb towards the boy in the corner. "He'll get used to it, or he'll get sent home. His father won't be pleased, after he's spent a pretty penny to get him taken on. So toughen up, boy," he shouted as he headed, none too steadily, towards the door. "If you want to stay in His Majesty's Navy."

Another group of seamen, who had been listening to the conversation, took over, moving onto the bench where Heinrich and

Moretto were sitting, and Heinrich called for another flagon of wine. They recounted that the loss of the flagship, the *Orient*, took the heart out of the French. One by one, the enemy ships began to strike their colours. All fighting had ceased by the middle watch and by dawn almost all the French fleet had been captured.

"But we lost the *Artemise* and the *Timoleon*. Their crews set them on fire, rather than let them fall into our hands and then *La Genereux* and the *Guillaume Tell* managed to sneak away – they still had their masts, sails and spars intact, you see. The *Zealous* went after them but they escaped. They would have made a fine prize. But no matter! None of our ships were lost and Nelson was satisfied with that!"

Moretto had been absorbing all this information so that he could report to the Cardinal. "What kind of a man is your commander?" he asked.

"The best! He's always at the front of the battle. Fears nothing – but he doesn't require of us anything he won't do himself. We men would follow him through the gates of hell!"

This statement was followed by a rousing chorus of assent. "Listen! He's lost an eye and an arm for the Royal Navy. He'd lay down his life without thinking twice about it, I swear. But he lives under a lucky star. They haven't managed to kill him yet. Did y' hear he got hit in this action as well?

"It were a bit of shrapnel cut open his forehead, right down to the skull. He thought he was blinded. The loose flap of skin had fallen down over his good eye, you see. But when he goes below decks to get stitched up, he refuses to pass before the brave fellows waiting to have their wounds seen to. 'I'll take my turn,' was what he said. Then he was back up on deck immediately in the thick of the fight. I swear I got this first hand from the crew of the *Vanguard* and it didn't surprise me one bit. A lion, he is – never thinks of savin' himself. You don't get many commanders like that – and I should know. I've been on the sea for upwards of forty years!"

"They certainly hold this Nelson in great esteem," Moretto remarked to Heinrich as they walked back towards Via Toledo together. "However, I'm thankful that my commander deals in peace, rather than war."

"Don't be too sure," Heinrich replied. "These are strange times and the world seems to be revolving in reverse. Some Cardinals are grinding their teeth for war – Ruffo di Calabria, for instance. He's well past his youth but he's clamouring to lead an army to defeat

Napoleon. I think in the end the King will content him. The Queen believes in him and is all in favour…"

"Well, let's hope the great Victory of the Nile will be sufficient to prune the Corsican's ambitions," Moretto said with a sigh. "He's stuck in Egypt and he can't get his army out. This could, indeed, be the end of him!"

Part 3
Sicily

December 1798 – March 1799

Maria Carolina was galvanized into action by the Victory of the Nile. She held councils of war with Nelson, Acton and Hamilton, urging them to press forward the advantage gained against the hated French. Ferdinand, however, was reluctant to be drawn into action. He was no fool, despite the low opinion his wife and many of his subjects held of him, and he knew that his army was no match for Napoleon's polished war machine. The decision, however, was largely taken out of his hands.

With Bonaparte momentarily stranded in Egypt, the French Directoire recalled much of its army from central Italy to defend the conquests on the northern frontier with Austria. Fifteen thousand French troops under General Championnet, a veteran of the Italian campaign, were left to guard Rome. They were camped at Civita Castellana, some thirty miles north of the city, while only a skeleton garrison remained in Rome itself, entrenched within the walls of Castel Sant'Angelo, the papal fortress.

The members of the Directoire were jittery. Elections had been held in France in the spring of that year, and the Republicans had come out badly. Royalist support had increased and plots were afoot for a restoration of the French ruling house, with the active corroboration of other European monarchies. Undecided on how to meet the crisis, the members wasted time quarrelling among themselves.

From every point of view, in fact, this seemed the ideal moment to put an end to Napoleon's dreams of further expansion. The British government was confident that the Austrian Emperor, Francis II, France's archenemy, and also Ferdinand's son-in-law, would jump at the chance to send troops to support Naples and Nelson was ordered to persuade Ferdinand to launch an offensive and free Rome from the French.

Caught between his nagging wife and the coldly contemptuous Nelson, the pleasure-loving and easy-going Ferdinand was at last convinced that he had no other option but to comply and set about raising an army.

Nelson, who was still smarting from the slights he felt he had been dealt by the British government, was furious when he learned that the Austrian General Baron Karl Mack von Leiberich had been recalled by the Naples court to organise the campaign. He despised Mack, who had in fact made some messy military blunders in the past, and he had such little faith in the indecisive baron's ability that he wrote to Emma, advising her to pack her possessions and be ready to flee as soon as a first hint of bad news reached her ears. At the time, he was at the port of Leghorn supervising repairs to the *Vanguard*, but he assured her that he would be ready at the drop of a hat to convey her and the royal family to safety.

Emma told Maria Carolina, who interpreted the message as meaning that an invasion of the kingdom by the French was imminent. She became hysterical, raging at her husband and his advisers and she quarrelled with the prudent Acton, who flatly declared that without the backing of the Austrian empire, the Neapolitan campaign was sure to be a disaster.

Ferdinand was pestered anew into pressing Vienna for a firm commitment, but Francis kept putting him off with one excuse after another. The Emperor was reluctant to break the peace treaty with France that he had laboriously achieved only the previous year, after five years of bitter warfare.

While awaiting Francis' answer, Ferdinand went ahead with mustering an army. All the men in the kingdom between the ages of seventeen and forty-five were conscripted. Naturally, these recruits were not professional soldiers. They were mostly peasants, shepherds and humble tradesmen who did not understand military tactics and were not used to handling arms. To make matters even more complicated for the commanding officers, the men did not even speak the same language. The Sicilians, the Calabrians and the men from Apulia all had different dialects, which were incomprehensible to the Neapolitans.

Every day, the new recruits were drilled for several hours in the vast open space in front of the royal palace, observed by the curious population. A group of Henry's men strolled down several mornings to watch the proceedings. While the young soldiers hopped around, confused by the orders barked by the Neapolitan commanders, Annibale, who had spent some time in the papal army, did not hide his contempt.

"These clod-hoppers don't know their right foot from their left!" He fixed his gaze on a scrawny young boy, who stood staring around, clearly bewildered. "They've never worn a pair of boots in their lives, by the look of them."

"If this is the defence of Naples, the Lord have mercy on us," muttered Garani, crossing himself.

"Here comes King Beaky in person to sort them out!" exclaimed Moretto, as Ferdinand emerged from the palace courtyard, mounted on a white charger. He was resplendent in red and blue dress uniform, with large gilded epaulettes on his shoulders and rows of medallions and loops of golden tassels covering his chest. The guard of honour, lined up on either side of the archway, saluted while the trumpeters and drummers struck up a rousing march.

Maria Carolina rode out directly behind him. She was smartly dressed in a blue riding jacket and a flowing cape that fell over her horse's flanks. She wore a general's tricorn hat capped with a white ostrich plume perched on top of her wigged head. The soldiers stared at her open mouthed and the officers forgot to call them to attention.

"Do you see she's wearing breeches!" exclaimed Garani in a state of wild excitement. "She's a queen but she behaves more like a harlot. She's showing off her legs without modesty or shame in front of all these men!"

"Maybe she is planning to lead them into battle herself! That could be a weapon the Neapolitans could use to effect," commented Moretto with a snigger.

Voices from the back of the crowd drew their attention. They turned around to see Lady Hamilton, rosy and smiling, seated opposite Nelson in an open carriage. After a few weeks of rest and relaxation in the congenial atmosphere of Villa Sessa, the Admiral had recovered his health. His pale white skin had acquired a touch of colour and he wore his hair longer and combed down over his forehead in an attempt to hide the long scar he had acquired in the recent conflict. He was wearing full dress uniform, with a chestful of medals and awards.

MacLaren nudged Garani. "You know what I heard from an Englishman I was with last night? He said his general had met Nelson here, for the first time, and the Admiral was so covered in stars, medals and ribbons that he looked more like a prince from an opera than the Conqueror of the Nile! You can see what he meant!"

There was some half-hearted applause from the crowd and Emma smiled, raising her hand in salute, but Nelson continued to survey the sea of heads bobbing around the carriage with a haughty stare. Then he urged the coachman to drive on, forcing the press of people to move smartly out of the way.

"Well, if the Neapolitans don't love him, it's his own fault," remarked MacLaren. "They had him up on a pedestal, like a god, but he makes no attempt to hide the fact that he despises them. I've been told that he says this is a nation of musicians, poets, whores and brigands. That means he thinks the poets and musicians are as low as the brigands and the whores. That doesn't go down well with the *Lazzaroni*. You know how they love their poets and their music! So now they think he's a churl!"

Garani shrugged. "Well, he's disgruntled because his own government hasn't given him the honours he thinks he deserves and he's turned sour."

The discussion spread to other spectators who were standing by listening.

"If he doesn't care for the life here, why doesn't he go home?" chipped in an elderly man with a pile of books under his arm.

"Are you blind? The reason for him lingering is sitting right opposite him!" chuckled a tradesman, with his tools poking out of his apron. "Did you ever see a more delectable chicken? I could eat her up in three mouthfuls!"

"Did you hear that they go to taverns together late at night, pretending to snuff out the Jacobin conspirators? And they've been seen gambling away great piles of gold. I got it from a reliable source at court." This was a woman's voice, relayed in an audible whisper.

"Well, you would believe anything the old gossips have to say!"

"As to my fine Lady Hamilton, her own compatriots wouldn't let her touch the hem of their gowns if it weren't for the fact she's the Ambassador's wife. They call her vulgar and ill mannered. I'm in service with a lady who says she has no taste in dress."

"Well, knowing her origins, what else could you expect? I've heard that before she married Lord Hamilton, she was his nephew's floozy. The nephew had run up a mountain of debts and the uncle settled them. The girl was part of the deal."

"I'd keep a more careful tongue in my mouth, if I were you! She's now become a great lady and the Austrian woman adores her. Now she also has the Hero of the Nile eating out of her hand. There's more to little Emma than her pretty face, I can tell you!"

At that point, the crowd, becoming bored with the repetitive drilling exercises, started drifting away. Garani and Moretto lingered a little longer and then headed back to Via Toledo.

After weeks of dithering, Austria finally sent a definite refusal to be drawn into the fray. Maria Carolina, who examined all official dispatches, intercepted the letter and, seething with fury, kept the contents hidden from her husband. Thus, Ferdinand remained blissfully unaware that he was on his own and proceeded to organise his campaign to reconquer the Papal States.

With Nelson patrolling the coast to prevent any surprise attacks from the sea, Ferdinand and Mack von Leiberich set off with their army for Rome.

Seated in his carriage, Henry watched the forty thousand men of the Bourbon army march resolutely out through the city gates in seemingly endless file, headed by King Ferdinand and General Mack, riding side by side and saluting the wildly cheering crowds. The gold and crystal royal coach followed behind them, empty so that the King could dismount when he got tired and take a seat in his carriage. The new recruits looked proud in their new uniforms. They tried hard to march in time, holding their heads high, but many of them were limping because they were unaccustomed to wearing shoes and the ones they had been issued with pinched their feet.

On the twenty-ninth of November, after a brisk march of two weeks, the Neapolitan army arrived at the gates of Rome. There had been no official declaration of war, and the French were taken by surprise. They had not been expecting any trouble and General Champoinnet was still camped with his army thirty miles away. So the Neapolitans met virtually no resistance when they marched into the city. The King of Naples was welcomed with open arms by the Romans, who were tired of the rigid regulations and the new taxes imposed by the French regime. Joyful crowds rushed to knock down the Tree of Liberty on the Capitol Hill. In their enthusiasm, they also killed any unfortunate republican soldiers they happened to come across in the streets.

The peace-loving and indolent Ferdinand heaved a sigh of relief and settled himself comfortably in the luxurious Palazzo Farnese, a property that he had inherited from his Italian D'Este relatives. He believed that the war was over and that he would now be able to relax and enjoy the fruits of his triumph.

He celebrated his victory by addressing the people of Rome from the summit of the Capitol in a grandiose speech larded with rhetoric. "The Neapolitans have rung the death toll of the French! We are showing Europe the way! The time has come for the return of the King of France!"

Five days of banquets and lavish festivities followed.

While the French were hastily re-organising their forces at Civita Castellana, General Mack was revealing just what lengths an occupying force could go to in order to arrive at full control. In order to winkle out the besieged garrison in the papal fortress of Castel Sant'Angelo, he issued an ultimatum: the injured French soldiers in Roman hospitals would be held hostage and every time a shot was fired from the fortress, one of them would be executed.

Knowing that his army was more than twice the size of Champoinnet's, Mack felt confident that he would be able to confront the French and win an outstanding victory. At the beginning of December, he marched towards Civita Castellana. Ferdinand instead remained in Rome with six thousand chosen men in order to continue the siege of Castel Sant'Angelo.

The general, however, had seriously miscalculated. Champoinnet was a veteran of Napoleon's campaigns and a skilled strategist. Despite the numerical disadvantage, the experienced republican soldiers decimated the bewildered southern Italian peasants, who flung down their arms and fled. The glorious Neapolitan army that had marched so proudly out of Naples only a few weeks previously was routed in minutes. The retreat was chaotic, with every man out for himself. Mack risked being lynched by his irate troops and fled to Capua to surrender to the French, where he tried to negotiate a safe passage back to Austria.

As soon as Ferdinand heard of Mack's defeat, he abandoned Rome and headed back to Naples as fast as his coachman could carry him.

The Romans accepted the turn of events with an ironical resignation. Ferdinand and Mack were ridiculed mercilessly. Within hours, a series of satirical poems had been attached to Pasquino, the 'talking statue', where the Roman populace traditionally left anonymous messages and complaints against the authorities.

"Del Tirreno dai liti/	*From the shores of the Tyrenne/*
con soldati infiniti/	*to Rome with many men/*
venne in Roma Bravando/	*came swaggering King Don Fernando/*
il Re Don Fernando e in pochissimi dì	*/and in a few short days*
/venne, vide, fuggì/	*he came, he saw, he fled."*

The news of the disaster reached Naples in the early days of December, when the first deserters came scuttling furtively through the gates. During the last few weeks, Henry had slept little. He had been dubious from the start about the ability of the improvised Neapolitan army to confront the French. Anxious and restless, he had sat by his window for long hours in the night, watching the urine gatherers scuttle from house to house, followed by the water carriers and the street sweepers. He was dismayed, but not surprised, to see the first straggling groups of men in torn uniforms slipping like shadows along the sides of the buildings.

It was only the beginning. Throughout the following days, increasing numbers of ragged and dejected soldiers began to flow back wearily into the city, trundling carts heaped with the wounded. From his window, Henry continued to observe the steady procession of bowed, exhausted and limping men, accosted every few yards by groups of women, who came running out of the alleyways to look for sons and husbands.

As the days wore on, a strange noise began to issue from the bowels of Spaccanapoli. At first it sounded like a dog's low growling. Then it gradually increased in volume until it grew into the muted roar of a wounded bull. This, he thought, was the city's cry of rage and it was a fearsome sound. His heart swelled in his chest till it became painful to breathe and his vision blurred. Immediately, he realised all the implications of this defeat. It meant that they would not, after all, be going home. Instead, they would become fugitives again, in flight towards some unknown fate.

He looked around at his servants. His valet, Ridolfi, the youngest man in his retinue, was weeping openly. Eugenio, he knew, had left a sweetheart behind in Frascati. They'd had news that she had borne him a son, whom he now feared he would never see. As if he had read his thoughts, Ridolfi threw himself down trembling on his knees.

"What is to become of us, dear master?" he cried. "We are exiles from our homes. Today I had to leave the market in haste because the porters were grumbling against the Romans and giving me black looks. They say we are using up all their food – this after the thieves made us pay three times the usual price for bread and eggs."

Henry found nothing to say. Latterly, he had become increasingly aware that his resources were dwindling. His see in Frascati had been taken over by the French and his revenues impounded. Other incomes from the Apostolic Chamber and his benefices in Spain had been confiscated. He realised that he would not be able to meet the expense of supporting such a large number of people for much longer. If, as now seemed likely, Champoinnet would take advantage of the Neapolitan defeat to invade the Kingdom of Naples, they would have to move on.

For the first time since his illness at the Olivetan monastery, Henry felt his age.

Flight to Sicily

December 23rd, 1798 – January 1799

Messengers had ridden in all haste to the royal palace where the Queen's advisers had tried to keep the tragic news secret while they debated what to do. Even John Acton hesitated to approach the royal apartments and give Maria Carolina the report of the ignominious defeat. Later, when Heinrich met Moretto, he told him that the Queen had been beside herself with fury and despair. The entire palace had resounded with her shrieks, curses and lamentations while her trembling maids tried unsuccessfully to calm her. She raged against her inept and bungling husband and the cowardly and treacherous General Mack, while tearing at her clothes, wringing her hands and smashing mirrors and precious ornaments.

When the royal coach arrived, Ferdinand did not attempt to confront his wife. Instead, he rode out onto the streets, urging the people to arm themselves and defend the realm against the invaders, who would soon be arriving at the city gates. The *Lazzaroni* rallied to the call. They rushed to set up barricades, turning carts and barrows on their sides and heaping up piles of debris to obstruct the roads. They wheeled cannons and guns into the piazzas and primed them ready to fire at the invaders. The clergy were in a state of panic, knowing that the heathen Jacobin republicans hated the Church and the French would be set on destruction and plunder. During mass, the priests read out declarations of war from the pulpits, inciting the population to rise up and take arms, while at night, under cover of darkness, they brought out the church gold and treasures from the sacristy, taking them to secret hiding places.

Eventually, Ferdinand and Maria Carolina, united at least in appearance, headed a procession to invoke the divine protection of the Virgin and saints. They carried the venerated relics of San Gennaro through the streets, among hundreds of men, women and children who fell on their knees offering up desperate prayers for the saint's intercession.

The *Lazzari* sacked the abandoned houses of the noblemen and merchants who had taken flight, tearing out beams and floor planks to reinforce the barricades. Meanwhile, the peasants outside the walls drove their animals up into the hills in the hope of saving them from the invaders. Food became scarce. The markets were empty. Only the taverns were busy. Gigi reported that all kinds of rogues had sprung up like beetles from under the stones and were sitting drinking from morning to night, clanking their rapiers and waving their daggers. Many of the brigand bands had come down from their mountain lairs, summoned by the warrior Cardinal Ruffo di Calabria. It was rumoured that even condemned criminals like Gaetano Mammone and Fra Diavolo had joined Ruffo's army.

The news became more and more disquieting. Champoinnet was marching south and had met little resistance. He had conquered Pescara, Gaeta and Capua. Very shortly, they realised, he would reach the gates of Naples.

Henry knew that they had to leave. Acton had advised him that the royal family was planning to flee to Palermo, their capital in Sicily, and he advised the other Cardinals of the Sacred College who had taken refuge in Naples to do the same.

Summoning Moretto, Henry gave him a gold ring and a set of silver salvers he had brought with him from Frascati, instructing him to sell them to the jewel merchants in the Decumanus. Gigi reported back later that he had gone from one dark shop to another but not one of them would give him more than a fifth of their value.

"It seemed as if they had made an agreement among themselves to profit as much as possible from the desperation," he lamented. "The goldsmiths and moneylenders were besieged with people. All shouting and haggling. Men and women, all clamouring to sell. Small wonder the usurers get rich! I pray their greed will send them straight to rot in…"

The sight of Henry's nose twitching halted him from saying more aloud, but he continued under his breath. "I hope the rebels round them up and slaughter them like the animals they are!"

Annibale was entrusted with finding a ship to carry them to Sicily and this proved no mean task. After combing the harbour and the taverns, he could only get an old cargo boat that was not big enough to hold the Cardinal's entire Family. He had to negotiate a second passage with the surly captain to pick up the rest of the company a few days later.

At that point, hearing that he would not be travelling with his master, Giacinto Belisario, the cook, fell weeping on his knees. He begged His Majesty to release him from his service and allow him to go home. Henry was alarmed, knowing all the dangers the man would face travelling alone though the bandit-ridden mountains of Campania, and the lands of the Church, which were now patrolled by the French. He urged him to reconsider carefully. But Giacinto replied that if he was destined to die, he'd prefer it to be at the end of a rope rather than at the bottom of the sea.

Henry begged him to wait at least until the following morning so that he could have time to reconsider. Instead, he stole away secretly during the night, without a word of farewell to any of his lifelong companions. Henry was grieved. Till now, his Family had stuck together, facing all kinds of hardships and the uncertainty of the future without complaint. Belisario's defection was a sign that their faith in his ability to lead them eventually back to their homes was wavering. But what other alternative did they have except to follow him?

"They are nothing more than a flock of helpless sheep," he thought in exasperation. "Most of them have never been out of Frascati. The wider world is a frightening place for them. I have no idea of what lies ahead of us either, but they depend on my authority. I cannot let them see me weaken or in doubt. Their faith in me would crumble totally. Although, God knows, I have no better idea than they have of what lies ahead of us!"

Acton sent him a message to say that Admiral Nelson had arrived with a small fleet of ships and that the *Vanguard* was anchored in the harbour, ready to convey the royal family to safety in Sicily. General Champoinnet's army was hard on the march south and camps had already been set in the hills a few miles from the city walls. Henry knew there was no time to delay and gave his servants orders to pack and make all their preparations.

He had to pay one of his hardest farewells to his prize team of horses. The master of the boat he had hired had been adamant that there would be no room for them on board. He stroked Nero's silken neck, thinking how patiently and courageously these high-bred animals had bourne the hard journey south and how he had felt proud to show them off to the haughty Spanish nobles at the Naples court. As he talked softly to them, they turned their heads towards him, twitching their ears. He handed a large pouch of money to the stable boy, making him swear on his holiest oath that he would look after them well. Silently, he prayed they would be taken by some French officer who would appreciate their beauty and that they would not end up as butcher meat.

There were other incidents that filled him with grief. During the last few days before their departure, they were increasingly disturbed day and night by urgent knockings on the door of the palazzo. Many of those who came to ask for help were clergymen and monks in fear of their lives. On the night before the Cardinal's departure, three ragged figures arrived. The gatekeeper did not want to let them in, but Henry heard their pleas from his window and commanded him to open the door while he went down the stairs to meet them. They fell on their knees, weeping and kissing his ring.

In halting Italian they explained they were French refractory priests who had refused to swear the oath of loyalty to the Republic. They had fled from France during the time of the Terrors and after wandering for months in Austria and Veneto, they had finally arrived in the Kingdom of Naples where they had been sought refuge. They had been living in a monastery outside the city for the past five years, but now they feared that they would be killed when the godless Jacobins invaded.

"Your Grace, we do not even dare to speak our native language in the streets any more in case the common people turn on us because we are French!"

They begged the Cardinal to take them with him to Sicily. They said there was not a single boat left for hire in the whole of Naples and, in any case, they are too poor to pay the high fees that the fishermen and boatmen were demanding.

Henry took pity on them. He gave them a purse of silver and told them to meet him on the quay when his party was due to sail. However, his attempt to save them ended badly because the ship's master doggedly refused to take them on, saying that his ship was already overloaded and he would not take any further risks. Before Henry could protest further, he ordered his crew to cast off, leaving the three poor priests standing on the quay, downcast and forlorn.

Henry had planned to sail at the same time as the *Vanguard*, but, looking at the enormous pile of trunks, packing cases and bundles heaped on the quay, it was plain that stowing the court's possessions was going to take at least another day. Squinting through the darkness, he made out the outlines of the *Sannita* and the *Archimede*, the escort vessels commanded by the Neapolitan Admiral Francesco Caracciolo, hovering behind the *Vanguard*. Small boats were being rowed back and forward between the two ships, conveying passengers and goods.

As they drew slowly out of the harbour, Moretto scrutinized the crowd of courtiers and servants bunched together on the quay, looking for his Austrian friend Heinrich. They had met briefly the previous evening and Heinrich had described the incredible scenes of panic at court.

Initially, he said, Ferdinand had not planned to leave. He had been confident that his faithful *Lazzaroni* would protect him and he drove around the streets distributing ducats lavishly to ensure their loyalty. The Neapolitans, however, did not respond with their usual demonstrations of affection. Although the preparations to evacuate the court had been carried out in great secrecy, the word had got around that the royal family were planning to slip away to save their skins. As the rumours spread, resentment mounted in the alleyways of the poor of Spaccanapoli, who became convinced they were being abandoned without defence, left at the mercy of the invading revolutionary forces.

The King changed his mind about staying on in Naples when a royal courier, bearing a letter from Acton to Nelson, was brutally lynched in the street and his severed head was set on a pike in the market place. This grisly incident, which evoked the dreadful excesses of the French Reign of Terror, acted as the necessary spur that convinced him to sail away with the rest of his family, without further delay.

Their departure was delayed, however, because of the huge amount of baggage that the royal couple insisted on taking on board. In addition to the clothes and personal effects of the family, which included a six-week-old baby grandchild, they were carrying off the crown jewels and the contents of the royal treasury, amounting to twenty million gold ducats and stacks of gold ingots from the mint, as well as numerous paintings and antiquities from the royal collections in the palaces of Naples, Capodimonte, Portici and Caserta.

In order to avoid incidents, it was decided that the royal fugitives would be conducted in secret to the port at night. Their passage led through a maze of cavernous service tunnels infested with bats and rats that lay under the palace apartments and led out to the harbour, where Captain Hardy, Nelson's second-in-command, would be waiting with three boats to row them to the *Vanguard*.

The cargo boat that Annibale had found had only one cabin with two wooden bunks where the Cardinal and Don Angelo Cesarini could rest, but the roof was so low that the occupants either had to sit or lie down. The rest of the party huddled on the deck among the heaps of nets, coils of rope and fish barrels, covering themselves as well as they could with cloaks and blankets and trying to ignore the nauseous smell that rose from the bilge. The crew told them to tie themselves securely with ropes to whatever strong support they could find. A storm was threatened and they could easily be swept overboard and lost.

The boat master grumbled and cursed throughout, saying he regretted agreeing to take them, that this was not the season to making a journey on these seas, that a storm was threatening and that the waves would be wild. The sky was as heavy and black as lead, with a wind howling across the surface of the water as he sniffed at the air and predicted a 'devil of a storm about to blow'.

They were barely out of Naples harbour, in fact, when the tempest broke, with lightning splitting the dark sky open and thunder cracks that deafened the panic-stricken passengers. The frail little boat keeled from side to side, as helpless as a bobbing float in a torrent. As they plunged up and down among towering walls of waves that seemed certain to engulf them, the Cardinal's men clung to the ropes in terror. This was the first sea voyage that most members of the Cardinal's retinue had ever experienced and they did not expect to survive.

"I think I'm already in hell and paying for my sins!" Moretto shouted over the shrieking wind to Eugenio Ridolfi, who lay huddled beside him, soaked through and retching helplessly onto the deck.

To add to their distress, they seemed to be making no progress. As soon as the boat had gained a mile or two from the Gulf of Naples, the wind reeled it in again, like a cat playing with a mouse when it lets its prey run forward to give it the illusion that it can escape, and then pulls it back. The waves became mountains as high as a church steeple, looming over the masts while the boat dived into deep dark troughs in the bowels of the ocean. After a very short time, the Cardinal's men did not care if they lived or died. None of them, not even the devoted Moretto, was able to make his way to the cabin to see how their lord was faring.

The two prelates had to cope not only with seasickness. They were thrown mercilessly around against the walls and beams and were covered in knocks and bruises. Henry's head was bleeding and Cesarini lay curled up on the floor, unable to rise.

The miserable voyage lasted for twenty-three days, with only brief lulls when the storm abated. But even in the periods when the sea was calm, the men seemed more dead than alive. They lay around in their sodden clothes, covered in vomit, without even the will or strength to try to get up. To add to their discomfort, they were subjected to the mockery and jibes of MacLaren, the only one of the Cardinal's men who had been unaffected by the adverse conditions.

He strode around the deck with his plaid wrapped firmly round him, laughing at their wretched state. "Weaklings! You're women – the lot of you! You think this was a storm? You think this was a high sea? Where I come from, we sail in all weathers – we sail through snow and fog so thick the helmsman can't see an inch in front of his nose. We slide like seals round our rocky islands. They're lashed by waves, summer and winter. You've never seen St Elmo's fire ablaze on the top mast. That's a sight to put fear into the toughest sailor. You need to sail around my islands. That way, you'd soon get your sea legs, instead of puking like women every five minutes!"

"Look at him!" Moretto said through clenched teeth. "His chest puffed out like a bantam cock!"

"He doesn't know what he's talking about anyway!" muttered Annibale, whose father had been in the Cardinal's service before him. "He was but a bit of a boy when he came to Rome. Old King James was still alive. I wager he doesn't remember anything about this country of his he's always going on about."

The conversation was interrupted by Henry's appearance on deck. He surveyed them with a cold look. "So this is what I find? Instead of praying to the Blessed Virgin for your salvation, you waste time quarrelling among yourselves!"

The coast of Messina, he told them, was in sight on the horizon. He told them to make themselves ready and sent a chastened MacLaren to assist Cesarini.

Although they all made an effort to obey him and stand up, most of them had to be carried to the boats waiting to row them into the harbour of Messina and when they put their feet on dry land, they stumbled and fell around, as if they were drunk, .

Henry gave the boat master gold to go back to Naples to collect the rest of the Family, promising him a large reward when he returned with them all, and sent MacLaren to hire litters to carry himself and Cesarini into the city. Before he left Naples, he had arranged for his household to lodge with three other Cardinals who were also taking refuge in Sicily. None of the prelates had anticipated that they would be barred for so long from returning to their homes, and the financial resources of all of them were shrinking. Henry and Don Angelo therefore moved into a single large property, to be shared with Braschi, Doria Pamphilj and Pignatelli. Although the house was capacious, it was an uncomfortable arrangement that inevitably led to bickering and complaints, especially among the kitchen servants.

The next few days passed gloomily with long vigils of prayer in the nearby church. The storms returned, even worse than before, with no word either of the *Vanguard* or the boat carrying the rest of the Cardinal's servants and Henry spent long and anxious hours on the roof of the house, scrutinising the sea through the telescope he had acquired from one of the sailors in the port.

The little merchant ship arrived late one night and downloaded its exhausted passengers. Henry, who had been awake for several hours, called out to Eugenio to come at once and dress him, while Moretto was dispatched to get a carriage to take them to the harbour.

He found his servants stretched out on the rocks trying to recover from their ordeal. None of them had touched food for days and some were so weak that they were unable to rise. Henry however, was relieved to see them at all. He had had doubts about the boat master keeping his word, despite the lure of generous compensation. Thankfully, despite all his misgivings, the man had kept faith and the Family was safe. He signalled Moretto to hand over the promised purse of ducats.

Garani struggled to his feet and staggered over to kneel at the Cardinal's feet.

"I hope I'm not dreaming, sire," he said. "And this is really you. We were certain we were dead. We were ghosts in purgatory, expecting to end up at the bottom of the sea."

"You are indeed safe now, my friend," Henry replied. "And if you can rally the others, there is shelter and food awaiting you not far away in the town, just over there."

Annibale had meantime arrived with some of his guards and Henry instructed him to put the oldest and weakest into the carriage and to send a man on ahead to organise food for the new arrivals and pallets where they could rest. He walked alongside the carriage, along with the others, leaning on his cane.

He was anxious for news, but he curbed his impatience till he could hear a murmur of voices rising from the kitchens and he summoned Garani.

"What about the *Vanguard*?" he asked. "It hasn't arrived yet. Did you get any news of it?"

"We left together with Lord Nelson," Garani said. "His ships were supposed to leave just after you, but there were endless delays. All these courtiers and officials with their families had to be taken out to the two ships Admiral Caracciolo had brought to escort the *Vanguard*. Then Caracciolo found he was left without a crew. Over two hundred of them had deserted and slipped away. So he had to ask Nelson to lend him some of his seamen to man his ships. But even then they couldn't up anchor because of the winds that kept them blocked in the harbour.

"We were waiting all that time for your boat to come back and get us, so we saw everything that was going on. They were held up for over two days and all that time there were delegations of citizens being rowed out to the ships to beg the King not to abandon them. But he wouldn't receive 'em. Too scared. He knew if he went back on land, they might kill him! Not that they can be blamed, I'm sure you'll agree, sire."

"Continue!" Henry cut short.

"Well, it was almost the Feast of Christmas. The twenty-third of December. We heard that the French had arrived and Nelson said there was no more time to lose, even though a storm was threatening. Our boat had arrived as well and we set off along with them. Our captain said it was better we stick together. He'd keep near the *Sannita*. She was in better condition than the *Vanguard* and she'd be able to pick up any survivors if we sank. That's what he said. Laughing, he was the devil!

"You can imagine how we were. We'd never been on the sea before. We were all scared to death. And then the storm hit. I never could have imagined anything like it. We were sure our last hour had come. We'd end up at the bottom of the sea with no graves for our loved ones to weep over…"

Henry interrupted him impatiently. "What about the *Vanguard*? Did she come to grief?"

"That I can't tell you, my lord! We lost her and the other two ships. It was black, day and night. We couldn't see more than a yard in front of us! The only one that kept calm was that rogue of a captain. He kept telling us that the next wave was sure to swallow us. But in the end we stopped listening to 'im.

"One thing we did see! It was on the Feast of Saint Stephen. For the whole night, the sky over the Bay of Naples glowed fiery red. The captain wept when he saw it. He said they were burning the Neapolitan war fleet. It'd been hidden away in the Grotto of Posillipo but either the French had found the ships, or the Bourbons had destroyed them so that the French wouldn't get them. These fine ships were the pride of the kingdom, he said. It broke his heart to see them ending in ashes."

Just at that moment, Moretto burst into the room, in a state of great excitement.

"Sire," he cried. "The *Vanguard* has been spotted. She's coming into harbour now. They say she's a sorry sight – masts broken, sails torn, but still afloat."

Henry at once struggled to his feet. "We must go and meet her!" he said. "Come with me, both of you! Tell Annibale to get carriages if he can and litters. Alert the kitchens. Tell them to get ready hot food and wine!"

Henry was at the harbour when the *Vanguard* dropped anchor. Slowly the boats were lowered and passengers were carried or handed in. Among then, he glimpsed the dwarf, Don Rodrigo, who scuttled off quickly without looking to left or right as soon as his feet touched dry land. He had lost his wig and he hastily pulled up his cape to hide his bald head.

One boat contained only two women and as it drew near, Henry recognised the Queen of Naples and Emma Hamilton. They were both sitting motionless, shrouded in heavy cloaks. Maria Carolina was carrying a bundle, laid across her lap. She was deadly pale. She held herself rigid, her gaze fixed before her, empty of expression, with the eyes of a sleepwalker. One of the seamen came forward to help her out of the boat. He tried to take the bundle out of her arms, but she clung on to it fiercely, and Henry, who had also come forward to help, saw with a shock of horror that she was holding the dead body of her youngest child, the little six-year old Prince Alberto.

Emma Hamilton got out and waded up onto the beach, dragging her wet skirts. She drew Henry aside.

"My poor lady! She is totally distraught. She hasn't spoken a word since it happened." She spoke very quietly, so that he had to strain to hear her. "Little Albert! He was my favourite. Everybody loved him, but he was always a delicate child. He was seized with convulsions. We took turns to hold him – his poor little body was racked with spasms for hours. He died in my arms on Christmas Eve."

Henry moved instinctively towards the Queen, who was being lifted into a carriage, but Emma laid a hand on his arm.

"Forgive me this liberty, Your Grace, but she will not understand anything you say. Give her a little time to rest then she will be glad of any comfort you can give her."

Henry glanced sharply at her. He detected a new tone of determination in her voice. She had always given him the impression of delicacy and fragility, but now he glimpsed a will of steel that lay behind her outward show of simplicity and innocence. He began to understand the power that gave her such a hold over her husband, the Admiral her lover, and the Queen.

"Tell me, my Lady, where is her husband, the King?"

Emma shrugged. The briefest expression of contempt crossed her face, but her voice remained low and even.

"His Majesty is visiting his Kingdom of Sicily for the first time and he is aware how important it is to appear before his subjects like a king. He is therefore making his preparations."

"Pardon me, but I do not see your husband either."

"He is recovering from his fright on the high seas when he was convinced he was going to die. He had two armed pistols at the ready. His intention was to shoot himself if the ship sank."

For the first time, she allowed a small, dry smile to cross her face.

"We owe our lives to Lord Nelson. It was only thanks to his skill and seamanship that the *Vanguard* survived. The ships of Admiral Caracciolo, which were escorting us, were blown off course. I don't know where they have ended up. The voyage could not have been worse – and not just for the storm – my Lord Nelson said it was the worst storm he had ever encountered in all his life at sea – but the servants were so incompetent that they forgot to load many of our supplies. We were without firewood or candles. Salted anchovies was all there was to eat after the first day or two! But of course, by then most of us were unable to eat anything at all."

They were joined by an older English lady wrapped in a white wool shawl who bent her head and curtseyed deeply.

"My mother," Emma explained, introducing her to the Cardinal, who bowed. He had not seen the lady before, although he knew that she lived in seclusion at the Ambassador's villa. "She has been a tower of strength. The women Her Majesty brought with her from Naples were totally incapable of giving us the minimum assistance. My mother and I coped alone, giving what help we could." She raised her chin and looked him full in the eyes. It was a look that told him she considered herself the equal of anyone and she would not be put down:

"Lord Nelson himself told us of his admiration for our efforts."

Emma's mother touched her daughter's arm, indicating that they should go on. Henry realised that the two women were shivering in the cold morning air and that their capes were wet. He immediately offered them his carriage and hospitality at his lodgings.

Emma thanked him, but she said that as soon as the King had descended and greeted the Sicilian nobles who had come to meet him, the entire court would be moving to Palermo, where preparations to receive them were already underway.

Dawn broke and the morning advanced. From his vantage point on the roof of the villa, Henry observed Ferdinand's descent from the *Vanguard* through his telescope. The King seemed to be fully recovered from the recent ordeal. He was freshly shaved, wigged and powdered and clad in an elegant blue velvet coat and a waistcoat embroidered in gold thread, white breeches, silk stockings and gold-buckled shoes that glinted in the sunlight. He was a tall man, only slightly overweight, and Henry had to admit that he cut a princely figure. A group of local noblemen had meanwhile assembled on the quay to meet him. Henry observed how he greeted them all jovially, clapping them on the shoulders. No doubt, the Cardinal reflected disapprovingly, he was accepting invitations to partake in hunting trip on their lands.

If it had not been for their circumstances of homeless refugees, their new life in Sicily would have been easy and pleasant. The city was known as Messina the Noble, due to its privileged position on the Straits that linked the Ionian Sea with the Mediterranean. After the nightmare flight from Naples, the Cardinal's men felt they had arrived in paradise. The climate was consistently mild. The high steep cliffs enclosing the city were covered with pomegranates, grapes and oleanders, as well as exotic plants from the Americas, like the giant cacti sprouting red, orange and yellow fruits on their fat round branches. Gardens and orchards flourished in every corner. The Messina of the period was one of the most charming and prosperous cities in Europe, full of aristocratic palaces, decorative fountains, spacious piazzas, theatres and libraries. Every evening, at sunset, a gentle breeze blew in from the sea, refreshing the air, and the townspeople gathered together in the squares and along the seafront. Henry watched them strolling back and forward under the stars until late at night, chatting, singing and reciting poetry.

He was astonished when he learned that this splendid city had been almost completely destroyed by an earthquake less than twenty years previously. To add to their suffering, the population had had to cope almost immediately afterwards with a second calamity, when cholera spread its deadly fingers among the ruins. Over sixty thousand people died before these twin scourges ended their course.

King Ferdinand had met the emergency with unstinting generosity. He immediately sent ships to Messina, loaded with food, medicines and clothing, which he paid for out of his own private purse, as well as doctors and military engineers, thus earning the eternal gratitude and love of his Sicilian subjects. The same could not be said for his wife, 'the Austrian Woman'. Maria Carolina had made a serious tactical error by refusing to let the starving survivors accept a shipload of grain sent from the hated land of France. As a result, she had become one of the most unpopular sovereigns in the island's history.

It irked Henry to live in close proximity with his brother cardinals and so he went out for most of the day, with Moretto as his only companion. He liked to stroll down to the harbour and talk to the fisher-folk, as he used to walk around the workshops at Frascati, watching the blacksmiths, knife grinders, tailors, shoemakers, carpenters and bakers busy at their trades. He often told Moretto that he admired their skills. As a royal prince, he said, he had been taught nothing useful, apart from shooting, dancing and Latin. As always, Moretto demurred, saying that, on the contrary, His Majesty had many skills that befitted his station and Henry would laugh and shake his head, as if the Boy had said something amusing.

Most of the city had been rebuilt. The public buildings and the palaces of the nobility and the wealthy merchants had been restored but the backstreets still bore many scars. Most of the houses of the poor had been roughly patched up and were only half finished. He was struck by the odd appearance of the fishermen's cottages along the seashore. They all seemed to be levelled off, as if a giant axe had cleanly lopped off their roofs and upper floors. He walked over to an old man sitting on the sea wall, repairing his nets, to ask him the reason.

"Ah, my Lord, you may well ask. It was the earthquake. A terrible time, Your Honour. All our homes were lost. Nothing left but piles of stones as high as – as that church steeple over there. But fisher folk stick together. We prayed to Saint Rosalia and Saint Barbara to give us strength and we got together and built back as much as we were able. It's enough to shelter our families." He waved his hand towards the row of truncated cottages. "In time," he said, "we'll build the rest. In time, we'll finish our homes – make them good as new again."

Henry asked him gently about his family. The old man spread his hands: "It was the will of God to take my wife and my son – a fine lad he was, already coming out with me in the boats. Then the fever got my Tina and my Rita – fine girls too, just about ready for marriage. I only have the one daughter left now to care for me in my old age."

He shook his head and bent down over his nets. Henry gestured to Moretto, who was waiting nearby, to bring the pouch of money he always gave him to carry at his belt and to hand it over to the fisherman, but, to his surprise, the old man refused.

"I thank you, Your Honour," he said gravely. "But I do not want to be favoured over my neighbours. In our community we all help each other. We share our daily catch with those that have had less fortune. We look after our widows and fatherless children and make sure they are not left in want. We are all equal before the good God, who will continue to look after us and grant us his aid and protection."

Henry was humbled and moved by these words. He told Moretto to lay the pouch on a nearby stone, and said, "Share this then with your community. I will pray that the Blessed Virgin will take you under her protection and ease your sufferings and misfortune."

Messina to Palermo

Spring 1799

They had been less than a month in Messina when a messenger arrived with summons to attend the Queen at Palermo. Henry was not keen to undertake the journey. He disliked being singled out in this way, fearing it could arouse suspicion and resentment among his brother cardinals. However, after some thought he decided that he could hardly refuse since his Family had enjoyed the generosity and protection of the Bourbon court for many months in Naples.

Leaving most of his entourage in Messina, he took Moretto as his personal servant and Garani and Annibale as his escorts, as well as a grumbling Don Angelo Cesarini, who said he had heard of the dangers of bandits and highway robbers on the road and since, purely by the grace of God, they had managed to avoid attacks on the road to Velletri, they should not tempt God's providence yet another time.

The journey to Palermo was long, uncomfortable and tedious. Over a hundred miles separated Messina from Palermo and much of it was over mountainous terrain. They were obliged to use mules rather than horses on the roughest tracts. There were sixteen staging posts between the two cities, but they found some of them closed and others without inns. However, they were able to find hospitality at religious houses near the towns of Tindaro, Santo Stefano di Carnastra and Cefalù where they could stop for a night's rest. It was a slow, exhausting journey that took them almost five days, due to delays at border points where bored officials took their time studying their documents, passes and the contents of their baggage. Fortunately, they did not come across any brigands on the road and they progressed without mishap.

Their hearts lifted when at last the towers and domes of Palermo appeared on the horizon and they were able to make their way to the Benedictine monastery where they had rented lodgings near the Cathedral. Henry hoped that their sojourn would not last more than a couple of weeks.

The arrival of the Bourbon court, along with some two thousand high-ranking refugees with their servants, goods and paraphernalia, had given the sleepy provincial city of Palermo an unaccustomed boost. The streets were suddenly filled with courtiers, diplomats, merchants, soldiers and members of the exiled clergy. A babel of tongues in Russian, German, Spanish and English filled the streets and piazzas. Within a short time, various nations had installed their official representatives in the Sicilian capital, along with their merchants and spies. As a result, the city was booming. Trade was brisk. Work opportunities abounded. The number of beggars at the church doors dwindled.

While Naples, meanwhile, was being transformed into the Parthenopean Republic, another of France's 'sister' republics, the Bourbon royal family set about creating their new court in Sicily. Suitable quarters for a royal household, however, were limited in this remote and hitherto neglected province of the great Kingdom of Naples. To make matters more difficult, it was an unusually cold winter, with snow and ice lying over the city. The best accommodation Ferdinand could find for his family was a dreary and neglected mansion that had been uninhabited for some time. The rooms were small, damp and sparsely furnished. The cold tiled floors added to the chill of the atmosphere and there were no carpets or comfortable upholstered armchairs and couches.

Maria Carolina was horrified to find herself in this situation. She complained bitterly that none of the doors or windows closed properly and that they let in draughts in every room. Accustomed to a climate that was normally mild all year round, the Sicilian houses and palaces rarely had fireplaces, and in Palazzo Colli the Queen and her family had to huddle around braziers for warmth. Ferdinand was not totally indifferent to his wife's laments, but he said she must have patience for the moment, until he found another solution. In actual fact, he had other priorities that did not include home-hunting. The Forest of Ficuzza, less than a morning's ride away, was home to abundant game and he was spending his days there, riding or hunting with the local aristocrats, who were only too delighted to be in the company of their King.

The Hamiltons had fared better. After they had had a careful look around, they took over Palazzo Palagonia, a luxurious villa near the port, where they soon began to hold their customary lavish receptions, with Emma starring as the leading light of local society. Admiral Nelson continued to stay with them and Emma and Nelson no longer bothered to hide their relationship. The elderly and studious Hamilton either seemed unaware of what was going on or else he simply did not care. He spent his time observing the glowing fires of Etna through his telescope. Palermitan society latched onto the scandal immediately. The tales that circulated became more and more outrageous. Emma, they whispered, disguised herself as a sailor when she accompanied her one-armed lover on his inspection tours of taverns and brothels suspected of harbouring spies and republican sympathisers.

While he was waiting for a footman to announce him, Henry looked around the reception hall of Palazzo Colli, frowning. He saw stains of damp around the walls and patches of crumbling plasterwork. The fresco of saints that decorated the ceiling was badly faded and flaking.

As if reading his thoughts, Cesarini remarked in solemn tones, "These proud Bourbons have come to a sorry pass! This is a poor substitute for their grand palaces in Naples. This is a lesson for all the mighty – how far they may fall!"

"You are too right, Angelo!" Henry replied. "And the same may be said for ourselves!"

His tone was mild and ironic, but Cesarini was offended. He drew himself up, with his hand on his crucifix. "I see you are making fun of me, Henry! But there is little to joke about. Our present situation is, I agree, undesirable. But we can be sure of a reversal of our fortunes. We have right on our side and it must prevail. Our God of Mercy and the Holy Virgin will crush the evil serpent of disorder and our Holy Mother Church shall rise again. I pray for this day and night, as I believe you do too – when you are not out wandering around associating with low people and beggars!"

His last remark rang with a hard tone of disapproval. Henry's nose twitched but before he could reply, the footman returned to escort them upstairs to the *piano nobile*. The Queen was sitting in a corner of a vast, largely empty room, with her ladies gathered around her. The dwarf, Don Rodrigo, was seated apart, on a little stool in the opposite corner, as if he preferred not to be noticed. He had regained his habitual composure. He was dressed in the same rich clothes he had worn at the royal palace of Naples, with a small, neat wig on his head.

He appeared to be absorbed in a book, but Henry was aware that the small eyes had flicked momentarily in his direction, sizing him up. His visit, he realised, would not be private. Every detail would be relayed to the King, the court, the foreign spies, or whoever else the dwarf sold his services to. Henry was familiar with the ways of spies. He had grown up among them. Palazzo Muti had buzzed with them like a hornet's nest. They had spread rumours that had caused an irreparable rift between his mother and his mild-mannered father. They had besmirched his brother's reputation. They had slandered and belittled him as well and had cast doubts on the sincerity of his vocation. He had learned, however, how to deal with them and lead them off the track they were avidly sniffing out, by feeding them deceptive hints and false leads.

At this point of his life, however, Henry did not consider spies a threat. In Rome, in fact, he had barely been bothered by them. He knew that there was little in his way of life as Archbishop of Frascati that could interest the Hanoverian informers who had troubled his father and exasperated Charles, his brother, and that was why they dismissed him as a simple old man with airs of piety. Charles, unfortunately, had never learned discretion. His tempestuous relationship with his wife, Louise of Stolberg, had been the talk of Rome. Even the Pope had lent his ear to the slanderous tales that had painted the Young Pretender in the very worst light, while his adulterous wife was idolised by the common people as 'the Queen of Hearts'.

Henry turned his back on the dwarf and gave his full attention to the Queen. He was shocked at the change in her. She had aged. All traces of the haughty beauty of her youth, that had still been visible when he had last seen her at Caserta, had vanished. Her eyes were inflamed and swollen with weeping. Stray strands of grey hair escaped from under her wig and her dress was dishevelled, despite the efforts of her ladies to smooth the folds of the skirts she kept grasping and twisting in her hands.

"My Lord Cardinal, dear brother, look at me!" she implored. "I am the unhappiest of queens, mothers and women! I don't know if I can go on living after all I have suffered!"

Henry sat down beside her and laid a hand gently on her shoulder.

"Dear Lady," he said quietly. "I heard of your loss. The little Prince Albert. Believe me, I share your grief!"

"You think this is the only cause of my misfortune? So many of my children have come and gone! Eighteen times – yes, eighteen times – I gave my kingdom a child. But how many are left? How many were taken before they could grow into men and women? I did my duty to the realm, the duties of a queen. I submitted to the obligations of marriage, although my husband was crude and obnoxious and every act was hateful to me!"

Maria Carolina's ladies put their hands up to their mouths, twittering, while Cesarini hastily walked away and stood looking out of the window, his back turned. Henry felt his face grow hot but he did not remove his hand.

"Madame," he said softly. "You are distraught. What you are saying should be reserved for your confessor."

She gave a low, harsh laugh. "Lord Cardinal of York, you are a priest. Don't tell me you do not hear the confessions of women or that you do not give them absolution. My husband dares to tell me that my sufferings are the reward for my sins. He, who only thinks of his own amusement! He who does not think of protecting his wife and his daughters! He who does not believe our lives are in danger here!"

"Take heart, dear Lady," Henry said in the same soft tone. "The people of Palermo are loyal to your royal house. They will give you protection and help as long as you need it!"

But Maria Carolina was not to be comforted. Her face darkened.

"These people are too silent. They look at us without a word when we pass. The nobles who should be out to greet us and see to our needs hold back. They stay inside their homes. They are cautious. They are waiting to see which side they should throw themselves on!"

She clenched her fists and rubbed them up and down the side of her skirt.

"I can see that soon we will be thrown out of Sicily," she went on, her voice dropping lower till it became almost a hiss. "It may end even more tragically. Must we give these vultures everything we possess – all our jewels, our clothes, our finery and laces? Perhaps then they will leave us alone to live and die in peace."

"Do not torment yourself, Madame," Henry went on quietly. "The people will not rise up against you. Your husband the King is well loved."

Her lips turned inwards and she bared her teeth.

"Don't speak to me about my husband. He only thinks of himself. He never considers us. He has lost the best part of his crown and his kingdom, but he fills up his days amusing himself. We have lost most of our income, but what does he care? What about my children? What about my daughters? What will become of them? I can only pray they will be allowed to go to Vienna where they can find husbands, or else they take the veil and live under the protection of the Church."

Her eyes filled with tears. "I wrote to my daughter in Vienna and her husband the Emperor begging them to send us troops to fight the Corsican pig. But they did not even reply. They don't care at all about us! Their hearts are cold!"

There was little Henry could say to this. It was well known that Francis II was reluctant to enter into another war against Napoleon, who seemed, in fact, to be invincible. It was also true that Ferdinand seemed to think only about entertainment and diversions. Some of the court gossip had reached him. The King had grown tired of his wife's constant nagging and complaining and he had gone off to live in a villa near the sea where he could hunt and fish in peace. When his time was not taken up with these pursuits, he entertained the local nobility with soirées, receptions and theatrical performances. The Sicilian aristocrats were captivated by his friendly, easy-going ways and competed with each other to spend time in his company.

When Henry finally rose to go, Maria Carolina implored him to stay near her in Palermo.

"My dear brother, you alone can understand me, apart from my dearest Emma. We are both outcasts from our rightful kingdoms. We are fugitives, without help or support. I have such a great need of friends!"

Henry sighed. It pained him to refuse her plea. She was so ill and distraught. He had heard that Emma Hamilton, her only friend, did not come to see her as much as in the past, busy as she was entertaining Horatio Nelson. He knew too that her children avoided her because of her frequent scenes and outbursts. He was filled with pity for her and he also felt a strong sense of obligation. The thought of the generous asylum she had given him and his entourage in Naples weighed on his conscience. After a moment's hesitation, he promised to stay in Palermo as long as she needed him.

The House of Bells

During the next few days, Henry went out very little. He followed the rituals of the Benedictines, with their disciplined days, and confined himself to taking the air by walking round and round the monks' orchard and vegetable garden. He was tired and low in spirits. Cesarini too was doleful, anxiously awaiting news. Moretto, however, felt free to go out as his master seemed to have forgotten about him. He met up again with his old friend Heinrich, who kept him supplied with the latest court gossip.

One afternoon, a letter with the royal seal arrived saying that the following morning the King and Queen planned to go out into the countryside for a day excursion and that they desired the presence of their dear brother Stuart. At the bottom of the page, Maria Carolina had scribbled a couple of lines, begging him to come along. Henry, avoiding Don Angelo's disapproving expression, sent back his reply accepting the invitation and told Moretto to be ready to accompany him.

When they arrived at Palazzo Colli the following morning, they found the forecourt humming with activity. A great company of lords and ladies were gathered, while servants were running in and out of the cellars and kitchens, loading tables and chairs, flasks of wine and foodstuffs wrapped in cloths onto brightly painted donkey carts.

Henry had not really believed that husband and wife would be together, as they notoriously avoided each other's company. However, they were already seated in their separate carriages, with the royal children.

Francesco Gennaro, the Crown Prince, sat in his own coach with his wife, the Princess Maria Clementina, and their baby girl, cradled in the arms of her nurse. Ferdinand was in another coach. The ten-year old Prince Leopoldo, the couple's only other surviving male child, sat opposite his father, a bored expression on his face. The King was excited and animated. He was standing up, relaying orders to the servants and chatting amicably with the coachmen and footmen. By contrast, the Queen sat silent in her own carriage, with her two unmarried daughters. She kept her face averted and her parasol raised, although the sun was still low in the sky. It was obvious, Henry thought, as he went forward to greet her, that she had somehow been induced to submit to an experience she would have preferred to avoid. Looking around, he was surprised to see that the Hamiltons and Lord Nelson were not in the company

"We have a surprise today for you, Madame!" Ferdinand shouted over the heads of the crowd to his wife. He spoke in Italian rather than his habitual Neapolitan for the benefit of the Palermitan nobles, who did not understand the Naples dialect. "As you are dissatisfied with our house in Palermo, I have found us another residence. I requested the Prince of Aci, our Viceroy, to find us more suitable lodgings and he has obeyed my instructions with commendable efficiency."

Maria Carolina looked down at her hands. She was clearly distressed and she did not reply. Her daughters stared nervously at their father and clasped each other's hands.

They finally set off in a long and leisurely procession, wending their way slowly through the crowded streets and market places, where the people cheered and waved as they passed and Ferdinand threw handfuls of coins and comfits over their heads.

Once they were out of the city outskirts, the King's coach took the lead, heading along a well-beaten track through pastures and farmland. It was still mid-morning and the sun was pleasantly warm. The early Sicilian spring had arrived and almond trees scattered their soft pink blossoms along the route. Groves of lemon and orange trees stretched into the distance on either side, filling the air with their heady pungent perfume. The countryside was prosperous, gently undulating and pleasant, watered by streams and little pools. They passed several imposing summer residences belonging to the Palermo nobility, surrounded by extensive estates.

After a few miles at a leisurely pace, they reached a wide plain ringed by hills. Ferdinand became impatient and urged his coachman to drive on ahead till he finally halted and turned around to wait for the Queen and the princesses. Finally, the carriages drew up in front of a building that drew a gasp from the company. Henry stared. He had never seen anything like it before.

At the end of a wide driveway, that traversed a formal garden with palm trees and topiary animals enclosed in geometric plots edged with box hedges, stood a gaily-painted building of oriental inspiration. It was on three storeys, with a high columned porch and wooden balconies running all along the length of the first and second floors. A slender minaret rose on one side and the roof was topped by a Chinese-style pagoda. Hundreds of little bells, tinkling merrily in the morning breeze, dangled from the wrought iron railings surrounding the house.

The overall appearance was so odd and comical that many of the courtiers burst out laughing.

King Ferdinand was unperturbed. He stood up in his carriage and flung out his arms.

"This is Villa Campanelle, the House of Bells," he announced to the entire company. "Bells bring luck. They keep evil spirits away. This is a house of a good omen."

"*Che orrore!* What an abomination!" exclaimed Maria Carolina, her eyes wide with shock and consternation. She was horrified, not only at the eccentric appearance of the building, but also at her husband's open declaration of superstitious beliefs she considered fit only for the ignorant peasantry.

He paid no attention to her but went on happily. "This was the villa of Baron Lombardo. I have persuaded him to sell it to us. We shall make our new capital here and we shall be the envy of Europe. No other building like this exists. Look!" He spread his hand towards the vast expanse of woods and countryside that extended uninterrupted far over the horizon. "My desire has been to find a place similar to our palace at Caserta, with plenty of land around and good air.

"This is a healthy place. The air is good and clean for you and the children!" he insisted, dropping his voice to a coaxing tone. "You will lose your sickly look, my dear. This place will be beneficial for our little Leopoldo here who is always ailing. And Maria Amalia – she's been coughing ever since we left Naples."

Maria Carolina had sat motionless throughout this discourse, her face rigid with shock. But she recovered herself quickly and said in an icy voice, "I am not interested in toys, Sir, and I marvel that you, in such a grave moment, with your kingdom in peril, should allow yourself to be distracted with such a bauble. Your duty is not to create toy castles but to reconquer your throne and crush the invaders and the rebels!"

Ferdinand was unperturbed. "We shall call it La Favorita," he said, stretching wide his arms as if to encompass the entire building before him. "Like our beloved palace at Portici. We shall feel its loss less!"

He turned to her again, making a last attempt to placate her.

"I know, Madame, how sensitive you are regarding matters of our royal purse, so you will be pleased to know that this was a bargain. The Baron had contracted debts he was unable to honour and he was glad to sell it to us at a price far below its true value. I have many plans for this charming residence. I intend to start work right away. I have already contacted Giuseppe. Our dear Marvuglia is the best architect in our kingdom. He's busy right now with the Prince of Belmonte, but I won't have difficulty winkling him away from my friend the Prince.

"You shall see what this will become! It will be a marvel of the world. Don't be afraid that it won't prove worthy of us. I have informed the landowners nearby that it is our wish to expand our territory and they have all sworn that they are delighted to favour us by donating the land they possess along our borders.

"Look," he went on. "See how near we shall be to our capital. We are only a short distance from Palermo. It will be easy for our ministers to go back and forward and for you to go to the theatre as you liked to do in Naples."

He pointed back the road they had come. The Cathedral dome of Palermo, in fact, was just visible on the horizon.

He waved a hand again towards the house. "I have it all planned. You shall have an entire floor to yourself to decorate as you wish, since you do not care, I see, for the Chinese style, although, I can assure you, Madame, it is greatly in vogue in other countries. We shall live as a family, taking our meals together, without servants around. Marvuglia is to make us a mathematical table, where we can have our dishes hoisted up on ropes from the kitchens."

But Maria Carolina continued to look coldly away. Ferdinand shrugged and gave the signal to descend from the carriages. The servants jumped down and began to unload the wagons, setting out tables and chairs in preparation for an alfresco meal. The young people and children began to play and run around on the grass. While the food was laid out, the King, in high good humour, took it on himself to pour out the wine for the Sicilian nobles who had joined the expedition.

Henry took the opportunity to go and greet Maria Carolina, but she did not look at him or acknowledge his presence. Throughout the entire meal and the rest of the afternoon, she stayed in her carriage, biting her lip and twisting her gloves. Not even her daughters could persuade her to come and join in the revelry. Her husband ignored her. Her ladies brought her morsels of food from time to time but she refused them all. She remained seated, a mournful figure in the middle of the carefree gathering, as the fugitives from Naples put the painful memories of their recent trials and terrors behind them.

A few days later, the dwarf arrived unexpectedly at the monastery. He was carrying two letters. One was from his friend, Cardinal Albani. Henry inspected the seal. He suspected it had been intercepted by spies. However, he said nothing. He opened it and read that Albani was in Messina:

"I hope you will return here soon. I have important news for you concerning the Sede Vacante that I dare not put down on paper in case this letter ends in the wrong hands. I do not have any of my own men with me whom I can trust, so I shall say no more except to

warn you to be ready as I am hopeful of developments in our favour in the near future."

Henry folded it up without comment and handed it to Moretto. He saw that the second letter was from the Queen. Knowing that the dwarf was observing him, he was careful to show no emotion as he opened it, expecting to find a string of reproaches because he had not visited her as he had promised. However, the contents were quite different. Maria Carolina was jubilant.

"Dearest Cousin," she wrote, *"Rejoice with me! We hope to return soon to our kingdom. The hero, Cardinal Ruffo di Calabria, has mustered the Holy Faith army. Thousands of the right-minded are rushing to join him and fight under his banner.*

"Can you believe that this noble priest, already advanced in age, has taken upon himself to cast the hateful enemy out of our realm? He came to the King only days after we poor miserable outcasts arrived in Palermo and asked his leave to lead an expedition to recapture our rightful throne. My husband, who is, as you know, an idiot, gave him only one ship and eight men-of-arms in support. Undaunted, this great and courageous Cardinal sailed with this miserable small force to Calabria, which is his home territory, and proclaimed a Holy War in the name of the Bourbons and the Holy Roman Catholic Church.

"We hear that the people have flocked eagerly to his banner, encouraged by their parish priests, who support our just cause against the godless republicans. I so wish I could see him. They tell me he cuts the figure of a hero, in flowing white robes and mounted on a snow-white charger, like the knights of romances. The Holy Faith army is advancing at this moment through Calabria, sweeping all before it.

"Dear Admiral Nelson is patrolling the coast to protect them from attacks by sea and King George has also given his support. His government has arranged to send reinforcements of desperate men from the prisons of England to swell the ranks of the Sanfedisti, the fighters of the Holy Faith, as they are called.

"Before this year is passed, I hope to enjoy your company once more in our beloved gardens of Caserta."

Henry read no more, but folded up the letter and looked coldly at the dwarf, who was squinting up at him, eager to read his expression.

"Don Rodrigo," he said. "I thank you for bringing me these communications. I would now ask the favour of you to take back my message to Her Majesty the Queen."

He sat down at the monks' table and ordered Moretto to bring him pen, paper and ink. He wrote to Maria Carolina saying that circumstances forced him to return to Messina, but that he would come back to Palermo as soon as possible. He did not bother to elaborate. Her dwarf, who had certainly read Albani's letter, would be able to explain the circumstances he mentioned, if she had not already read the letter herself. He had been warned that, terrified as she was of conspiracy, all correspondence, official or private, that arrived at the Palermo court passed through her hands.

After the weary trek back to Messina, he found that Albano had already departed on a mission north, leaving Henry word that he had received a vital communication from Monsignor Consalvi with news that he would reveal as soon as possible.

Henry at once announced that he was going back to Palermo and he sent Moretto to sell two jewelled cups and a gold crucifix to meet future expenses. Don Angelo was full of indignant reproaches when he heard of his plans.

"Henry!" he said when they were alone together. "Have you lost your senses? Have you forgotten your station? Have you forgotten your vows and obligations to our Holy Mother Church?"

Henry looked at his old friend, half amused and half angry.

"What exactly are you implying, Angelo? Have I heard you correctly? You forget my age, which alone would be sufficient to defend me from gossip and evil wagging tongues! I have even more grey hairs than the Queen's own chaplain."

Cesarini glowered. "Don't believe you are safe. These courtiers are so idle that they find nothing better to do than throw filth around. The Queen is not loved. They will invent anything to put her in a bad light. Look at the Englishman, Lord Acton! They are convinced he is her lover but..." his voice faltered and he ended hastily in a lower tone. "I have been told this is untrue."

"Ah!" Henry retorted. "You have been talking to Lady Hamilton, I see. Take care of your reputation. We know that she is not a respectable woman – certainly not one to exchange confidences with a priest!"

Don Angelo withdrew, red-faced and defeated. But he came back shortly, contrite, and offered to accompany Henry back to Palermo.

"We can consider this journey as a penance to expiate our sins," he said in his most sanctimonious tones. But Henry gently refused his offer. He said he would only take Moretto and his valet Eugenio with him to Palermo and he needed Don Angelo in Messina to look after the others and manage his dwindling finances until he got back again. He did not bother to explain that he was not motivated by the desire to gratify the Queen's whim, but that he had other, more urgent, reasons for being in Palermo. The hints in Albani's last letter had convinced him that he needed to be in the capital city because that was where the news arrived. The letter had led him to hope that the war against Napoleon was finally taking a new direction and that the winds were beginning to blow in their favour.

Bonaparte was still in Egypt. His fleet had been destroyed by Nelson and he could not bring his grand *Armée d'Orient* back to France. His Italian army had suffered setbacks and the Directoire was recalling troops back up north to defend the conquered territories in Milan and Turin. Rome might soon be liberated. Meanwhile, it was time to think of a new papal election. He knew that his former protégé Ercole Consalvi was negotiating with the Holy Roman Emperor to hold the conclave in Venice.

But Henry never got back to Palermo. Not long after that, while he was preparing to leave, he had an accident. He had rented a couple of carriages to take his luggage and his attendants to Palermo. Both Moretto and Eugenio were busy supervising the operation and they did not notice that he was climbing into the first coach unassisted. He slipped on the steps and fell, striking his shinbone hard. Eugenio came running, but he waved him impatiently away, saying it was a trifle. But by that evening, his leg had swollen and was giving him a lot of pain. Despite the best efforts of his doctor to dress the wound it did not heal. An open sore developed that caused him a great deal of discomfort and limited his movements.

He had always been very active, despite his years, but now he was confined to his room, as his leg was suppurating and the dressings needed to be changed frequently. Moretto spent long hours with him, reading aloud to take his mind off his frustration at not being able to depart for Palermo. He dozed off frequently under the effects of the laudanum the doctor administered. While he slept, he tended to ramble, confusing incidents in the past with their present situation. He muttered prayers for his parishioners and expressed his fears of invaders, confusing them with the threat of an earthquake like the one that had destroyed Messina.

After a couple of days, when his fever finally subsided, he became lucid again. He told Moretto he had been dreaming about a miracle that had saved him in the past.

"Our Saviour rescued me when the floor collapsed in La Rocca. I was unhurt, but my poor secretary Gandolfi – do you remember him? He lost his life."

The fatal accident had happened many years earlier, not long after he had taken possession of the fortress of La Rocca. He was entertaining twenty eminent guests in honour of the Reverend Simonetti, canon of the Vatican Basilica, who had just been ordained a subdeacon. The banquet had barely begun when he noticed that the footmen arrayed along the wall were exchanging perplexed glances.

Calling one of them over, he asked what was wrong. The man said that they had all felt a strange shifting movement under their feet. His guests seated around the banqueting table, talking loudly and toasting each other's health, had noticed nothing, but suddenly, with a great roar, the centre of the floor gave way.

A huge gap opened up and the table, complete with all the diners, vanished before the servants' eyes. The main architrave had split apart, hurling Henry and all his guests down into the carriage room below. This had been his salvation because he landed on the roof of one of the coaches, breaking his fall, and he was unhurt. Many of the other guests were not so fortunate. Most lay stunned among the piles of masonry, broken chairs and furniture, shards of porcelain and buckled silverware. As soon as they had recovered from the shock, all the members of his household rushed to their aid but the thick cloud of dust and plaster hampered their vision and made them choke and splutter with fits of coughing.

Henry meanwhile had regained his composure and directed the rescuers from his perch on the carriage roof, sending for doctors and surgeons to attend to the wounded. The word of the disaster spread fast and within minutes all the citizens of Frascati had come rushing to their aid, giving loud thanks that the intervention of the Blessed Virgin had saved their beloved *Cardinale degli Organi* from harm.

Sadly, a fragment of marble had pierced the side of the secretary Gandolfi, who died of his injuries two days later. Don Bruni, his Master of Ceremonies, lay between life and death for many weeks. Others had broken limbs. Some were blinded by the dust and did not recover their sight for days. It had indeed been a miracle that they were not all dead.

He woke up agitated and Moretto tried to soothe him. "That is all in the past, sire. There is no need to distress yourself with these sad memories. The masons you called in afterwards to restore the pavements said that the beams were over three centuries old and should have been substituted much sooner. In fact, you remember that you had all the floors of La Rocca replaced and made safe. This happened five and twenty years ago and there have been no further incidents."

Henry finally smiled. "Well, if I did not do a good job," he said. "Perhaps the floors will collapse on the French!"

Part 4
Corfu

March–Summer 1799

Towards the middle of February, the long-awaited news arrived. Francis II had finally agreed to allow the conclave to be held in the Serenissima Republic of Venice, which was now under the dominion of the Austrian Emperor. Cardinals Pignatelli and Braschi-Onesti immediately made plans to sail, while Doria Pamphilji said he could not face another voyage and would go overland.

Despite the wound in his leg, which continued to trouble him, Henry was determined to go with them. First, however, he had to face the painful task of telling his Family that he would be leaving them behind. His finances were now so low that he realised he would not be able to cover the expenses of taking his retinue with him to Venice. He decided, in fact, that he would only have Moretto accompany him. All the others would stay on in Messina under Don Angelo's care until he was able to fetch them.

When he summoned them all together to convey his decision, they were stunned. Then the room rang with their protests.

"Lord," cried Annibale, forgetting to use the royal title in his agitation. "How can you think of such a thing? Travelling to a foreign land without protection! I have been your guard and protector for over twenty years. You can have no doubts of my loyalty. I would gladly give my life for you! You know that! Have you forgotten how I saved you from that assassin Oligomer? He was determined to kill you – lying in wait outside the church of the Capuchins…"

Garani broke in. "My sword arm too has always been at your service. Who is to drive your carriage over the broken roads, with outlaws on every side? How can you face the dangers of an unknown road without your men to guard you?"

Henry sighed. Even his valet, the normally timid Eugenio Ridolfi, was remonstrating in reproachful tones. "Sire, who is to dress you? You cannot dress yourself. Who is to look after your robes and hats? Who will ensure your shirts are clean when you have to meet the Holy Roman Emperor of Austria?"

Meanwhile, the rough old Scots warrior MacLaren was stamping around the room in agitation, muttering audible recriminations. "So it's come to this? I have served the House of Stuart all my life. I served your father, your brother and yourself. And now I'm to be cast aside, abandoned on this accursed island among strangers? It's come to this! I would never have believed I would meet such an end!"

Henry's nose twitched. His voice cut coldly across all their protests.

"Silence! Since when have you disputed my orders? Since when have you challenged my decisions? My mission to Venice is urgent and none of you can come with me. You are not being abandoned. You are simply to wait here with Monsignor Cesarini, who is to take my place during my absence and whom I expect you to obey without question, as you should obey me, your lord."

His men fell silent and stood with surly faces. Many of them glowered resentfully at Moretto, who was standing staring out of a window, plainly embarrassed. Cesarini too looked uneasy. He had argued with Henry the night before and had seen that it was useless to try to change his mind. Keeping only a small amount to pay for the journey to Venice, Henry had given him the bulk of his gold and jewels to cover his Family's expenses in Messina for the next few months. He had confided in his friend that he was optimistic the war would soon be over and the new Pope would be able to return to Rome.

Two days later, the three Cardinals and their servants crossed over to the Calabrian coast where they hired a sturdy Greek merchant ship to take them round the heel of Italy and up the Adriatic. The voyage started well. The ship hugged the coast, propelled by a gentle wind, but when they entered the Gulf of Taranto, they sailed straight into a violent tempest. Once again, they found themselves tossed around helplessly, at the mercy of winds that seemed to change direction every few minutes. For several days, the ship floundered among monstrous waves, unable to keep on its established course as it was blown backwards and forwards between the coast of Apulia and the shores of Albania.

The travellers were shortly laid low with seasickness. Henry and Braschi kept to their cabin but Pignatelli said he did not wish to die like a drowning rat caught in a hole. He stayed up on the heaving deck, staggering about and losing his balance, clutching on to ropes and railings, while he prayed loudly all the time for their salvation. His wandering hindered the work of the crew, who cursed him repeatedly as he got in their way.

Henry lost count of time before the storm finally abated and he was able to leave the cabin. He made his way slowly up the narrow wooden stairs to the deck, taking deep breaths of the salty breeze to clear his head. Dawn was breaking and black clouds were separating and drifting away in long fragmentary streams to reveal a pale pearly sky. He gazed around in all directions but he could see nothing except the endless ocean. However, he realised almost at once that something was wrong. The captain was steering due east towards the rising sun, rather than north as he had been ordered.

Henry was immediately alarmed. He had not liked the look of the captain from the very start. He had seemed a shifty fellow, dirty and ignorant. He had grabbed their gold too eagerly, stuffing it at once inside his shirt without bothering to count it. Henry looked around at the crew and noticed that they did not meet his eyes, going about their work as if their passengers did not exist. He wondered uneasily if they had landed among pirates. They had been so eager to leave on their mission to Venice that they had hired the first ship they came across in Reggio Calabria without checking the owner's credentials. He had heard of unscrupulous merchants who did not trade only in goods, but also in Arab slaves. They roamed round the Mediterranean, attacking any African fishing boats they came across and took the crews prisoner. Those too poor to be ransomed were sold in the market places of the towns and islands in the Adriatic.

The fear flashed through his mind that they were being betrayed and that they would be handed over as prisoners to the French. He knew that they controlled the Island of Malta and most of the Ionian Islands. Three cardinals of the Holy Roman Church, he thought, would be considered a juicy prize if the republican rebels were bent on retarding the conclave to elect a new Pope!

The captain was at the helm, whistling tunelessly through broken yellow teeth, and Henry made his way over to demand explanations. The fellow did not seem surprised or put out by Henry's angry tone. Spitting sideways into the wind, he turned his head round and with an ingratiating grin he explained in a few words of mongrel Italian that they were heading for the Island of Corfu. He said that his ship had suffered damage during the storm and needed to be repaired.

Henry's alarm deepened. He had no way of knowing whether this change of plan was due to the adverse winds and the helmsman's incompetence or if it had been the scoundrel's intention all along to consign them to the enemy.

At that moment, the faint outline of the island appeared on the horizon. Pignatelli joined them, holding his spyglass. He exchanged a questioning glance with Henry. The captain, reading the expression on their faces, attempted to reassure them of his good faith. He began by apologising profusely for all the discomfort and inconvenience they had suffered during the voyage. Their Lord Cardinals, however, could not blame him in any way for that, he insisted. No one could control the whim of the sea! It had been a hard crossing. He would have advised them to wait had he expected bad weather. But it had been tranquil when they had set out from Reggio. How could he have foreseen such a change – such a wild storm! But storms were not unusual in these parts, even in spring – in fact, often in spring.

Henry cut him off. He wanted to know about the political situation in the Greek island they were heading towards. The captain seemed to have trouble understanding the question, which made the two Cardinals more suspicious. He kept repeating, vigorously nodding his head, "Corfu no France. No France! Russi, Turki!"

They did not know whether to believe him or not. They had had no news since they left Messina. At last, seeing that they remained sceptical, the captain called over the ship's *mozzo*, a young lad of about twelve, who spoke English reasonably well.

The boy assured them that what the captain said was true. The island was no longer in French hands. Only the day before it had been captured by the Russians and the Turks, who were the enemies of General Napoleon, and so they could land there safely. Yesterday evening, his captain had sent a tender on ahead to advise the esteemed British Consul, Monsieur Spiridion Foresti, of our imminent arrival and the gentleman would certainly be at the harbour to greet them.

The boy went on to tell them that he was himself from Corfu. During the battle, he had been very worried because his mother and his small brothers lived on the other side of the island. Now, however, he had been assured that they were safe. Since, according to what they had been told, the victory of Corfu had been so recent, Henry wondered how the lad could have received this information, but then he noticed the scores of little fishing boats that had come out to meet them. They were clustering like bees around the hull, shouting out excited and jubilant messages in various tongues to the mariners who were swarming up the masts to lower and furl the sails as they headed for the harbour.

All the confusion woke Moretto, who had fallen asleep exhausted on the deck. Contrite, he rushed forward to help his master prepare for the landing, but Henry waved him impatiently away and turned to the rail to watch as they approached the island.

As they drew near, Henry realised that the island of Corfu was a citadel, cut off from the sea by massive walls reinforced by buttresses. The town was dominated by a high rock crowned with one of the most formidable fortresses he had ever seen and the surrounding hills bristled with batteries. As they slipped slowly past a fortified island that stood guard over the harbour approach, Henry wondered how it had been possible to take such a well-defended city.

Meanwhile, the boy was tugging at his sleeve. "Signore," he said, pointing to the two mountains rearing up behind the township. "Look! Those are Abraham and Salvatore. They have always protected us and saved us from disaster. That's Fort St Rocco between them. Over there is Vido Island. Our enemies had to take that first before they could advance."

The captain came up to them, owing and showing his teeth in a wide grin, and offered Henry his telescope. As the Cardinal scrutinised the horizon, moving the glass back and forward to take in the whole scene, the man began to point out various items he believed would be of interest. Henry trained the lens for a long moment on the fleet of ships crowded in the harbour and then moved it up to scrutinise the flags hoisted above the citadel.

"Tell me," he demanded. "Who is now in command of this island?"

The captain squinted sideways and stroked his chin.

"Why, of course, your lordship. You are without news. There has been a siege and the French are vanquished. My valiant people withstood them. I have just learned that a whole quarter of our city was burned down because the people refused to surrender their weapons to General Chabot."

"You have not answered my question," Henry said sternly. It had not escaped him that the rogue's command of Italian had greatly improved in the last few minutes.

"Well, now we are ruled by the Ottomans, with the backing of the Russians. They say, however, that Vice-Admiral Abdul-kabir Bey is a just and temperate man, although, of course, he's an infidel and not a Christian. However, have no fear. You will be under the protection of Monsieur Foresti, who represents the government of Britain and is the enemy of the Corsican."

"And who might this gentleman be? His name is Greek or Italian, not English."

"Ah, your Grace, put your mind at rest. He is a man of great importance. He has the ear of the great Lord Nelson himself and, they say, also of the English King George. He was arrested and imprisoned by the French invaders but he sent off his dispatches just the same – right under their noses! Nothing happens in our islands that Monsieur Foresti doesn't know. He is the greatest man on the islands – as cunning as a fox and a lion in courage. He is already waiting for you. Just look there – on the quay."

Henry put the telescope to his eye and looked in the direction of the captain's pointing finger. He was able to make out a small delegation of waiting citizens, surrounded by an escort of soldiers. It was too far off for him to tell if they were wearing Russian uniform. Standing in the front of the group, he could just make out a tall figure in a blue cape, whom he took to be the extraordinary foxy and leonine Monsieur Foresti. His curiosity was aroused.

Meanwhile, Braschi-Onesti came up on deck, supported by two of his valets, his face a sickly pallor. He went to stand beside Pignatelli, who informed him of the change of destination. Both men then turned and looked apprehensively towards the harbour.

The ship dropped anchor and a fleet of small rowboats arrived to take the party ashore. To his consternation, Henry found that his injured leg was so weak that he was unable to descend the ladder that the crew had thrown over the side of the ship. Finally, the captain called over a robust seaman who was commanded to carry the Lord Cardinal down on his back. Henry took a look at the mariners gathered round the deck rail, eager to see the undignified spectacle and refused this solution. After some confabulation, the captain agreed to lower him in a sling made from a piece of sailcloth tied at the four corners. This method was, if anything, even more uncomfortable because he was continuously knocked against the hull but he bore the discomfort in silence. In the meantime Moretto had scrambled down the ladder and onto the boat so that he could help his master out of the sling and safely to his seat.

After a short time, they reached the harbour, where the townsmen rushed forward to help them step onto the quay and they stood waiting to meet Signor Spiridion Foresti.

Henry looked him over. He noted that he was taller than most of the Greeks he had met. His long, black hair was oiled and tied back at his neck with a black ribbon, in the style of a corsair. His skin was swarthy and he had a sharp protruding nose and chin. He was elegantly dressed and carried himself with ease and confidence. Had Henry not been warned by the captain, he would have taken him for a courtier and gentleman, rather than a professional informer.

While the three prelates tried to compose themselves and assume an appearance of dignity after their hard voyage, Foresti's dark, alert eyes flicked for the briefest moment over each one of them before he bowed deeply and reached out to kiss their rings. Henry reflected speculatively that not much missed Monsieur Foresti's quick-moving and penetrating glance. It was easy, in fact, to see why he was compared to a fox.

"My Lords," he greeted them. "On behalf of His Britannic Majesty, whom I represent, it is a great honour for me to welcome you to our poor island, which, alas, has suffered a great deal of damage and hardship in the recent conflict. However, we feel we can offer you adequate hospitality until you decide to proceed upon your journey. For now it is better that you rest."

With a wave of his hand, he summoned three Venetian sedan chairs to convey the exhausted guests to the place where they were to reside. Moretto hurried to take up his position trotting by his master's side, but not before he had seen the Greek sea captain, who had been waiting in a doorway nearby, go up to Foresti and speak quickly in his ear. Foresti listened gravely and nodded, then he took a leather pouch from his belt and gave it to the man. Afterwards, the Boy swore that he had been near enough to hear the clink of coins and had glimpsed the captain's satisfied and crafty expression.

They travelled through a maze of streets lined with buildings that bore clear signs of the recent bombardments. Some houses had great gaps in their walls; others had been reduced to rubble. At every turn they saw groups of citizens hunting among the ruins for their possessions. Russian soldiers were posted on street corners, guarding the palaces of the wealthy from looters. Despite the scenes of devastation, however, the city was already beginning to return to life. Little stalls were set up in the open spaces and piazzas with peasant farmers selling vegetables and fruit and they glimpsed a butcher under an arcade, cutting up the carcass of a horse.

Finally the bearers stopped in front of a wide courtyard, flanked on three sides by palaces in the Venetian style. Fragments of ancient Greek and Roman sculptures lay around the gardens, which had been stripped of all their fruit trees and rose bushes. Henry spotted a cannon ball embedded in the roots of a broken pomegranate bush. The buildings, however, were intact.

Foresti had accompanied them on horseback and now he dismounted and bowed.

"My Lord Cardinals, Eminences, the Governor of our island has ordered this residence to be prepared for you. You will find it a little bare of furnishings. We are just emerging from a war, as you know, and it is not possible to keep a guard on everything. However, the buildings have not suffered damage and we hope we have installed everything you will need. You will find the servants obedient and willing, even if they do not all speak your language. But I am certain that Men of the Church of your standing and experience will have no trouble making your commands understood."

The palace had once belonged to a rich Venetian merchant and during the siege it had hosted the French governor, General Chabot, who had surrendered it to the Russian commander Fyodor Uschakov. It had therefore suffered little internal damage. It was spacious enough to allow all three Cardinals and their servants to have separate lodgings. While Pignatelli and Braschi-Onesti hurried inside to rest after the trials of the sea voyage, Henry lingered to thank Foresti for his courtesy and for the trouble he had taken to ensure that their stay, although short – he emphasised the word short – would be as comfortable as possible. During their passage through the war-stricken city, he had had an uneasy thought that since the political situation was so unsettled they might not be able to leave whenever they wished.

However, Foresti gave no sign of having understood his hinted query. He bowed and said the new governor, the Vice-Admiral Bey Abdul Kabir, would be honoured to meet them and that an invitation would be delivered soon.

Days passed. It was difficult to rest as the noise of hammering, sawing, rattling and the trundling of barrow wheels went on day and night, all over the town, as the islanders worked to restore their homes and public buildings. Henry went out frequently. He hired a litter if his leg was giving him too much pain to walk. On better days and if he was going only short distances, he walked, leaning heavily on Moretto's shoulder. He was curious to see the city, where the winged lion of St Mark still crouched defiantly on the walls of the fortress, mute stone attestation to the four centuries-long dominance of the Serenissima Republic of Venice. He liked to stop and rest at Platia Dimarhiou where the nobles and wealthy merchants congregated in the Loggia before they were cast out by the French.

He also explored some of the churches of the Greek faith, admiring the jewelled icons of the Virgin and Son. He noted sadly that the lower walls, the altars and presbyteries had all been stripped of their gold leaf and decorations, leaving empty patches and cracks. He watched the black-robed priests scurrying to and fro, carrying objects wrapped in canvas and cloths. They were bringing back the church treasures – the gold and silver chalices and candelabra, the jewelled crosses and the crowns of the Child and the saints, the precious caskets of reliquaries, the golden mitres and chasubles embroidered in gold and silver thread. The fact that they were being brought out of hiding and returned to their rightful place was, he thought, the most concrete sign that the great fear of war and pillage was over.

Not long after their arrival, Henry reached his seventy-fifth year. The previous year, his birthday had occurred while they were staying at the monastery of St Erasmus and he had forbidden his servants to mention it. This year again he was in no mood to celebrate. War went on, with no end in sight. They were stranded in Corfu when, instead, they urgently needed to reach Venice. His health had deteriorated. His leg would not heal. He could no longer ride and he walked with difficulty. When he looked in the glass, he saw that he was no longer the same man as before. In Frascati, he had been energetic and vigorous and he had still been able to ignore his years. But the trials of the flight from Napoleon had taxed his body. He now walked with a permanent stoop, leaning heavily on a cane. Pain had drawn deep new lines across his brow and down the sides of his mouth.

The Siege of Corfu

October 1798 – March 1799

One morning, as he emerged from the Cathedral of St James, he met Spiridion Foresti. He was sitting at a table in the shadow of a marble portal, drinking a minute cup of very black coffee and he immediately rose and invited him to join him. Henry accepted immediately, thinking this would be a good opportunity to find out when they would be able to proceed on their journey to Venice. Moretto, knowing that his master never touched coffee, waved away the girl with the copper coffee pot who had come forward to serve the Cardinal, and helped him to sit down on a nearby chair, before taking up his watchful position a few paces behind.

Foresti, however, did not give Henry the chance to speak. Instead, he launched into an account of the French occupation.

"You will remember, Your Highness, the Ionian Islands were handed over to France a couple of years ago. Bonaparte was convinced that he could use Corfu, Zante and Cephalonia as stepping stones towards the conquest of Egypt and the Ottoman Empire. As you can observe, Corfu occupies a vital strategic position between the Adriatic and Ionian and he hoped thus to block British shipping and break your country's trade monopoly in the Orient and India. The Venetians had also understood that control of our island was essential to protect their trade routes."

He leaned back in his chair and waved a hand towards the massive stone walls of the castle that loomed, grim and impregnable, on top of a rock on one side of the port. "You see how strongly they built the defences of the island. That is Palaio Frourio, the Old Fortress. Venetian engineers rebuilt it four centuries ago and dug out a channel to separate it from the town. After the Ottoman siege – that was in 1537, if I'm not mistaken – they built the New Fortress on the Hill of St Mark up there, on the other side. The two strongholds are joined together by the great boundary wall you saw running right along the seafront when you arrived. We have the mountains in the back that give us a natural barrier defending the town. And we also have our two vanguard islands, Vido and Lazaretto. They are both heavily fortified and can repel anything but major attacks."

Henry's interest was captured.

"I am astonished that the island could be taken at all!"

"It was our misfortune that Venice was forced to give up the islands as part of the conditions of the Treaty of Campo Formio. It was a great disgrace for the glorious Venetian Republic. The Doge Manin was reviled by his people. Here in Corfu many of us were not happy to see the end of the Serenissima. We had been part of it for four centuries and it had brought us prosperity. I am born a Greek, but I am a Venetian at heart.

"The French administrators moved in. They tried to introduce order in our untidy little state. But we Levantines do not care much for order and discipline. It is against our nature. I won't deny that the new ideas they brought – the doctrines of equality and brotherhood – appealed to some, especially the young people, the poets, the dreamers, the men of letters, who rushed eagerly to raise the Trees of Liberty and wave the French tricolour around the streets."

He shifted slightly in his chair, his restless eyes running over the people in the square.

"But the wiser ones among us recognised the truth. The free will they preached was only a chimera. The fact was that we were an occupied country with no control over our destiny. The French behaved arrogantly. They believed us their inferiors and treated us accordingly. We became disillusioned when we saw that the equality they preached was little more than pretence and that they were demanding we pay all the costs of their occupation. We had to feed and billet their soldiers at our expense and they taxed us heavily for the privilege."

He took a slender, long-stemmed pipe out of his waistcoat pocket and made a gesture towards the Cardinal. "You permit?" Henry nodded. After Foresti had lit his pipe and taken the first long meditative pull, he fixed the Cardinal with a penetrating look.

"You are possibly short of news, Your Highness. Britain, Austria and Russia have formed a Second Coalition against Napoleon. The Ottomans have joined forces with the Russians. The Sultan is anxious, of course, to halt Bonaparte's conquest of Egypt, his protectorate. Together they retook our island."

He tipped back his head and blew out a thin waving curl of yellowish smoke.

"You are wondering about my part in all this? You have heard tales about me, of course! I am constantly in touch with Lord Nelson, who has always favoured me with his trust and friendship. I was able to report to him when the French commandeered the Venetian fleet and sailed out of Venice loaded with booty stolen from the Republic. Much good will it do them! Venice had been at peace for so long that her ships were all old and in a bad state of repair. I advised the British Admiralty that they were not battle-worthy and that the French would be unable to incorporate them into their fleet. I believed that had probably been their original intention because I got information soon after that there was a suspect build-up of French war ships in Toulon harbour. That was how Nelson got his clue as to Bonaparte's intentions – that he was planning to invade Egypt."

Henry sat back and studied Foresti. He had met several spies, hanging around the Stuart court and the Vatican. He had always looked down on them as fabricators of gossip and untruths. He thought of them as eels, slipping round corners at receptions, listening in to conversations, always obsequious and self-effacing. But Foresti had none of these traits. His manner was bold and direct. His eyes glowed with an almost fanatical light. He plainly saw his work as a mission. He was proud of his role as gatherer of vital information. Henry thought that it was fortunate Foresti was on the side of the Alliance against Napoleon. He would make a dangerous enemy.

Foresti seemed to read his thoughts. He smiled at him, with a hint of mockery.

"The French were suspicious of me, of course. They imprisoned me a couple of times but they were never able to pin anything definite on me. It was easy enough to run rings around them. I have my informers in every port in the Mediterranean – merchants and traders, simple people who come and go as part of their regular business. They don't always understand the importance of the things they tell me."

He sat in silence for a moment, his eyes flickering round the square. Henry saw his chance to interrupt and ask when they could leave, but Foresti seemed not to notice and launched into an account of the recent siege of Corfu.

"I escaped. I went to Venice. I came back on the flagship of Admiral Uschakov, the Russian commander. I can assure you that no nobler or more generous man ever lived. During the siege, he took fleeing French soldiers into his ranks to save them from being butchered by the Muslims and the Albanians mercenaries in the Turkish army.

"We arrived at the beginning of the month of November and we saw that the harbour was well defended. Have you ever witnessed a sea battle, my Lord? I think not. It's a sight to stir the blood. The *Généreux* and *Brune* were in position, their cannons primed and pointed towards us, as well as the *Leander* (you may remember she was the Royal Navy ship that had been captured by the French. She has now been sent back to her rightful owners). My sources had informed me that the French had 3000 men and 650 guns on Corfu. They had other troops and artillery batteries set up as well on Vido and Lazaretto.

"Uschakov decided that we did not have a big enough force to mount an attack and we should wait for reinforcements. So we set up a blockade and bided our time. For some reason – and I still don't understand why they did this – the French abandoned their positions on Lazaretto. We were therefore able to land the first Russian troops a few miles up the coast. They found no opposition and they set up their guns and began battering the forts to keep the invaders hemmed in till the Russian ships we were waiting for finally arrived."

His eyes sparkled with excitement as he warmed to his story.

"At that point we had a total battle force of twelve ships-of-the-line and thirteen frigates. Seeing that there was now no hope of holding out against us, the *Généreux* decided to cut the cord and make a run for it. She painted her sails black and slipped out of the harbour under cover of darkness. She made it across to Ancona, which was – and still is, I believe – under French control.

"We made the final assault on the 28th February, just days before you arrived. We had a combat force of four thousand Turks and Albanian mercenaries. Vido Island fell first. The surviving French militiamen jumped into the sea and swam over to the mainland. But of course there was no respite for the poor devils there. We bombarded the port for hours. All five shore batteries were put out of action. All the forts – St Rocco, St Salvatore and St Abraham – capitulated. The *Leander* and the *Brune* were crippled.

"And so the siege finally ended. It had lasted four months. You can imagine the suffering my people went through during that time. They lost everything. They were starving. The French had burned down the entire suburb of Madrouki thinking it harboured rebels."

He knocked out his pipe, which had gone dead as he recounted his story.

"When Louis Chabot, the French governor, surrendered, Admiral Uschakov treated him with compassion and honour. He sent him and his surviving troops safely back to Toulon. I can tell you that the prisoners taken by the Turks will not be so fortunate. They will be force marched in chains to Constantinople. Not many of them will arrive, I fear."

He gestured towards a group of men and women in a corner of the square, labouring to remove a pile of rubble.

"That is war, Your Grace. Not medals. Not conquest. Not the glorification of nations. War means the aftermath; the long, long struggle to rebuild what was lost in a few brief days and weeks of chaos and destruction."

He turned and looked Henry straight in the eyes. "You will hear many things about me. They call me a spy, an agent serving several masters. I have many enemies who wish to discredit me. But, my Lord Cardinal, remember what I have just said and understand that I see my work as my duty. I do not like war and I fear the tyranny of one man who sets himself up to become master of the world."

When Henry got back to the residence, he found the two Cardinals Braschi-Onesti and Pignatelli seated in the atrium, waiting for him. Braschi was plainly irate and Pignatelli would not meet his eyes.

"Well, Stuart, you have been out wandering, we see, in a strange and hostile city, full of infidels," Braschi began in belligerent tones.

Henry did not reply. He stood waiting, leaning on Moretto's arm.

"My servant tells me that he saw you conversing most amiably – these were his words – most amiably with that pirate and blackguard Foresti. We cannot believe that you can forget your station and sink so low as to tolerate the company of persons of dubious loyalty and moral convictions!"

Pignatelli put in nervously, without raising his eyes. "Dear Henry, you must remember we are representatives of Holy Mother Church. This island is peopled by heathens who rejected the true faith at the time of the Great Schism. The present governor is a Muslim and he holds us prisoner here. Our situation is delicate, very delicate. We must all be cautious."

"I thank you both for your concern," Henry cut in coldly. He could feel his nose twitching. "But I do not care to be spied on by your servants and be made the object of gossip of two elderly priests who are unable to fill up their time in a more profitable way. May I suggest you would be better in church praying for our delivery from evil!"

He turned away and jerked Moretto's supporting arm to show that he wished to be helped up the stairs to his private quarters.

The following day, an Arab doctor arrived at the palace to treat Henry's leg, with a letter of introduction from Foresti, who had noted Henry's limp and his grimaces of pain as he moved. Although they could only speak to each other through an interpreter that the doctor brought with him, Henry realised at once that he was in the hands of a skilled and experienced physician, who examined the leg carefully and asked a number of questions regarding his symptoms and general state of health. The doctor was back within the hour, bringing poultices of herbs that he wrapped carefully around the swollen leg. He had also brought medicine for Henry to drink. Moretto was horrified to see his master swallow the potions without question or complaint.

"That heathen is probably poisoning you! I don't think you should touch any of his medicine. I have heard that some poisons take many days to invade the body. That the victim feels no ill effects till it is too late. If you die here, in a foreign land, my lord, what shall I do?"

His eyes were filled with tears. But Henry waved him away and forbade him to dispose of the medicine.

"The true poison is in my leg, Boy," he said gently. "That is what will spread through my body and kill me in the end if I do not follow some cure."

A few days later, Henry was already feeling better. He was sitting in the shade, his bandaged leg propped on a stool, when Moretto brought some letters that had just arrived on a ship from Sicily. One bore the seal of his friend Albani and was dated almost a month back. He opened it eagerly, hoping for good news concerning the negotiations with the Austrian Emperor.

"My Dear Friend Stuart," Albani wrote. *"I have finally returned to Messina and to my distress I found that you were gone. I had hoped you would be there to comfort me, because I have a tragic story to tell. All the brothers who so kindly and selflessly sheltered me at the Abbey of Casamari are no more. I left them only a few weeks ago and now I have learned, to my great sorrow, that they have been slaughtered by a wretched band of republican soldiers hunting for plunder.*

They came to the Abbey just before the start of the Great Silence and the community was gathered to chant the compièta. Father Simone welcomed them with the kindness the monks show to all-comers, bringing them food and drink. But they were set on treasure and when they did not find gold or precious things they lost their heads and turned into monsters, howling insults and profanities. The poor brothers fled, seeking places of concealment in the kitchens, the cellars, the barns, outside in the hills. But the Prior, the blessed Reverend Father Simeone Cardon and five other brothers stood firm, determined to protect the holy Eucharist from defilement. All six of these blameless men were mercilessly murdered. They died in horrible suffering, stabbed with bayonets and hacked with sabres. The soldiers were like rabid dogs. They demanded the money and jewels they believed were hidden away but all that they could find were the sacred chalices of the mass that the brothers died clutching to their bosoms.

Several of these monks, including Father Cardon, were refugees who had fled to Italy to escape the purges of the French Revolution, but here they have found only temporary sanctuary. Death has pursued them, like the huntsman that follows the stag and never gives up the chase till he has slaughtered his prey."

Henry read the letter twice, overcome with incredulity and distress. He could not believe that the great French army, renowned for its discipline, could have sunk to the level of bandits and felons. Things must indeed be going badly for the invaders if the officers were unable to prevent the rank and file from committing the kind of atrocities that would forever leave a bloody stain on the ideals preached by the Revolution.

Finally, he turned to another letter, which was from Cesarini. It said they were all anxiously awaiting his return to Messina. The Family was idle and restless. He had had no word from the court at Palermo or from Cardinal Albani. Only a brief missive had come from Ercole Consalvi. He said the situation now seemed more secure since the Emperor had apparently reconfirmed his willingness to hold the conclave in Venice. The French army in Italy had suffered several defeats and many of the Cardinals who had fled or had been exiled believed that they would be able to attend.

It now became urgent for them to leave as soon as possible. He sat down with pen and ink to request an interview with the Ottoman commander, Bey Abdul-kabir.

The Governor of Corfu

Rather to his surprise, the invitation came the next day, carefully penned in formal diplomatic terms: the three esteemed Representatives of the Supreme Pontiff of the Church of Rome were respectfully invited to the residence of His Eminence the Bey for a visit of courtesy and friendship.

When Henry showed the invitation to his fellow Cardinals, their reactions were mixed. Braschi grumbled and worried about protocol. Pignatelli refused to go. He said it was a trap and that the infidels would cut their throats and no one would be any the wiser. He could not be persuaded to change his mind, so Henry wrote their acceptance, but excusing him on grounds of illness.

The Bey lived in palatial house, which had also once belonged to a rich Venetian merchant. They were met at the door by an escort of ten servants identically dressed in robes of richly flowing silks and embroidered conical headdresses, who went down on their knees in greeting, touching the floor with their foreheads. They were conducted through a succession of high-ceilinged halls with silk-draped walls and tall windows overlooking the gardens and the sea. Fountains of tinkling water flowed from walls of rock, decorated with seashells. The rooms were paved in brightly coloured ceramic tiles and scented with jasmine and roses. Servants slipped silently away as they passed, disappearing like ghosts through concealed doors.

Finally, they were ushered into what looked like a study, furnished in the Venetian style, with an elaborately carved desk, a wall-length bookcase full of tooled leather volumes that Henry thought looked like ledgers, and a number of high-backed gilded chairs arranged along the walls. The Bey was seated on cushions on a low couch set on a splendid Persian carpet that covered the entire floor. Henry judged that he must be approaching his sixth decade. His skin was scored with the deep lines that came with a lifetime exposure to the sun and he had a waxed moustache that curled out on each side of his face and a long beard streaked with grey. He wore a long, richly embroidered silk robe and a voluminous white turban swathed around his head. A jewelled dagger hung from the gold silk cummerbund that was wrapped several times around his midriff.

His expression was serious and he did not smile as he invited them to approach. Instead, he called an elderly and distinguished-looking man who had been standing near the window to come forward. He bowed to them and introduced himself, first in French and then in English, as Mahmud Raif Effendi.

"Gracious Lords," he said. "I learned the English language in London, where I had the privilege of holding the position of Chief Secretary to the Honourable Yusuf Agah Efendi, who was, as you may know, the first permanent Ottoman Ambassador at the court of King George. The Bey greatly regrets that he speaks none of your languages, but it will be my humble task to interpret for you to the best of my ability."

Servants arrived with golden trays containing long stemmed Venetian glasses filled with sweet mint tea and plates piled with a variety of bonbons. The Superintendent explained that their religion did not allow them to drink alcohol but if their guests desired Greek wine they had only to ask.

While the Bey remained seated on his low divan, his legs tucked under his robe, the servants brought forward two chairs for the Cardinals and arranged them in front of him. Henry felt a little embarrassed as in that position they were looking down on their host. However, his injured leg, plus the rheumatism that had begun to afflict him, made it impossible for him to attempt to sit on one of the other low couches that were strewn around the room.

There was, however, nothing subservient in the elderly Bey's manner. He sat proudly, openly scrutinizing them with an intense expression of curiosity. Both Cardinals had come for the visit in the sober black cassocks they wore for non-liturgical occasions and Henry wondered if perhaps they should not rather have set out to impress, appearing in *cappa magna* with voluminous scarlet train sweeping the ground behind them and *mozzetto* of ermine fur over their shoulders.

Just as the servants were beginning to serve the tea, Spiridion Foresti was ushered into the room. He bowed deeply to the Bey and the Superintendent, pressing his two palms together and then turned to the guests, saluting them likewise. Braschi turned his head away, refusing to acknowledge the greeting, his right hand gripped tightly round the gold crucifix that dangled on his chest, but Henry inclined his head gravely. He found he was glad that Foresti was with them.

After they had exchanged the usual courtesies, the Bey began to speak, in a slow ringing tone, as if measuring every word. Henry strained to interpret his mood, which seemed to him not so much one of hostility, but rather of recrimination and reproach. Finally, he paused and gestured to Mahmud Raif, who turned to them with a grave expression.

"Our esteemed General," he said. "Would have you note that our civilization is much older than yours. Our scientists, our doctors and our mathematicians were making new discoveries for the benefit of mankind while you of the European continent were little more than disorganised primitive tribes fighting among yourselves. I beg your pardon if this offends you, but it is a historical fact."

He continued, "The Bey would have you know that the glorious Ottoman Empire lived in peace. We did not trouble our neighbours. But General Bonaparte, with no provocation, invaded our land of Egypt – the land of the Pharaohs that goes back to the dawn of time. He even set up a scientific institute to study the great achievements of the ancient Egyptians, of which he was apparently ignorant."

Foresti raised his hand, asking permission to speak. He continued in English, which Henry had spoken since childhood. Braschi, however, understood very little and sat glowering, his lips tightly pressed together.

"Bonaparte," explained Foresti, "considered Egypt a backward country. In many ways he was right, of course. He wanted to transform it into a modern nation according to the new French ideals. It was to be part of the great empire he wished to create following the footsteps of Alexander the Great. He dreamed of making France the cultural centre of this world, so when he embarked in Egypt with his *Armée d'Orient,* he took along with him a hundred and fifty of his country's best brains, experts in all fields of the sciences. He has founded an *Istitut d'Egypte* in Cairo, where these Savants work together. Even now, they continue to work through all these months of conflict and they have apparently produced a great number of important studies. Isn't this so, Mahmud Raif Effendi?"

Mahmud Raif nodded and explained what was being said to the Bey, who reacted with an indignant expression and a sharp reply.

"Our General says that Bonaparte's soldiers shot at the Sphinx, causing great damage. He tried to violate the Great Pyramid, but he failed to penetrate its secrets. He also planned to dig a canal that would connect the Mediterranean with the Red Sea and create a new sea route. Were the French not aware that in ancient times the Pharaohs had already built such a channel and Queen Cleopatra was able to sail across her land from the Red Sea to the Nile?"

The Bey sat silent for a moment, frowning, and then he launched into another long angry discourse, that Mahmud Raif translated.

"Your people make many bad reports about our people. Much of it is untrue. When Corfu fell, we gave the garrison safe conduct. By the Bey's orders, two thousand and three hundred French soldiers were sent home unharmed to Toulon and Ancona. The Sublime Porte, our High Command, sent winter clothing and food for the prisoners that were transported from Corfu to Constantinople. We showed more compassion towards our enemies than the French.

"We share booty and prisoners with our allies, as is normal in war. Your people say that we cut off the heads of the dead and carry them in sacks to Constantinople. There is nothing strange in this, my Lords. War is war. But we do not cut off heads simply to have them as trophies. It is merely for practical purposes, so that the guards can prove how many prisoners have died.

"The Bey also says that if you believe Christians are so much more civilized than we, we would remind you that General Napoleon, much revered as a hero by his own people, cut the heads off thousands of Muslim dead on the battlefields in Egypt and that he did this with a much more wicked purpose. He rolled the severed heads out of the sacks in front of peaceable townsmen of Cairo in order to terrorise them."

Foresti made a move to speak, but the Bey silenced him with an abrupt gesture of his hand and continued in even angrier tones.

"You are priests. You are no doubt shocked to hear about the iniquities of war," Mahmud Raif translated. "General Bonaparte, after exterminating our courageous Mamluke cavalry, has now set his sights on conquering Syria. His army is on the march. But they will not pass. Our valiant Commander, Al-Jezzar Pasha, has courageously and successfully defended the Fortress of Acre, blocking their advance. You call him 'The Butcher', but you do not refer to General Bonaparte in these terms, even though he massacred four thousand five hundred captives, including women and children, after Jaffa fell. He had them killed like animals, without pity, with knives and bayonets, saying his soldiers should not waste bullets."

Mahmud Raif became progressively ill at ease as the torrent of indignation continued. His voice dropped and he avoided looking at the Cardinals in front of him. Henry too was disconcerted. He had not expected to meet such hostility and he began to worry about the Bey's true intentions. Fortunately, Abdul Kabir began to calm down. He beckoned to his servants to serve his tea and intimated that his guests should do likewise. The unhealthy flush faded from his face.

At last he gave a dry smile. "Already the wrath of Allah, blessed be His name, has fallen on them. At Jaffa, bubonic plague struck them down. His men are dying of the disease. The British do not allow new supplies to get through to him. His army is in retreat and the desert is a hard master. Many will die of thirst and hunger. Soon his great campaign of conquest will be buried under the sands."

Henry glanced at Foresti, looking for confirmation of this news, but the Consul gave no sign. Realising that this turn of events made their mission to elect a new Pope even more urgent, he turned to the Superintendent and asked him to speak to the Bey on their behalf. In his most diplomatic turn of phrase, he said that they could not thank the Bey enough for the hospitality they had received on the island, but that they had business of vital importance awaiting them in Venice and they would be extremely grateful if he would tell them when they would be allowed to leave.

Unexpectedly, at that point Foresti smiled and both the Superintendent and the governor began to laugh. Henry was mystified and turned to Foresti for an explanation, while Braschi scowled and cast an uneasy glance over his shoulder.

"My dear Lord Cardinals," Foresti said. "But what have you understood? You are not prisoners here. You are free to go whenever you wish. But the Bey is concerned for your safety. He says there are many dangers in your path and you should wait until times are more favourable."

Before they could say more and without further explanations, the Bey dismissed them with a grave nod of his head.

More days went by with no news of a ship that could convey them to Venice. Henry's leg improved to the point that he was able to walk with his cane as far as the port, where he scrutinized all the vessels that came and went. He looked out for Spiridion Foresti but the Consul had departed on a mission. Desperate for news, he would send Gigi to interrogate the sailors that arrived on ships from Sicily.

One day, when he was sitting on the sea wall overlooking the bay, Moretto arrived in a state of great excitement.

"My Lord, sire!" he cried. "I have news that will bring you great happiness. My own heart is almost bursting with the joy I feel!" And he laid his hand on his heart in a dramatic gesture.

Henry smiled indulgently. He knew the Boy often play-acted to amuse him. This time, however, it turned out that he was not exaggerating. Walking up the harbour slipway, a bundle over his shoulder, was a familiar figure. It was a member of his Family, whom he had left behind in Messina; Annibale, his captain of the guard, who now dropped on his knees before him.

"Monsignor Cesarini sent me to get news of you, Your Majesty. Since your first letter, when you informed us you were here in Corfu, we have heard nothing and we are all anxious. I thank God to see you are alive and well."

The suspicion that his letters to Sicily had been intercepted flashed at once through Henry's mind, confirming his fears that their departure from the island was being deliberately delayed, despite the assurances they had received to the contrary. He felt anger rising in his chest. He was Sub-Dean of the Sacred College and the Conclave could not be held in his absence. Not for the first time, he suspected Spiridion Foresti of playing some double game, perhaps on the request of the British government which would prefer to keep the Roman Catholic Church in its present state of disorder.

Annibale had a bundle of letters for him. One was from his friend Don Angelo, who told him that Cardinal Ruffo di Calabria was chasing the French out of Naples and that the Bourbon monarchs would soon be restored to their rightful thrones.

"It would seem," he wrote, *"that finally heaven has answered our prayers. It cannot be long now before we can go home.*

"I have another piece of news that will give you pleasure," he added at the foot of the letter. *"Our cook, Giacinto Belisario, who so disgracefully abandoned you in Naples, has arrived safely back in Frascati. I was informed by Canon Altobelli, who also told me that, praise be to God, the Cathedral and La Rocca have not suffered damages that cannot be repaired."*

Another letter came from Ercole Consalvi, telling him that he was now in Trieste. The Cardinals of the Sacred College were beginning to arrive and he urged Henry to delay no longer.

A disquieting letter came from the Queen of Naples:

"You cannot imagine the depth of my despair. My dwarf Don Rodrigo is dead. I believe he was poisoned as he complained for two days of severe pains in his belly. Nothing could ease his suffering. My physicians could not save him. He was a good servant and invaluable to me as he kept me informed of the intentions of my enemies. I do not think I can ever replace him. I feel his loss ever more keenly as I have no friends left. My Emma talks of going back to England with Nelson, even though they can never be man and wife. Acton is too busy controlling the situation in our beloved and unfortunate city of Naples.

"We are anxiously awaiting news of the victory of our heroic commander, Cardinal Ruffo di Calabria. I have heard accounts of the transformation of the city under the republicans that make me shudder. They called our realm the Parthenopean Republic. They

changed the names of the streets that were called after saints or the royal family, re-naming them for their ignominious heroes and commanders. They even forbade the ringing of church bells, under pain of death. Innkeepers and tavern owners have been urged to become spies, reporting to the police any suspicious remarks they happen to overhear.

"My former friend and royal librarian, the Marchioness Eleonora Fonseca Pimentel, has betrayed us in the most shameless manner. She publishes a newspaper called 'The Monitor' in which she slanders my family and publishes invented stories about 'the ferocious Cardinal Ruffo'. The people are disillusioned. The splendid dawn of liberty and equality preached by the republicans has brought no improvements to their daily lot."

Henry closed the letter at that point and handed it to Moretto to burn. He had no desire to become this unhappy woman's confident. He had more impelling problems to deal with at that moment.

The fourth letter, from his protégé, Ercole Consalvi, rekindled his hopes of an end to their present situation:

"I have had information, in the strictest confidence, that Bonaparte has been forced to retreat. He does not have sufficient troops left to attempt the conquest of Syria. The army is depleted in numbers and crippled by disease. They failed to take the fortress of Acre and so they had no option but to head back to Egypt. By the time they reached Jaffa (which they had conquered only a short time before), his men, tormented by heat and thirst, began to rebel. The Turkish army was hard on their heels and their progress was held up by the sick and wounded they were carrying with them – I was told these numbered well over a thousand. Napoleon gave orders to abandon all those who were unable to walk or ride and give them laudanum so that they could kill themselves and be spared the rough justice of the Turks. Those who did not die were fortunate, however, because the Turks turned them over to the British who sent them back to France.

"When the army reached Cairo, Bonaparte tried to pass his campaign off as a great victory. He entered the city with flags flying, a military band playing and the men all waving palm branches. He deceived no one, however. The Directoire had got wind of the extent of the disaster and once he gets home, he will be taken to account. We can hope at last to see his wings clipped and a reversal in our fortunes."

As they waited anxiously for news of a ship to take them to Venice, Henry's eyes became painfully inflamed. Moretto was anxious and distressed.

"If only we were back with the monks at St Erasmus! They cured you well and saved your sight!"

Henry ordered him to go and recall the Arab doctor. As his leg wound had been healing so well, the physician's visits had been reduced to a couple of times a week. Moretto objected, but with less conviction than before. Even he had had to admit that the Arab cures had been efficacious.

Once again, Henry found himself reduced to inactivity, lying in a darkened room, with his eyelids covered with cloths dipped in rose water and Moretto watched fascinated as the doctor squeezed the juice from the fleshy leaf of an aloe plant and prepared the poultices he gently applied to the Cardinal's eyes.

It was while he was in this condition that permission was finally given for them to proceed on their journey. However, the doctor advised him that he risked going blind if he did not complete the cure. For now, he could not leave. Braschi-Onesti and Pignatelli were forced to depart without him.

Trieste – Padua

June–July 1799

A few days later, Henry called Foresti, insisting that he could not delay his departure any longer. Foresti tried to persuade him to stay, saying that he was not completely cured and he risked falling ill again, but the Cardinal was adamant. His presence was needed at Venice where the new conclave had to be organised. Removing a ruby from one of his rings, Henry asked him to present it to the Bey in gratitude for his hospitality. He wanted to give another jewel to Foresti to thank him for all his help, but the Consul refused, saying he had only done his duty as his Britannic Majesty's representative on the island.

Since Henry was so determined to go, Foresti stopped trying to talk him out of it. It was early summer and they could be sure of fair winds. This time, the weather was fine and the sea calm. Henry embarked with his two servants, Moretto and Annibale, on a Venetian merchant ship. The voyage was pleasant and uneventful and they arrived in Trieste two days sooner than anticipated.

Nevertheless, Ercole Consalvi, the Cardinal's protégé, had had advance warning and he was there at the harbour to meet them. Although the weather had changed and it was raining heavily, he knelt on the wet stones of the quayside to kiss the Cardinal's ring,

Moretto pulled a long face when he saw him and muttered to Annibale, "I can't say I'm glad to see him. I believe our master thinks all too highly of him."

Annibale poked him in the ribs, chuckling. "Everyone knows you are jealous of him. But there's not a doubt he is very capable. He'll certainly rise high in the Church. I can remember when you were both in the seminary together. He was always a young gentleman, top of the class, while you were a donkey from poor peasant stock!"

Moretto was silent. He knew that what Annibale said was true. Consalvi came from a wealthy and noble family, while he, the foundling, had had to depend on his master's charity to pay the college fees of four barrels of wine and a *rubbio* of grain. It was also true that Consalvi had been a brilliant student, while poor little Gigi had struggled with Latin and Greek and puzzled over mathematics.

Moretto's ill-feeling towards Consalvi stemmed from the fact that he had realised that Ercole, to a large extent, had supplanted him in the Cardinal's affection. The feeling of hostility between the two men was, however, reciprocal. Monsignor Consalvi's lip curled as he watched the Boy help his lord descent from the ship's boat and Moretto knew that he did not consider him a fit companion for a royal prince. The resentment dated back to when they were boys studying together at the Herboracum. Even then Consalvi was careful to keep his distance from the Cardinal's orphan.

Moretto knew that Henry intended to promote Consalvi to a high position in the coming conclave. Cardinal York had been impressed by the fact that Consalvi had stayed on in Rome when the French invaded. He had, at great risk, travelled twice to Florence to visit Pope Pius VI while he was being held prisoner in the Carthusian monastery there. At a certain point, the French had imprisoned him in Castel Sant'Angelo and condemned him to be transported to the dreaded Devil's Island. Fortunately, the sentence was suspended, thanks to the intervention of his wealthy family. He was sent instead to the fortress at Terracina, and then finally released and allowed to proceed to Naples. Moretto knew all this from some dispatches that had reached Henry in Sicily and his master had confided his concern for his protégé's safety.

Meanwhile, Henry urged Consalvi to rise and embraced him warmly. Outside the Cardinal's Family, Consalvi was one of the few people who addressed him as a king, which had greatly contributed to winning his favour

"Your most Gracious Majesty," Ercole said. "I have been waiting here for days, ever since I got the news that you had set sail from the Island of Corfu. Thank God for your safe arrival. The Lord Cardinals Pignatelli and Braschi-Onesti preceded you by only three days, as they were delayed by a storm. I know you must be fatigued after your journey so I have arranged for you to rest for a few days in a monastery here in Trieste before we proceed to Venice."

In the meantime, he continued, he would be occupied meeting and assisting the other members of the Sacred College as they arrived.

That evening, he came to dine with Henry at the monastery, so that he could bring him up to date with the developments regarding the conclave.

"Unfortunately," he said. "The Emperor is not such a good friend of the Church as we initially supposed. He has agreed to hold the conclave in his territory, but he refuses to name a suitable place. He rejects all our suggestions. At the moment, those members of the Sacred College who have arrived are housed in Padua, where it would be convenient enough, but he objects. Between you and me, sire, I believe he wants us under his nose so that he can manipulate the vote."

"Dear Ercole, that would be nothing new!" Henry replied. "Do you know how many conclaves I have attended? Every time the ruling houses of Europe have fought each other to elect their chosen candidate. Every time, the secret vote is influenced by outside forces."

"I know well that your own election was unfairly rejected for political reasons," murmured Consalvi. "The British made it known more than once that they did not desire a Stuart on St Peter's throne."

Henry leaned back in his chair and stretched out his injured leg, which was becoming stiff.

"That is an old story," he said. "In any case, I do not believe that the Ring of the Fishermen would have fitted my finger. I am not a lover of ceremony. Nor am I a diplomat. A Pope has to be adept at both!"

"I believe, sire, that you would have made a fine Pope!" Consalvi insisted in heated tones, but Henry merely shook his head and asked how things were in his see at Frascati.

Consalvi became animated. The people, he said, had rebelled against the republican Jacobins and desired nothing more than the return of their dear Cardinal and benefactor. He then recounted an incident that had taken place at the shrine of Galloro, which was only a few miles away from Frascati.

"A courier told me that the citizens were outraged when French soldiers stabled the regimental horses in the nave of the church and set up the Tree of Liberty in front of the sanctuary with the venerated image of the Virgin. The abbot and monks of Galloro, who were cowards, went off meekly and obediently to pay homage to the new French administrators and while they were away a group of parishioners pulled the Tree down and tossed it into the valley below."

This tale restored Henry's good humour and they sat down together to enjoy the supper of bean soup and roast meat that the monks had prepared for them.

Henry, as usual, ate sparingly. Consalvi knew this. Unlike the Cardinal he enjoyed his food, and as protocol did not permit him to continue eating after his superior had finished, he made quick work of his meal, cramming large portions of meat and bread into his mouth and swallowing rapidly. Henry appeared not to notice. He sat lost in thought, his head bowed. Finally, he asked if Cardinal Ruffo di Calabria would be attending the Conclave.

"Why, I believe so," Ercole replied, wiping his mouth. "He sent word that he would come north as soon as he had finished his business in Naples."

"So, how is his war going?" Henry asked, anxious to have news. The Queen's last letter had made him uneasy.

"Well, by all accounts. His Holy Faith army has been marching all through the spring, sweeping all resistance before them. The fortified towns of Calabria have all fallen. The citizens have been quick to change allegiance." He shrugged his shoulders with a deprecating smile. "It's said they're republicans at sunrise and magically turn into royalists at sunset."

Henry laughed, but a knot of anxiety remained in his stomach. "I heard that everything does not go so smoothly, however. There have been disorders. What information do you have?"

"Sire, this is a war, not a social meeting in a coffee house. Most of his soldiers are simple peasants. Many are criminals that the King and Queen of Naples released from the jails in Sicily, as well as a rabble of cutthroats the King of England obligingly sent over. The brigand chiefs have also joined his ranks – no doubt in the hope of gain.

"Obviously, Ruffo can't keep a pack like that in check. They've been swarming all over the countryside, plundering, looting and killing. The countryside was in an uproar and the peasants started to desert and go home to protect their families."

Consalvi leaned back in his chair. He longed to reach for his snuffbox but he desisted, knowing that Henry thought it a dirty habit, unworthy of a high-ranking clergyman.

"Ruffo needed to re-establish order. So what did he do? He had the bandit chief Panzanera hanged in the public square as an example. Then he appointed that other brigand Panedigrano to a position of command, so that he would keep the discontented and rebellious Calabrian division under control. Panzanera was no worse a villain that Panedigrano – Panedigrano was just more fortunate!

"They arrived at the gates of Naples just before you got here. My informant told me that the main body of the French army had already marched north. There's only a small occupying force left, commanded by General Jacques MacDonald, Ruffo now has an army of 20,000 men and MacDonald can't hold out against them. If he's sensible, he'll negotiate a safe conduct and head off north as well."

At that moment, the door opened and one of the monks ushered in Cardinal Albani. Albani had arrived in a hurry and he was short of breath.

"Welcome, my dear Stuart. I am so thankful that you have arrived!" He panted, greeting Henry with the ritual embrace. "I'm at stalemates with the Emperor. I don't know what game he is playing but he is running rings around us all. I need you to accompany me and speak to him. He may be swayed by your royal blood and high lineage!"

His tone was gently mocking. When they were young men together and the Stuart cause was not yet lost, Albani had often needled him about his lost kingdom, asking him whether he believed that he, the son of a mere Duke and grand-nephew of a Pope, was an elevated enough companion for a Prince of three kingdoms. This time, however, Henry was in no mood for jokes. He said they would immediately request an audience. Albani, however, shook his head.

"It's no use, dear Henry. You must curb your impatience. Francis is off on a tour of the lands he acquired by the Treaty of Tolentino. He will not find a warm reception among his newly acquired subjects. The Austrians are quite different from the Venetians. They have banned Carnival and the people are seething with resentment. During Carnival everything was allowed, apparently. Men and women, rich and poor, noble and commoner, mingled together quite freely, with their faces hidden behind masks. The Austrian Emperor has forbidden the practice of wearing masks in the street."

"I can't say this is not a good thing!" interrupted Consalvi, pursing his mouth. "It isn't hard to imagine the deceits and abuses that were perpetrated. Not to mention the murders and crimes, where the culprit, concealed under his disguise, could not be identified and thus went unpunished!"

"Unfortunately, there were a great many workshops producing these masks," Albani went on in a level tone. "They've all been closed and many craftsmen have lost their livelihood. That alone causes discontent, but the Emperor has gone even further. He has banned many of the popular entertainments, like bull running and Jew baiting. He has even forbidden the new invention called the Magic Lantern, where you can see pictures that move, believe it or not! Everyone was in a frenzy to see it. I think it seemed harmless enough but the Jesuits say it has been invented by the devil!

"And then," he went on. "There are other reasons for their discontent. This city has been ruthlessly despoiled by the French. The citizens do nothing but grumble. All their luxuries have been taxed, first by the French and now by the Austrians, their new overlords. Many of their great works of art have been stolen and taken to France. The other morning, when I was strolling in Piazza St Mark, a gentleman passing pointed out to me the front of the Cathedral. He said it had used to be adorned with four splendid bronze horses with ruby eyes that the Venetians had brought from Constantinople many centuries ago. But these had been carried off to Paris, along with the most precious works of Venetian art.

"The people see their art as public property, belonging to all of them. They cannot bear to be deprived of the ancient sculptures and the paintings of the great masters that gave lustre to their city. The humble serving man that brought me my coffee in a coffee house could hardly speak for anger when he told me that the French had stripped all the gold from the *Bucintoro* and taken it off to be melted down into coins. The *Bucintoro*," he explained, seeing that Henry looked puzzled, "is the golden barge the Doges used each year when they presided over the marriage of the city to the sea. It was a custom that the Venetians held particularly dear!"

The End of the Serenissima

A few years earlier, the news of the ignominious end of the glorious Republic of Venice had been the subject of much debate at the papal court. Henry had followed the developments with a sense of foreboding as he feared similar tactics would be used to bring down the pontifical states. When Napoleon invaded northern Italy, Venice had declared itself neutral, in the hope of fending off the territorial ambitions of both France and Austria, the two rival nations pressing on its borders. But the strategy was doomed to failure.

Even before Napoleon and the Austrian Emperor had signed the Armistice of Loeben in April 1797, they had secretly agreed to carve up much of continental Europe between them. During previous months of haggling, chunks of territory were swapped around the treaty chessboard. Napoleon wanted total control of Lombardy, Milan and Mantua, as well as the Republic of Genoa and the Austrian Netherlands. He knew that if Austria was to be persuaded to agree, it would have to be compensated with a transfer of land of equal value and prestige. The obvious choice was the great maritime Republic of Venice – rich, admired, a storehouse of treasures and art and a dominant commercial power.

The Serenissima had tried desperately to avoid a takeover. The Venetian Grand Council attempted to mollify Bonaparte with offers of money and the pledge of a backup army should he decide to go to war once more against Austria. A magnificent diamond ring was sent to Napoleon's wife, Josephine. But Napoleon was deaf to all appeals and inducements.

The previous year, ignoring the Serenissima's declaration of neutrality, Napoleon had occupied the Venetian territories of Verona, Bergamo and Brescia. These cities had resisted the French invasion with all the determination they were able to muster. An uprising in Verona on the second day of Easter was initially successful. The populace poured out onto the streets armed with whatever weapons they could lay their hands on, from guns and sabres to pitchforks and clubs. A furious mob slaughtered hundreds of French soldiers, including the wounded lying helpless in the hospital.

The survivors fled and took refuge in the town fortresses, where they were besieged until the French army sent a rescue force of 15,000 men to crush the insurgents. Unfortunately for the Republic, this incident gave Napoleon the excuse he needed to bully the discontented Venetians into submission. He sent a threatening letter to the Doge, Ludovico Manin, swearing to avenge his dead and declaring that he would sweep down on Venice like Attila the Hun and put the city to fire and sword.

The Grand Council of Venice, frightened and cowed, offered abject apologies and lavish compensation. But Napoleon was having none of it. "Not all the gold of Peru would stop me from avenging the blood of our men," was his irate retort.

The French fleet invaded immediately afterwards and blockaded the port. The Venetians tried to put up a fight, but they were hopelessly outnumbered. Complacent and sluggish after centuries of peace, the Republic had virtually no army and the war fleet was reduced to four unwieldy old galleys and seven oar-propelled galliots that were no match for the modern and efficient French ships-of-the-line. Manin realised there was no hope of mustering any effective resistance. Venice therefore capitulated, hoping to avoid the worst reprisals.

The last meeting of the Grand Council was held on the twelfth of May, 1797, when it was agreed to accept all Napoleon's demands. Manin left the Doge's palace for the last time and surrendered the ducal insignia and the Golden Book that listed the names of the ruling Venetian families. A sullen and incredulous crowd gathered in St Mark's Square to witness Napoleon proclaiming the end of the thousand-year old Venetian Republic.

Trees of Liberty were raised all over the city, along with posters carrying slogans exalting Napoleon. Four thousand troops were billeted with Venetian families, ostensibly to keep order but effectively to save the army the cost of their keep. The merchants and noble families were heavily fined to cover the army's other expenses. The ringleaders of the rebellions in the Venetian cities were rounded up and executed. Bonaparte appropriated the gold reserves in the city mint, much of which was public money.

Venice's troubles, however, were not over. Only eight months later, in accordance with the terms agreed in the Treaty of Campo Formio, the Austrians arrived and took possession of the city. The Doge, Ludovico Manin, collapsed when he was forced once more to pronounce the words of the Act of Submission.

A few days later, Henry moved to Padua. He took up lodgings in a monastery, while waiting for the Cardinals of the Sacred College to assemble. Henry was worried that they would not be able to reach the legal number required for the conclave vote to be valid. So far, only a small group of cardinals had reached Veneto. There were other problems. Consalvi had been sent to Vienna to enrol the help of Gianfrancesco Albani's nephew Giovanni, who was the papal special representative at the Austrian capital. Although Francis II had given his formal consent to hold the conclave under his protection in Venice, he was reluctant to commit himself regarding costs. Since most of the cardinals had had their properties and benefices confiscated by the French, they would be unable to meet the expenses involved.

There was little to do in Padua except wait. The Cardinals were slowly arriving, but the negotiations for the conclave dragged on endlessly. Henry spent his time poring over the dispatches that arrived. He was ill at ease. The city seemed to be a hotbed of spies and he trusted no one, not even the friars. He did not approve of the way the religious house was run. Discipline was lax and the brothers seemed to be more interested in the affairs of the outside world than spiritual matters. He thought that they seemed suspiciously well informed and that they were too free with their information.

Although Henry held himself aloof, Moretto and Annibale had no such scruples. They hung around the friars, anxiously begging them for news. One morning, just before daylight, they were wakened by shouts of jubilation. They both jumped up and rushed to the refectory where they found the brothers gathered around the prior, who held a letter in his hand. The brothers were leaping around with joy, clapping each other on the back. Three of the older members of the community had fallen on their knees in prayer, unperturbed by the wild cavorting around them.

Henry, who was a light sleeper, had also heard the noise. He pulled a dressing gown over his nightshirt and hurried to the refectory. Afterwards, he told Cesarini, he had been almost afraid to hope that finally this was the glad news they had all been waiting for. Controlling his emotions, he took the letter from the prior and read it quickly.

"Call your masters," he cried to the servants who had come running and stood clustered in the doorway, rubbing the sleep out of their eyes. "Rome has been liberated. It has been retaken by the British and the King of Naples' army. Admiral Troubridge of the Royal Navy has also taken the port of Civitavecchia. The republicans have at last been defeated!"

He did not read out the rest of the communication, which had somewhat dampened his enthusiasm. It recounted that the British Admiral Thomas Louis had celebrated the victory by travelling up the Tiber in a state barge. Cheering crowds had gathered on the banks of the river hailing him as their liberator. He had then proceeded to the Capitol Hill, where, instead of the papal banner, he had hoisted the Union Jack on the summit.

Seeing him frown, the prior came forward. "Have no fear, Your Excellency," he said, in soothing tones. "We have been told – on good authority – that the British have pledged to allow the Holy Father to return to Rome, as soon as he has been elected, and that all his temporal powers will be restored."

Gradually, the other cardinals came into the room, while the cellarer ordered bread and wine to be brought from the kitchen and cellars to celebrate. It was some time before the excitement died down and a serious discussion could begin. Albani finally called them to order.

"Dear brothers," he said. "We now have a very grave task ahead of us. Despite the good news we have just received, the political situation is still full of uncertainties. We cannot take it for granted that Bonaparte is totally defeated. Our choice of a pontiff who is able to meet unknown difficulties and overcome them will be crucial for the future of our Mother Church. I therefore beg you to put aside all petty contentions and differences and direct your thoughts and inclinations purely towards the preservation of the Faith."

The cardinals seated round the table nodded in assent, but Henry noticed that several of them exchanged glances or looked down at their hands. The secret alliances were already forming, he thought. The conclave promised to be a stormy one.

Part 5
Venice

September 1799 – June 1800

Henry decided at that point that he would move to Venice, where he would be on hand when the choice of the conclave site was finally settled. Returning to his room, he summoned Annibale. Handing him some of his last ducats, he told him that he should now go back to Messina and prepare the Family for the journey back to Rome.

Annibale was thunderstruck. "My Lord, Your Majesty, do you speak in earnest? You are going to remain here with only one servant to take care of you? It's unthinkable for a prince – a king – of your elevated rank. What will the other lords think? They will think you are sending me away because you are dissatisfied with my service. Have I failed you in any way? How will I…"

Henry interrupted him, laying a hand gently on his shoulder.

"No, indeed, Annibale, you have always been my faithful servant. I have no complaint against you. I have only thanks for your devotion and constancy during these last two years. But now I must proceed to Venice. The conclave will open soon and I can only take one servant with me when we are locked inside. I need you to do something more important. You must take my message to Monsignor Cesarini and tell him to make his way back to Rome as soon as he sees fit. The safest way would be by ship to Civitavecchia. The British are in command of the port. From there, Rome is only a short distance away and the roads should be clear. Tell him not to go overland through Calabria and Campania. These regions are now overrun by bandits since the Holy Faith army has been disbanded."

Annibale continued to protest, but Henry cut him short.

"I have always been able to count on your loyalty. Will you begin to defy me now? I am entrusting you with an important mission, which I am unable to carry out myself. When I return to Frascati, which, God willing, may be sooner than we believe, I expect to find my Family there, safe and ready to welcome me!"

There was nothing his bodyguard could do except obey, but he went off shaking his head, with a sorrowful expression.

As Henry and his last servant, Moretto, were preparing to leave for Venice, a messenger arrived with letters. There was another communication from the Queen of Naples. After she had reproached him for not replying to her last appeal, she went on:

"We have returned to our kingdom but the people have become hostile towards us. Only a few weeks ago we were honoured and revered. But now I dare not go out into the street. In church I feel their black eyes bore into my back as I kneel to pray before the blessed St Januarius. They have even turned against him! They say that when the French invaded, he allowed his blood to liquefy, as a sign that he approved of the Republic, while street shrines and crucifixes sweated blood to show their displeasure. I believe that the French tricked them. They are capable of anything – even tampering with the sacred blood of the saint. However, many of the people have turned to St Andrew instead. He is the protector of the Holy Faith Army, which delivered us from the Republican scum.

"We have had to show great firmness in re-establishing our authority. It was regrettable, but we could not allow such shameless rebellion as took place in our absence to go unpunished. History shows us that indulgence towards traitors never pays. My husband is already tired of Naples. He says that shortly he intends to leave his capital and go back to Palermo, which he finds more to his tastes. I am not stupid. I saw he had his eye on the wife of the Prince of Partanna. Kindly do not think me jealous. My husband sits too low in my estimation to merit my jealousy."

Henry read no further. He crumpled it up and handed it to Moretto, telling him to dispose of it. He had heard rumours that the Boubon restoration had not gone smoothly as expected. Ferdinand and Maria Carolina had embarked on a campaign of reprisals, thus alienating the population that had originally welcomed them.

The Bourbons' Revenge

A lengthy epistle of several pages was addressed to Moretto. It was from his old friend Heinrich, who was now back in Naples.

After the ritual enquiries regarding health and circumstances, Heinrich went on to talk about affairs in the Kingdom of Naples.

"I no longer recognise my lady, the Queen. She was so affrighted by what befell us in Naples and how she and all the royal

family were forced to flee to save their lives that she is transformed into a fury. She will allow no mercy. I even heard her telling Lady Emma to urge Nelson to deal with Naples as if it were a rebellious city in Ireland.

"As for the King, he too is altered beyond recognition. He has become gloomy and surly. He wishes to leave this city of traitors (as he calls it) and return to Sicily. He wants to make his new capital, with his palace in that strange House of Bells – do you remember? The people have turned against their Majesties, because of all the acts of cruelty they have committed. The republicans were treated without pity. They are saying that thousands of political prisoners have been executed, and many others were deported or exiled or sentenced to life imprisonment. Many of these were the young heirs of noble houses, teachers and men of science. Their families were forbidden to wear mourning, on pain of death. The Marchioness Fonseca di Pimentel was hanged like a common thief in the public marketplace, even though she was a noblewoman and entitled to the axe.

"Even poets, artists and musicians have not been spared. You will remember Cimarosa, the court musician – the triumph of his 'Clandestine Marriage'. Alas, he had been foolish enough to compose a patriotic hymn to the Parthenopean Republic and for that he was condemned as a traitor. Fortunately, his powerful friends in the Russian court intervened and the death sentence was changed to banishment from the kingdom. He has gone to Venice. As your lord loves music, you may meet him. Giovanni Paisiello was also condemned to death, but at the last moment His Majesty pardoned him.

"But the act that has aroused most indignation and anger has been the execution of the noble Admiral Caracciolo. He had fought with valour alongside Lord Nelson at the Battle of Genoa and he had also helped to convey the royal family to safety in Sicily. But it grieves me to tell you that latterly he had adopted the ideas of the French Revolution, so he was pronounced a traitor. The Queen would show no mercy. Nor did Lord Nelson, who hanged him from the yardarm of his ship and left him to swing for over a day.

"If, my friend, you believe in divine retribution, you will interpret as I did what I now have to tell you. Just a couple of days later, the Admiral's body resurfaced right under the bows of the Foudroyant. The King and Queen, as well as Lord and Lady Hamilton, were all on board and saw this horrifying sight. King Ferdinand was overcome with remorse. He had the Admiral's body recovered and given a Christian burial.

"Other sad news I have to give you is that Cardinal Ruffo di Calabria has fallen out of grace as he had promised that the Republican prisoners who surrendered would be pardoned. Instead, they were all executed by order of Lord Nelson and my Queen.

"I regret to tell you that Their Majesties show great favour to the worst villains that fought with the Holy Faith Army. It would turn your stomach to see with how much honour these ruffians have been received at court!

"The criminal Gaetano Mammone was invited to court personally by the King and Queen, who addressed him as 'Our General and Good Friend, faithful supporter of the crown'. He was heaped with rewards and decorations. Francatripa (a lower fellow you cannot imagine!) was also presented to the Queen, who gave him, with her own hands, a costly trinket, a band of gold with a diamond and a white ostrich plume, which highly pleased him. Michele Pezza (that's the brigand they call Fra' Diavolo) had a banquet given in his honour by the First Minister, Lord Acton. He was elevated to the rank of colonel by the King's orders and given a large reward in gold.

"Naples," Heinrich went on to say, *"is not tranquil. The amiable capital that we knew, dedicated to culture and pleasure, has been transformed. No one feels safe. The Queen knows that she is hated by the people and she talks often of taking her daughters the Princesses, to Austria to place them under the protection of her son-in-law, the Emperor.*

"In that case, I shall certainly accompany them," he went on. *"I shall be glad to return to the country of my birth, though I have no family or friends there to welcome me. But I shall also be sorry to leave this land of sunshine after so many years, even though it is no longer the happy city where we used to stroll along the harbour among the fisher folk, who sang as they sat repairing their nets.*

"I fear, my good friend, that we shall not meet again, as you will follow your lord when he returns to his see and the distance dividing two aging courtiers, as we are, will prove insurmountable. We must each grow old in our separate worlds, far from the sea and the songs of the street sellers in our Bella Napoli. I fear I shall find Vienna far less congenial."

Moretto, with a sad smile, folded the letter and secreted it inside his waistcoat.

Cardinal Ruffo di Calabria had entered Naples on the thirteenth June, 1799, at the head of an army of 20,000 enthusiastic followers.

A charismatic leader, he ate and slept with his men. Unflinching under fire, he rode at their head into the battlefield, coming through time after time unscathed. The *Sanfedisti* were convinced that he was under divine protection. Apart from the risks encountered during engagements, he also survived a couple of assassination attempts, thus cementing his reputation as being indestructible. All these qualities were even more remarkable in a man past the flush of youth who suffered from recurrent attacks of kidney stones.

Ruffo had arrived at the city gates a few days earlier, but he waited, out of respect, for his sovereign to enter the city with him. This caused some delay as Ferdinand wanted to wait for the arrival of his son and heir, the Crown Prince Francesco. The hold-up cost the city dear. Riots broke out as Royalists and Republicans clashed. With no one to control them, the *Lazzari* ran amuck, murdering, raping, burning and destroying. The republican sympathisers and the French soldiers who had been left to hold the city shut themselves inside the three castles of Sant'Elmo, dell'Ovo and Castel Nuovo, bombarding the streets and houses from the battlements with a steady stream of cannonballs and musket fire.

Alarmed at the situation, Ruffo broke through the city gates. He rode at the head of his troops, attired in his Cardinal's scarlet robes and wide-brimmed *galero*. His right hand, flashing with rings, was held up high in the classic gesture of blessing. The church bells began to ring. The population fell on its knees as he passed. A couple of days later, he had negotiated with the insurgents, promising that if they surrendered they would go free and would not be held to account.

Nelson arrived in Naples ten days later with a fleet of seventeen ships, demanding that all the revolutionaries held in the city jails be executed. The two commanders had never liked each other. Ruffo considered Nelson haughty and cold. Nelson referred to Ruffo as the 'great devil' and 'that puffed-up priest'. They quarrelled furiously. Ruffo refused to follow Nelson's orders, saying he had sworn on his honour that the lives of the prisoners would be spared. He said that King Ferdinand had promised clemency.

"The word of a king is worth as much as that of an English admiral's!" he said, looking down his nose at the seething Nelson.

Ruffo held out for three days, but in the end he was overruled, mainly because the hysterical Maria Carolina put pressure on her husband to eliminate all the opposition to the restoration of the monarchy. The bloodbath that followed was to cast a long and lasting shadow that tainted Nelson's reputation and transformed Ferdinand and Maria Carolina from illuminated sovereigns into tyrants.

The Bridge of Tits

Immediately after these letters arrived, Cardinal Stuart left Padua for Venice. His funds were now so low that he had had to accept lodgings in the poorer part of the city, near the Rialto Bridge. The inn sat right on the waterfront and it was small and dark with low ceilings. A noisy market was held daily on the opposite bank of the canal, filled with stagnant, malodorous water. At sun-down, when the market was over, everything unsold and rotting got tipped into the canal, so that the surface became covered with bobbing cabbage leaves, wizened carrots, offal, blackened bread, wasted and discarded vegetables, fish-bones, bloody meat bones, bruised fruit, broken crates, baskets and all kinds of nameless objects.

Henry stood on the balcony of their room, watching the boatmen weaving to and fro, as if they were navigating through swamps. He thought that he had become accustomed to the stink of Naples but here it was infinitely worse. He felt a sudden pang of nostalgia, longing for the sweet, fresh air of his home in Frascati, with its comforting odours of hot bread emerging from the ovens, the must wafting from fermenting wine vats, the grilling of blood sausages and game in the kitchens, the honest country smells of earth, dung, cattle, sheep and horses.

Moretto was appalled and dismayed that his master had to live in such conditions. He had gone out at once to explore the maze of narrow alleyways that radiated from the Rialto. He discovered that they were lodged only a short distance away from the notorious Carampane district. From the bridges he peered into dark waterways that had no footpaths and could only be traversed by boat. He had realised immediately that they were in an area of ill repute. He saw gaming houses and taverns and brothels lining the canals.

Whenever a gondola passed under the bridges, whores leant out of their windows, beckoning and calling. They let their yellow shawls fall off their shoulders and propped their great white breasts, as round and smooth as melons, on their window ledges. Some of the windows were so low that men passing could reach out their hands and fondle the nipples which they painted red like cherries. Moretto sighed and prayed to the Blessed Virgin as he gripped the parapet to help him remember the vow he had made at the church of La Molara.

"The strumpets," he wrote in a letter to Heinrich, *"clamour for a coin to pay for this privilege and curse in the most horrible fashion those who do not pay the fee. This is not a good place for my lord to be. I have tried to suggest we go back to Padua, but he will not countenance it. He is too proud to live on the charity of the friars and he does not wish his brother Cardinals to know that he is sunk so low. He who has always been so liberal and generous with everyone – even his enemies – is reduced to this. I pray daily that the conclave may start soon and we can leave this place of sin and degradation!"*

Henry did not venture out of the inn for the first few days. The wound in his leg had flared up again and walking caused him pain. He sat with it propped on a stool, gazing out of the window at the activity in the market opposite. The weather continued to be unseasonably hot and they suffered from the heat, the stench and the swarms of insects that tormented them at night despite the garlic juice that Moretto rubbed over their faces, necks and any other exposed parts of their bodies.

Moretto became increasingly worried. Henry had always been full of energy, despite his age, but now he seemed listless and sat around, lost in dreams. When he talked, it was about old times, when his brother was alive and they were still on good terms. He talked about his niece, Charlotte, Charles Edward's daughter. She had died, he said, too young and without issue. Her father had forbidden her to marry and she had seemed in any case to have no inclination, so the noble line of the Stuarts had come to an end, not, as his ancestor James V had predicted, with the lass Mary Stuart, but with the lass of Albany.

Finally, after the landlord had knocked on his door for the second time to ask for his due, Henry roused himself and sent the Boy out to sell his last silver medallion. Since the sum offered by the moneylender was too low to cover their credit with the inn and inevitable future expenses, Moretto added the diamond-studded buttons from his livery coat and the gilded buckles from his shoes. He had them replaced with cheap imitations. To his relief, the Cardinal did not seem to notice. Over the last few days, Moretto had been reduced to haggling for credit at the shops and taverns to procure meals for them both.

"I take care to dress with a show of elegance when I go out to do dealings with the shopkeepers," he wrote to Heinrich. *"I am*

haughty when I address them and they do not dare as yet to question our ability to pay them. The more you insult these people – call them insolent dogs to doubt the integrity of the Cardinal, a Prince of the Church and of royal blood – the more they cower and are convinced their money will be coming to them.

"This is a lesson I learned in the streets of Naples from you, my old friend. I remember when you drank in the taverns and went with the whores without paying you would tell them, with a careless air, that you were in the service of the Queen and they would grovel instantly. These people are more subservient than the beggars who insult you if you don't toss them a coin. The beggar feels he is free to give you his lip because he does not depend on you. But the shopkeepers are obsequious because they know they must not set the rich against them or they risk their livelihood.

"Picture me therefore as I strut through the market in my best livery embroidered with my master's royal insignia, my brass buttons shined to look like gold, my ruffles snowy white and my boots well-polished and they all think I am a fine gentleman in the employ of a great prince who will look eventually look on them with favour when the right time comes."

As October progressed, the heat became less oppressive. Henry, however, remained lethargic. Moretto was worried. He racked his brains for some idea that could induce his master to leave his stuffy room and take the air. His wanderings had taken him to the more attractive side of Venice, where the great palaces of the rich looked onto the lagoon and the daily sea tides washed and purified the sluggish waters of the canals. He had enquired where the great musician Domenico Cimarosa lived, hoping that he could persuade the Cardinal to pay a visit, but when he went to the door of Palazzo Duodo, the footman told him that his master had never recovered from his terrible experience in Naples prison and that he was now too ill to receive anyone.

One morning, however, he had a stroke of luck. He was crossing St Mark's Square when he spotted the portly figure of Cardinal Stefano Borgia leaving the basilica and being lifted into his sedan chair with the combined efforts of the bearers and his two attendants. Cardinal Henry and Borgia were old friends and Moretto had often been with his master to Palazzo Altemps, Borgia's residence in Rome. The Cardinal was Secretary of the Sacred Congregation for Propagating the Faith, the Roman Catholic Church's proselytising organisation, and he had gathered a vast collection of antiquities sent to him by missionaries based in the Orient and the Middle East. As a young boy, Moretto had been fascinated and intrigued by the displays of pagan idols, sculptures, fetishes and various exotic *objets d'art* on display and Borgia had been touched by his interest and had often spent time with him explaining what they were and where they came from.

Henry, on the other hand, regarded his friend's collection with unconcealed disapproval that the good-natured Borgia took in good part, teasing Henry on his ignorance of the wider world. Henry's taste ran to classical Greek and Roman works of art and he found his friend's interest in the religious practices of heathen peoples incomprehensible. The shared interests of the two men were confined to their libraries. They kept up a friendly rivalry over who possessed the finest collection of rare books. Borgia boasted that he kept 4,500 volumes which he made available to scholars of all races and creeds. But Henry easily outclassed him in this field. His Herboracum Library at Frascati had almost three times as many books and was admired and envied throughout the papal territories.

With a beating heart, Moretto ran across the square and reached the Cardinal as he was being eased into his seat. He hoped he would be able to persuade Borgia to help his master out of his difficulties, and he also hoped he could count on his discretion. Henry was a very proud man and would not approve of his servant approaching his old friend to talk about his troubles.

Dropping on his knees, Moretto gripped the Cardinal's hand and pressed his lips to the ring before the two servants, who were busy re-arranging the cushions, could stop him.

Borgia started with surprise. "Why Moretto!" he exclaimed, recognising the Boy. "How is my old friend Stuart? We have been looking for him everywhere. Even his Eminence Cardinal Albani does not know how to get in touch with him. We have all been very worried. Is he unwell?"

"Alas, Your Eminence," Moretto said, not daring to raise his eyes. "He is indeed unwell. Allow me a few minutes of your time in private and I will tell you more."

Borgia looked at him keenly and then gestured to his servants to withdraw out of hearing.

"Well, Gigi, tell me all. We feared that something had befallen Cardinal York."

"Your Grace," Moretto said, in a trembling voice. "He could hardly be in a worse situation. He now resides in a place lower than Your Grace could possibly imagine. His fortune is totally gone. He has lost all his possessions. His benefices and assets have been purloined by the French invaders. You will recall his great generosity when our late Holy Father launched an appeal to buy peace from the grasping Corsican, who then betrayed all his promises to spare the city of Rome. My master is old and ailing. He travelled to Venice at great personal risk so that he could fulfil his duty to the one true Church. But the journey has been hard and his health has suffered. His trials have been too great for a man of his age. I fear he will not live long in his present state."

Borgia sat still, lost in thought for a long moment, stroking the rings of fat under his chin. Finally, he stretched his hand out gently over the Boy's head in blessing.

"Rest assured, I shall do my utmost to help His Royal Highness," he said. "Fortunately, I have friends who have the ear of the Hanover King. I am sure he will be sympathetic when he learns of the troubles that have befallen the ancient Stuart House. The same blood runs in his veins, even if from the female line and much diluted. After all, who can tell when fate might turn against him too! Be tranquil. You have my word that something will be done. Meanwhile, you must tell your master that the Emperor has consented to let us hold the conclave in the Benedictine Monastery of St George on the island of that name. He must therefore come back at once to Padua because he will have to help the Dean make preparations."

"Thank you, Your Grace," said Moretto humbly. "But I fear he will not listen to me. If you could pen a note in your own hand, I am sure it would have the desired effect."

"Very well," said Borgia. "Follow me. I reside nearby and I will write you a letter to take to his Grace."

Summoning his bearers, he had them convey him down a side street to a princely palace overlooking the lagoon, where the servants helped him alight. Moretto followed him as he laboriously made his way upstairs, panting and pausing at every step. He found Cardinal Borgia greatly changed from the robust man he remembered, full of vigour and good humour. It was evident that the trials of the journey when he had accompanied Pius VI into exile at Valence had taken a heavy toll.

They entered a study, where the Cardinal sat down heavily and called for pen and ink. He slowly and carefully wrote a letter that he closed with his seal.

"This should persuade him to come out, if he is still the old friend that I used to know," Borgia said as he handed it over. "I have things I must communicate to him face-to-face so in this letter I am inviting him to meet me this afternoon at the Hospice of Mercy where the orphans are singing. Do you know where that is?"

Moretto nodded. By now he was familiar with most of the city.

"I know your master loves music," Borgia said. "The orphans' choir is famous and going there will not attract suspicion. With this excuse, we can meet and I shall be able to speak to him personally. I know I can rely on your fidelity. Not a word to anyone of this!"

With a lighter heart, Moretto hurried back to their lodgings, ignoring the pimps and peddlers who tried to waylay him in the darker alleys. He found Henry seated at the window as before, his missal lying open on his lap unread, his eyes fixed on a large black beetle that was scampering across the floor.

Moretto concealed his excitement and assumed a casual air.

"Your Majesty," he said. "This morning I had the great good fortune to meet His Grace, Cardinal Borgia."

Henry stirred and raised his head. "Borgia has arrived? He is here in Venice?"

"Yes, indeed, sire, He is most anxious to meet you. He gave me this letter for you."

He pulled it out of his waistcoat and handed it over. Henry took it and examined the seal carefully.

"No, sire, no one has opened this. His Grace gave it into my own hands and I have brought it straight to you."

Henry continued to turn the letter over in his hands. "So you have met Borgia!" he said finally. "Is he lodging here in Venice?"

"Oh, indeed, sire. He took me to his house – a fine palace near St Mark's Cathedral. He is most anxious to meet you."

The Cardinal frowned, lost in thought, while Moretto bustled around the room trying to conceal his impatience. Finally, Henry broke the seal and read the letter in silence. Then he gave a heavy sigh.

"He wishes to meet me this very day, Moretto. He says he has important information for me, but we must exercise great caution as Venice is full of our enemies and also many false friends, who pretend to support our cause but are really out to betray us." He studied the letter again. "Do you know where this Hospice of Mercy is?"

"Oh, indeed, sire," Moretto replied eagerly, thankful to see that the Cardinal was finally showing interest after days of silence and indifference. "It is a much respected institution, caring for abandoned female children. The choir is said to be the finest in Venice. The Red Priest, the great Maestro Vivaldi, whose music I know you love, was the first choirmaster. He set up the Hospice conservatory to teach these unfortunate girls to sing and play musical instruments so that they may honourably earn their living when they come of age. When the orchestra and choir perform, the church is always crowded with listeners."

For the first time in days, Henry smiled. "I see you are well informed! You have put your time to good use here while I have been languishing in this place surrounded by rats!"

Full of relief to see his master coming back to life, Moretto rambled on in enthusiastic terms.

"Yes, indeed, my Lord, I have been exploring this strange city set on water. And I can assure you it is not all as ugly as this place we find ourselves in. There are many splendid buildings, palaces and churches that I am sure would delight your eyes. These canals all lead to the sea with fine open views."

"Well, we shall see!" Henry interrupted him. "His Grace has kindly said he will send his own gondola to fetch us. We shall have to wait on the dock near the bridge. I do not wish the boatman to carry tales to the Cardinal about how he found us in this hovel."

"No, indeed, Your Majesty," said Moretto, nodding his head in agreement. Obviously, Borgia had been tactful enough to make no mention of their conversation, in order not to wound his old friend's pride.

"So, sire," Moretto continued in a cheerful voice. "We must make you ready. I have instructed the washerwoman to bring your fresh linen within the next two hours and I have also summoned a barber. You would not like to meet his Excellency looking like a wild barbarian!"

The Orphans' Choir

Shortly before sunset, Borgia's gondola picked them up. Henry did not like having to travel everywhere on water, even though the boat glided very smoothly along the waterways and under the bridges and he was able to thank God that they were spared the wild heavings and torments they had suffered on the high seas.

As they moved into the Grand Canal, the setting sun bathed the palaces of the nobles in a soft pink light. The gilded embellishments dazzled and glittered. Gondolas plied to and fro. They were painted black and unadorned, in contrast with the rich and colourful clothes of their wealthy passengers, who reclined on red velvet cushions, exchanging languid greetings with acquaintances who glided slowly by.

Moretto was enthusiastic. "This is such a strange city!" he commented. "I do not think there can be anything like it in the world!"

Henry, however, was not impressed. He sniffed. His taste ran to the neoclassical style, derived from the principles of Greek and Roman antiquities.

"There's no order or harmony here," he commented. "The perfect rules of mathematics and architecture, established by the great classical builders have been totally ignored. I have the impression that here each owner built according to his whim, with too much attention to the oriental style. This city on water has been constructed by merchants ignorant of the noble forms of architecture, who merely wished to display their wealth – as if they were hawking their grand palaces on the market place."

Moretto ventured to disagree.

"I must confess, sire, that I do not find it entirely unpleasing. I think it is not without a certain unruly and exotic charm, like something from the land of the Moors that we can see in paintings of the Orient."

The Cardinal sniffed again and fell silent. But Moretto was anxious to keep him talking so he asked if it were true that before the Austrians came, the state of Venice was not governed by a king, but by a magistrate elected by a Grand Council.

"Ah, you are better informed than I would have believed, my lazy Boy. You take an interest now in politics. Yes, this is true. The Venetians believed that this system saved them from being ruled over by a tyrant. However, the magistrates all came from the great noble families."

"This is, I am sure, how our Lord God intended it to be," commented Moretto. "Since only those who are rich and powerful command in the world!"

"Amen!" said Henry in a level tone.

They disembarked at Sestiere Castello near the former Doge's palace and Moretto helped his master walk the short distance to the church at the Hospice of Mercy. Borgia's servant was waiting for them at the door and conducted them to his master, who sat apart, in a dark corner off the nave. The orphans' choir was not due to begin its performance for another half hour, but the body of the church was already full. The two Cardinals embraced warmly and then talked together in hushed tones. Borgia had important news. He said that thirty-three of the forty-six members of the Sacred College had arrived to attend the conclave and that they had thus reached the minimum number required for the papal election to be valid.

He also said that the Austrian Emperor had finally chosen the place where the conclave would be held. It was to be on the Island of San Giorgio Maggiore, where the Benedictines had a monastery.

"He believes he can keep us secreted there, away from outside interference," Borgia said. "We had requested the Basilica of St Mark's as more suited to our station and the importance of our mission, but he refused. However, he has given permission for us to hold in San Marco the solemn *Novendiales* in honour of our poor Holy Father, who died in exile almost a year ago, alone and uncomforted. The French have refused to return the body of His Holiness to Italy so our commemoration will be symbolic. However, it will send out an important message to the faithful that the Church has by no means been suppressed or confined, despite all the attempts by the godless Jacobins. The rites of commemorations will begin soon and you must be present."

At that moment, the choirmaster rapped his baton sharply on an iron grating as a signal that the choristers were ready to sing. Henry made a move to go forward but Borgia stopped him.

"There is nothing to see. The orphans sing and play their instruments behind these bars. They are in a gallery linked directly with their dormitories. This is so that they cannot be seen by evil-minded persons. They tell me that the pimps are always on the lookout for virgins to take, willingly or not, to the brothels, so the girls are well guarded."

The concert that followed was of the highest quality. The musicians were skilled and the bell-like voices of the choir rose and filled the walls and ceiling of the church. Henry was enraptured. "It's as they say. It's like the singing of the angels," he murmured to himself. His spirits had soared with the music and he had forgotten the privations of the past few weeks.

Observing that his friend had become animated, Borgia was well pleased with the impression the performance had made and smiled to himself with satisfaction. Moretto leaned back against the wall, relieved to see his master transformed into something like his old self.

"Dear Stuart, you must come to stay with me until the time comes when we can transfer to San Giorgio Maggiore. We have been advised that it is important that we stay together, as our situation is by no means secure," Borgia dropped his voice to almost a whisper, so that Henry had to move closer in order to hear him. "We have learned that Napoleon left Egypt in secret and has arrived back safely in France, eluding the British fleet. The man is under the protection of the devil, that's for sure! Who knows what he is planning next!"

He eyed Henry, who stood frowning in indecision, and grasped his hand. "Gianfrancesco Albani is here as well. He stays with me when he is not off to negotiate with the Emperor. You cannot refuse me. It will be my pleasure, as well as my obligation towards the Sacred College."

After a moment's hesitation, Henry accepted, to Moretto's great relief.

The Monastery of San Giorgio Maggiore

After that, events began to move fast. Ercole Consalvi arrived back from Vienna, confirming Francis II's agreement to house the conclave in the Benedictine Monastery on the lagoon. The next day, Henry, Albani and Ercole Consalvi hired a boat and crossed the San Marco basin to visit the monastery.

Henry brightened at the sight of the Church of San Giorgio – a masterpiece by the great classical architect Palladio. This was much more to his taste than the gaudily decorated palaces around the square of San Marco. The church rose like a vision of purity from the waters of the lagoon, white and gleaming, towering above the brown tiled roofs of the surrounding buildings. Its red brick bell tower rose on one side, like a beacon marker for the ships entering St Mark's basin.

The island of the Benedictines looked remote and inviolable, but when they arrived, they found it had not been spared. A contingent of Napoleon's army had invaded the monastery, which had been full of artistic treasures. The havoc they had left behind was evident as soon as they docked.

The elderly Abbot, who was too frail and stooped to be able to walk unaided, came out personally to greet them. As he led them inside, he told them that during the French raid the brothers had feared for their lives. The soldiers had burst in and ordered the entire community to leave at once, threatening them with death if they offered any resistance.

They were only able to return when the Austrians took control of the Venetian state, he explained, and they were still hard at work repairing the damage. The church had been stripped of everything of value and the few remaining sacred images were peppered with shot. The Abbot pointed out some of the mutilated carvings on the cloister columns.

"On their first night, the infantrymen got drunk and amused themselves, here in this sacred precinct, doing target practice. That is what the watchman told us – they had allowed him to stay as he was a lay member of the community."

Tears of indignation filled the old man's eyes and his mouth quivered so much that he was unable to say more. But no more words were needed. Everywhere they turned, they saw the signs of wanton destruction and desecration.

The Abbot took them out into the garden, an empty space of upturned earth and broken tree trunks.

"We found all our trees uprooted and our herbs and vegetables trampled on. They thought we had buried gold in the orchard but of course they found nothing. They made off with our pigs and hens and they raided our cellars. We have cleared the land but we must wait now for the spring to plant anew, God willing!"

He then led them into the refectory where, he lamented, the monastery had suffered its greatest, irreplaceable loss. Overcome with emotion, he pointed to the empty wall where a vast expanse of plaster gleamed paler than the surroundings.

"That was where we had our greatest treasure, the pride of our community, the splendid painting, which our predecessors commissioned from the great Maestro Paolo Veronese to adorn our dining hall. It portrayed the wedding feast of Cana, when our Lord performed his first miracle of transforming water into wine."

The old man shook all over as he recounted the outrage.

"Our porter told us how the French took it down from the wall. They had orders to send it to Paris but since it was so big they did not know how to transport it. Do you know how they solved this problem? They cut the Veronese masterpiece in half! When our brave porter protested, the officer simply waved his hands. He said he had his orders and the rest did not concern him. They would patch it up in France."

After a thorough inspection of the monastery and the adjoining church, the visitors realised that many repairs were needed before the buildings would be ready to house the conclave and that this would involve further delay. Consalvi said that the Emperor had agreed to bear the running costs but he was reluctant to commit himself to additional expenses. Albani had urged the Nuncio in Vienna to insist. The cardinals would at least need a dry roof over their heads when they were locked in the conclave chamber, but Francis

II only gave vague replies. Fortunately, help came from the Archbishop of Toledo, Cardinal Francisco de Lorenzana, who contributed 80,000 Roman *scudi* offered by the bishops of Spain.

The Cardinals York and Carafa were appointed *Fabricieri,* the overseers of the work in progress. Henry went to live with the monks so that he could be on the spot and ensure there would be no unnecessary delays.

During this period, Henry regained much of his former vigour. He saw himself in the role of shepherd, caring for his flock of cardinals, many of whom were confused and lost, far from their former homes and filled with fear and uncertainty concerning their future. He hobbled around under the scaffolding, leaning heavily on Moretto's arm, and shouted orders up to the workmen on the roof busy repairing the holes and replacing missing tiles.

Around the middle of November, alarming news arrived. Far from being in decline, Bonaparte had taken full power into his own hands.

He had lost patience with the Directoire. Albani's informer reported that the General had said he had no intention of taking further orders from a government he considered corrupt, incompetent and totally inadequate to fill the role of leading France on towards further glory. The Corsican had publically declared that he hadn't conquered half of Europe in order to remain a mere general. So on the ninth November, 1799 (eighteen Brumaire VIII, according to the republican calendar), he staged a coup d'état, with the backing of his army. He dismissed the Directoire and proclaimed himself First Consul with virtually unlimited powers. He was now absolute master of France as well as a large part of the European continent.

Henry, Albani and Consalvi got together to discuss the possible consequences. The Directoire had always been reluctant to pursue the conquest of Italy, believing that the central European territories bordering on Austria and Germany were more strategically important. But now, with the limitations imposed by the French government removed, Napoleon was free to follow his inclinations, which included the subjugation of the Kingdom of Naples and the invasion of Britain.

This could only mean even greater trouble. Bonaparte would be burning to avenge his humiliating defeat at Aboukir. He was already busy re-arming and was set on retaking the territories that had slipped away from French grasp during his absence in Egypt. And it seemed that nothing could stop him.

Help from King George III

Meanwhile, Cardinal Borgia had not forgotten the promise he had made Moretto. The day after his meeting with Henry at the Hospice of Mercy, he sat down and penned a letter to his friend Sir John Coxe-Hippisley, a British diplomat who had spent several years in Rome. The two men shared a passion for collecting ancient manuscripts and antiques and during that time Hippisley had also struck up friendly relations with Cardinal York. Sir John was known to be in great favour with King George III since he had successfully negotiated the marriage of his eldest daughter, Crown Princess Charlotte, to Frederick of Wurttemberg. Borgia wrote him an impassioned letter, describing the plight of the last of the Stuarts, who was His Majesty's blood cousin, living alone and in poverty:

"It is greatly affecting to me to see so great a personage, the last descendant of his royal house, reduced to such distressed circumstances, having been barbarously stripped by the French of all his property," he wrote, going on to explain that the Cardinal Duke of York, *"has been supported by the silver plate which he had taken with him, and of which he began to dispose at Messina... and in order to supply his wants during a few months at Venice, he has sold all that remains."*

Borgia continued, listing the Cardinal's lost revenues.

"The only income he has left is that of his benefices in Spain, which amount to 14,000 crowns; but this, as it is only payable in paper at the moment, is greatly reduced by the disadvantages of exchange, and even that has not been paid for a year."

He added that the Cardinal, despite his straightened circumstances, had continued to honour his obligations to support his brother Charles' widow, the Countess of Albany, as well as Clementina Walkinshaw, the mother of his late niece Charlotte. He was also required to pay out various annuities stipulated in the wills of both his father and his brother and he no longer had any credit to honour these obligations.

Borgia rounded off with a heartfelt appeal to '*English magnanimity*', trusting that His Majesty would not allow '*an illustrious personage of the same nation to perish in misery!*'

The letter touched a chord in the hearts of several British ministers, who immediately arranged a bank transfer of £500 sterling to meet Cardinal Henry's most urgent immediate needs. Many of them may also have suffered twinges of conscience. The fact was that Britain owed the Stuarts a great deal of money.

When Cardinal Henry's grandfather, James II and VII, had married Mary of Modena, a princess belonging to the rich and powerful Italian d'Este family, an Act of Parliament had ratified the marriage agreement. One of the clauses stated that, in the event of her husband's death, Queen Mary would receive the sum of £50,000 as part restitution of her dowry.

When James was deposed and forced to flee to France with his wife and infant son, his stepsister Mary and her husband, William of Orange, were invited to take over the throne. They had no surviving children and were succeeded by Mary's younger sister Anne. During both reigns nothing was paid out to the former dowager queen. In 1718, Mary of Modena died in poverty, living on the charity of the French court.

Meanwhile, the money accumulated in the London banks, ignored or forgotten by the Stuart heirs. It wasn't until some seventy years later that Henry's niece Charlotte, Prince Charles Edward's daughter, decided to look into the matter and realised that the British government owed the late Queen's grandsons arrears that amounted to well over a million pounds.

Charlotte was a determined young woman, and had she lived longer, she might have been able to make her case. As the matter stood, the British Prime Minister, William Pitt the Younger, had taken care to conceal the Stuart claims from the present king, George III.

Meanwhile, Borgia's appeal was conveyed through the correct channels till it arrived in the hands of King George himself, who at once arranged for Henry to receive an annual allowance of £4,000 from the state treasury.

The Times newspaper published the news of King George's magnanimous gesture, describing the Cardinal of York in sympathetic terms as '*placid, humane and temperate*'. The article went on to describe the tragedies and disasters in the life of the last Stuart, ruled by '*the malign influence of the star which had so strongly marked the fate of so many of his illustrious ancestors…*'

King George's gesture in granting a pension to the last member of the House of Stuart, which had once been a dangerous rival to the throne he occupied, may well have been motivated simply by compassion. He probably knew nothing of Mary of Modena's inheritance, locked away in British banks. However, many members of the British government certainly knew and they could congratulate themselves on having saved the treasury a lot of money.

Henry immediately wrote back long letters of thanks to the British intermediates who had helped him. Protocol prevented him from writing directly to King George, so his gratitude was expressed indirectly through the King's agents. Although it was a blow to his Stuart pride to be forced to accept charity from this remote cousin whose grandfather, George I, had usurped the Stuart's rightful throne, he sincerely believed that the Hanoverian king was unaware of the existence of the Stuarts' lost legacy.

He himself had known nothing about it until the death of Charlotte Stuart ten years previously, when she had passed her claim on to him, as the last of their line. But Henry had decided not to press his case. He had realised at the time of his brother's death, when Pius VI had denied Charles Edward a royal funeral and made it plain that the Church would no longer support the Stuart claims to the throne of Britain, that he would have little chance of recovering his inheritance. At the same time, he had felt no need to put forward any demands. Until the French invasion, he had been wealthy in his own right, surrounded by luxuries and comforts. He could not have foreseen the swift downward turn in his fortunes that had transformed him, almost overnight, from potentate to pauper.

The annual pension was a godsend in his present circumstances and he accepted it with joy and genuine gratitude.

The Venice Conclave

November 30th, 1799 – March 14th, 1800

On the 28th November, soon after the nine days commemorations for Pope Pius VI ended, Henry announced that all the preparations that could be made for the conclave were completed. The inaugural mass was held two days later in the Church of San Giorgio Maggiore.

Thirty-four cardinals in their scarlet robes filed solemnly into the conclave chamber. Each one was accompanied by two of his servants to see to his personal comfort. Henry, however, had only Moretto, who was mortified to see his master, the Sub-Dean of the Sacred College, diminished in this way.

"Never fear, Your Majesty!" he muttered in Henry's ear. "I shall do the work of two and you shall lack for nothing!"

"I would never doubt it!" Henry replied gently, patting the Boy on the shoulder with his free hand. He had refused to lean on his servant's arm as they walking in procession. His head held high, he made his way forward with the help of his cane, trailing his injured leg behind him.

Together with Albani, he had selected the Winter Choir for the Conclave. This was a discreet side room leading off from the monumental choir behind the main altar of the basilica. Small and unadorned, it had been ignored by the French. Plain wooden stalls ran intact round three sides of the walls. Notwithstanding all the efforts of the two *Fabricieri*, it was not an ideal place for a long, drawn-out assembly. Damp from the lagoon seeped up through the tiled pavement and the chamber was chilly, despite the many braziers Henry had had installed and the heavy curtains he had ordered draped over the walls. The windows had all been boarded up and the room was illuminated by dozens of flickering candles.

All the cardinals and their servants took the solemn vow of secrecy. Nothing that passed in the room must be revealed to the outside, though all of them were aware that this was purely a formality. This conclave, like many of its predecessors, would be infiltrated with spies planted by the rulers of Austria, France, Naples and Spain.

The traditional command was given: '*Extra Omnes* – Everyone Out', which was the signal that all those not directly involved in the voting process or in the service of their lords had to leave and Albani proclaimed the opening oration, '*pro electione futuri summi pontificis*'.

After that, the doors were sealed. Until the election results had been decided, the cardinals were shut off from the outside world. Their meals would be prepared by the monks and passed through a hatch in the wall.

Henry ran his eyes over the gathering. He had met most of the cardinals before. Some were his friends. Others, he knew, were his enemies, envying him his position as Vice Chancellor, the controller of the Vatican purse. He glanced over at Albani, who was taking the tally of the cardinals present.

"One of our members is not yet with us," Albani announced. "Word has arrived from Cardinal von Herzan that he intends to join us, but he has been held up by bad weather and lack of supplies. He has begged us to be patient and make the exception of allowing him entry when he comes."

Some of the cardinals muttered objections. It was no secret that Herzan von Harras, the former imperial ambassador at the papal court, was an agent of the Austrian Emperor, with instructions to direct the vote towards Austria's preferred candidate, Alessandro Mattei, the Archbishop of Ferrara, who had signed the Treaty of Tolentino with Napoleon in 1797. Since, under the terms of the Treaty, Austria had annexed territories belonging to the Papal States. Francis II wanted a Pope who would not create problems for him by demanding the lands back.

"Are we quite sure that Herzan is not delayed because he's made a detour to confer with the Archbishop of Seville?" said Braschi-Onesti, with a sly smile. "Despuig will give him opposing instructions from the Spaniards."

"Let us be careful what we say!" Albani interjected. "Remember that Monsignor Despuig is the Spanish Ambassador in Venice. He is in a delicate situation."

"I would remind you all, dear brothers in Christ," Henry put in. "That he also provided the money for the *Novendiale* in honour of our deceased Holy Father. So we all owe him a debt of gratitude."

Cardinal Francisco de Lorenzana, the Archbishop of Toledo and former Grand Inquisitor of Spain, who had put up the money for much of the restoration work, spoke up angrily, "That does not put us under an obligation to choose the candidate dictated by the Hapsburgs."

No one paid any attention. They all knew that Lorenzana was the King of Spain's representative in the conclave. Spain had allied with France in the war against Britain and basically wanted a pope who would be easily manipulated, like the mild-mannered and scholarly professor of philosophy, Cardinal Hyacinthe Sigismond Gerdil. However, Gerdil was already over eighty and the last thing the Sacred Collage wanted in these difficult times was a short papacy.

Henry sighed inwardly. He already knew, as they all did, that the conclave was divided into three opposing factions and that it would prove very difficult to reach the two-thirds majority required for any candidate to be successful. He could foresee weeks ahead of manipulation and arguments till one or other side was persuaded to back down.

It was no secret that Francis II had put a veto on the election of Cardinals of French origin, as well as any from Spain, Sardinia, Naples or Genoa. He had also banned an eventual election of Cardinal Henry York. Austria was allied with Britain against Napoleon and had no wish to upset George III by backing a papal candidate who might rekindle the aspirations of his discontented Roman Catholic subjects. These restrictions meant, of course, that a large number of cardinals were automatically excluded.

The Neapolitan government had made it known, however, that they would reject the Hapsburg Emperor's candidates. The Naples army had occupied Rome in Napoleon's absence and they feared that a Pope with Austrian support would force them to leave the Papal States. Henry knew that Lord Acton was monitoring events in Venice very closely.

The third group represented the French royalist party, which supported the exiled Louis Stanislas Xavier, Count of Provence and brother of the guillotined King Louis XVI. It was backing the election of Cardinal Jean-Siffrein Maury, who had refused to sign the Constitutional Oath that rejected the Pope's authority in France and was known to be a staunch defender of the *ancien regime.*

It was going to be arduous, if not outright impossible, to find a candidate who could reconcile all these differences. Before they had been locked into the conclave, Henry had discussed the situation with Albani and Consalvi. All three factions had a vested interest in the choice of the new Pontiff. Since numbers were so tight, pressure would have to be exerted to convince some of those present to change allegiance. This would inevitably create suspicion and bad feeling.

"We had best be prepared for a long session," Albani had said.

Meanwhile, they needed to appoint a secretary, since the Sacred College Secretary, Monsignor Pietro Maria Negroni, had been unable to join them. Gigi, who stood at the back of the room with the other servants, was galled to see Henry put forward the name of his former schoolmate Ercole Consalvi, now an auditor of the Sacred Roman Rota. Henry's proposal was accepted without discussion. Consalvi was well known and respected as a clever and capable lawyer and diplomat.

Moretto leaned back against the wall, crossing his arms with a scowl. The nomination meant almost certain promotion at the end of the conclave. He hoped that in future he would not be obliged to go down on one knee and kiss the ring of his haughty former fellow student.

The cardinals settled down to their new life of enclosure. Three times a day the hand-bell rang outside and the servants rushed to the hatch to collect the meals for their masters. Morning and evening, another bell rang for the servants to pass out the chamber pots. Henry fretted at not being able to stretch his legs. His injured leg got stiff if he sat around too much. Leaning on Moretto's arm, he hobbled up and down the chamber, attracting irritated comments from groups in earnest discussion, who were forced to move aside to let them past.

Campaigning had begun immediately. In between ballots, the cardinals huddled in little groups whispering together. When Cardinal Herzan von Harras was admitted on the twelfth of December, he found the Sacred College split into three litigious groups and he quickly realized that gathering enough support for Mattei was going to prove more arduous than he had previously imagined.

"Our Man from Vienna is apparently in difficulty," Albani murmured to Henry, from behind his wine goblet, watching an increasingly frustrated Herzan buttonhole one little group after another to expound his arguments.

As the weeks progressed, the atmosphere inside the boarded-up Winter Choir became more and more heated. At Christmas, new candidates began to emerge while von Harras continued to canvass for the Austrian Emperor's choice. The Spanish faction shifted its vote from the aged Gerdil to Cardinal Luigi Valenti Gonzaga, the former Papal Nuncio in Spain, but meanwhile, a new candidate, backed by a group opposed to Austrian domination, had come forward. This was the independent-minded Cardinal Carlo Bellisomi. His supporters included the Dean, Gianfrancesco Albani, York, Borgia and Jean-Siffrein Maury. Braschi-Onesti, realising that he had no backers and therefore no chance of election, was finally persuaded to add his vote to their list. At that point Bellisomi was close to the number of twenty-four votes required and was considered a likely winner.

A worried Herzan begged for time to consult Vienna to see what they thought of Bellisomi as Pope. Knowing that the Emperor could impose a veto if a candidate was not to his liking, Albani was forced to agree.

"It will take ten days or more to get a reply. Anything can happen in the meantime!" remarked Henry to Consalvi.

"That is true, sire," Ercole replied with a knowing smile. "I suspect this is all a ruse on the part of that cunning fox to wear down support for Bellisomi, your worthy candidate. If His Majesty the Emperor decides to apply an *esclusiva* there is little we can do."

Henry sat down, drumming his fingers nervously on the arms of his seat. He had known von Harras well when he was in Rome as ambassador to the Holy See and he had been impressed by his instinctive grasp of events. He remembered that Herzan had been one of the first to escape from Rome when everyone else still believed that the invasion by Napoleon could be averted. He had packed up his art collection in eighty-four trunks, so it was said, and headed for Austria.

While they waited, Herzan got on with his work of scuppering Bellisomi's chances. Henry observed him in a huddle with Cardinal Lorenzana who was trying to raise support for Valenti, the Spanish court's first choice. Making sure that all the cardinals could hear, Herzan raised his voice.

"We all know that Mattei is acceptable to Vienna, Madrid and Naples. That makes him the perfect candidate. The Emperor will only accept Valenti as second choice, if there should be no chance of Mattei being elected."

Secretly, von Harras had urged the Emperor to apply an *esclusiva*, or veto against Bellisomi. This tactic would have definitely blocked his candidature. However, Austria continued to play for time. Francis II did not want to commit himself to a gesture that would alienate many members of the Sacred College. No veto was forthcoming, despite Herzan's persistent recommendations.

By New Year, the conclave had reached stalemate. Support for Bellisomi had diminished, thanks to Herzan's hinted threats of a veto, but not enough to eliminate him as a possible successful candidate. Over the next two months, ballot after ballot, the votes remained substantially the same, with voters locked into their original positions.

In February, Napoleon, who was fast recovering many of his former conquests, began to take an interest. He dispatched a letter of protest to the Spanish Ambassador in Paris in which he complained that the conclave was being piloted by the House of Austria and he would therefore consider the elections illegal. This complicated matters still further. The cardinals realised that they would have to negotiate with France, as well as Austria.

"We don't need other problems!" Albani remarked to Henry, when the news of Bonaparte's initiative reached them. At that point, the Emperor's tactics had virtually eliminated Bellisomi, but the choice between Valenti and Mattei remained more or less even.

Henry looked round the room. The cardinals were exhausted and discouraged. They sat slumped in their seats, drained of enthusiasm and purpose. It was the first day of March. They had been in conclave for four months, and the end was not yet in sight.

Cardinal Leonardo Antonelli came up to them. He had been a fierce opponent of the Peace of Tolentino. He had protested against the terms of the treaty and at the time he had urged Pius VI to refuse all the conditions. He was anxious in case a French-supported candidate should step in and take centre stage. He therefore wanted the conclave concluded quickly in favour of Mattei, the Emperor's preferred candidate. This meant that he had to remove Valenti, by fair means or foul.

"My lords," he said smoothly. "Don't you think it is time that his Grace, Valenti Gonzaga, took his turn as scrutineer? We have all done it, except him."

"Why yes, of course," said Albani absent-mindedly. He called across the room. "My Lord Valenti, dear brother, would you do us the honour of taking the next ballot?"

Valenti agreed, but with a certain show of reluctance. His sight was failing and as he took each ballot paper and attempted to invalidate it by piercing it with the needle, his hands shook uncontrollably. Half of the papers slipped from his hands and scattered over the floor. The embarrassed cardinals had to stoop and pick them up, as the servants were not allowed to touch them. Valenti was trembling. He apologised.

"This is an affliction that struck me last summer," he said in a tremulous voice. "And no cure has been found. My doctors tell me it will pass with time…" his voice tailed off

The cardinals looked at each other and Henry could read their thoughts. It was obvious that Valenti Gonzaga was in no condition to occupy the Throne of Peter during the difficult times that lay ahead.

In the evening after prayers, Henry spoke softly to Albani, "We need another candidate," he said. "The Spaniards will continue to press for Valenti, despite his unsuitability. The votes will continue to cancel each other out. If we don't want to be here forever, under the protection of the worthy Benedictines, we need an outsider that no one can object to!"

Ercole Consalvi, who had been within earshot, spoke softly, "Your Majesty is right. If you will permit a suggestion, turn your attention to the quietest member of the council. The one who has never raised his voice or stated an opinion…"

They followed his glance, which was directed towards the quiet-spoken Bishop of Imola, Barnabas Luigi Count Chiaramonti, who sat unobtrusively in a corner. Chiaramonti was a Benedictine monk who had risen almost unnoticed within the ranks of the clergy. A small man, with delicate, almost girlish, features and fine hands with pointed fingers, he rarely expressed opinions. However, in 1797, when the French army invaded northern Italy, he had made the controversial announcement that good Christians could also be good democrats. Although the Vatican had criticized him severely for this imprudent remark, he had won the approval of Napoleon, who believed from then on that Bishop Chiaramonti had republican sympathies.

The Dean and Sub-Dean slept on it. In the morning, they were in agreement. Napoleon was on the march. It was only a matter of time before Austria and France were once more at war. In these circumstances, a pope who was acceptable to the First Consul of France could be vital for ensuring the survival of the Holy See. The cardinals were tired. At this point they only wanted the election to be over. They would raise no objections to a new candidate who had no special affiliations, who was not allied to either Austria or Spain and who would most certainly meet the approval of the most powerful man in Europe.

Consalvi was authorised to approach Chiaramonti to tell him that the majority of cardinals had decided to vote for him. The Bishop of Imola did not take the news well. He turned deathly pale and protested that he had no desire to become Pope. He merely wished to retreat quietly to his diocese once the conclave was over. It took all the powers of persuasion that the diplomatic Consalvi could summon up to convince him that there was no one else suitable to take his place and that, for the sake of the Church, he had to accept.

"You are throwing me into a stormy sea," he said, sad but resigned.

Von Harras made a last attempt to regain control of the situation.

"The storm will calm down if the Church is under the Emperor's protection," he insisted.

Chiaramonti listened politely. "What do I have to do to merit the Emperor's protection?" he asked in the mildest of tones.

"The Emperor has nothing against you personally," Herzan was excited. Looking at the placid little bishop, he thought that he had scored a half victory. Even if he had been unable to secure the vote for Austria's preferred candidates, he would be able to report that he had helped to find a substitute who would be malleable and compliant. "But His Majesty does not approve of your entourage. May I suggest a name for the position of Secretary of State – a worthy man whom the Emperor knows and trusts – the Cardinal Priest of St Mark's, His Excellency Cardinal Ludovico Flangini Giovanelli."

Chiaramonti remained silent, while the room waited in trepidation. When he finally spoke, he dropped a thunderbolt into the middle of the assembly.

"I am so sorry, Monsignore," he said quietly, compressing his delicate lips and folding his hands neatly in his lap. "But that will not be possible. I happen to know that Cardinal Flangini is a freemason, so he will not be suitable for such a sensitive position. I respect him and will consider him for another post that will be worthy of his talents."

Herzan's face flushed red. He was totally taken aback to hear the mild-mannered prelate's refusal but before he could say anything else, Chiaramonti added calmly, "I would respectfully bring to your attention that any nominees who are promised positions before a papal election are liable to suffer excommunication."

With that, the conclave was virtually over. On the fourteenth March, 1800, the Sacred College voted unanimously to elect Barnabas Luigi Chiaramonti the new Pope.

Barely a week later, he was crowned in the monastery Church of San Giorgio. Francis II was in a sulk because his candidate had not been chosen and denied the use of the Cathedral of St Mark's for the coronation.

The ceremony was untypically low key. The gold embroidered silken capes, the rochets in the finest Flemish lace, the jewelled triple tiaras and the other treasures of the papal regalia had been left behind in Rome, where most had been stolen by the invaders.

However, the noble ladies of Venice rose to the occasion. They made a triple tiara of papier-mâché and donated their own jewels and pearls to embellish it.

Chiaramonti chose the name of Pius VII, in honour of his predecessor. He could not have suspected that a strange destiny would link his life even more closely to that of his namesake.

Part 6
Return to Frascati

June 25th, 1800

A few weeks after the election of Pius VII, Napoleon made it known that he was willing to come to terms with the Church of Rome. Ercole Consalvi, who had been raised to the rank of Cardinal as a reward for his services at the conclave, was dispatched to France to begin negotiations. He had a hard task ahead. He not only had to obtain guarantees for the Pope's return to the Vatican, but he was instructed also to persuade the First Consul to re-establish the Church in France with all its former powers and privileges.

The following summer, after months of tough bargaining, Napoleon signed a Concordat with Rome. Pius VII had asked to have the Roman Catholic Church reinstated in France and the role of the clergy officially recognised by the French government. Bonaparte, however, was not prepared to concede status or too much power and the Pope only got a fraction of his demands. Catholicism was officially recognised, but with caution and reserve as 'the religion of the majority of French citizens'. Napoleon agreed to let seminaries re-open and saint's days be restored, but he refused to budge on issues like the appointment of bishops, which would continue to be controlled by the state. He also refused to return any church property that had been seized during the Revolution.

Despite all his diplomatic skills, Consalvi had been unable to wring any more concessions. Pius VII did not hide his disappointment and Henry also judged it a poor victory.

Afterwards, when he reported his laborious progress to Albani and Henry, Consalvi reported that Napoleon had even threatened him.

"He said to me, 'You realise that I could destroy the Church whenever I wish!'"

Henry and Albani looked at each other. "He dared as much, the devil!" Albani said hotly.

"But I didn't allow him to intimidate me," Ercole said. He paused to create more effect. "I told him that even we priests have not been able to do that in eighteen centuries!"

The talks had gone ahead with many interruptions because throughout the year, Napoleon had often been absent. In 1800, he had embarked on a campaign to regain the Italian territories that the Austrians had seized during his absence in Egypt. In May, he united his armies stationed on the Rhine and the Danube with his troops in Ligury and conducted them over the snow-bound Great St Bernard Pass into northern Italy, sweeping all before him and taking the Austrians completely by surprise.

On the second day of June, he entered Milan in triumph. Ten days later, he won a decisive victory at the Battle of Marengo, near Alessandria in Piedmont, putting an end to all Austrian opposition.

The worried cardinals followed these events with mounting trepidation.

"We thought the tyrant was finished!" Albani remarked to his friend Stuart. "But he has bounced back, more powerful than ever, the devil take him!"

Henry shook his head. "There must be an end to him sometime. His own people will tire of war. When too many of their sons have been killed in the name of his cause, their eyes will open. They will start to rebel. The whole book of history tells us this."

Henry's words turned out to be prophetic. That Christmas, an attempt was made on Napoleon's life. The Bonaparte family was on its way to attend a performance of Haydn's 'Creation' at the Paris Opera when a bomb detonated in a cart left parked on one side of their route. The First Consul's carriage had already passed and was undamaged, but the second coach, carrying his wife Josephine and her daughter, was hit by the explosion. Several bystanders who had come to cheer the procession were killed or injured, as well as one of the carriage horses. The windows of Josephine's coach were shattered and the two panicking women were showered with shards of glass. It was a warning that Bonaparte could not ignore. He realised he could no longer be sure of controlling the situation at home.

Napoleon had already sniffed the winds of unrest months before this incident occurred and he had also been astute enough to realise that he needed the Church's endorsement in order to carry out his plans to expand his empire. So far, the state's interference in religious matters had proved to be counterproductive. All the attempts that had been made by the Directoire to suppress Catholicism had failed. These had not ushered in progress and freedom of thought, as the humanist philosophers had hoped, but had produced the opposite effect. The majority of the population had stuck doggedly to the old familiar forms of worship and the position of the papacy had been reinforced.

After the election of Pius VII, the First Consul had therefore become more amenable to negotiations with the Holy See. He officially recognised the new Pope and the cardinals waiting anxiously in Venice felt that they would finally be able to return safely to their dioceses.

At the beginning of the summer, Pope Chiaramonti set off for Rome on an Austrian ship which conveyed him the port of Pesaro. From there, he made a leisurely progress down the Italian peninsula, greeted all the way by cheering crowds. He arrived in Rome to a triumphant welcome on the third of July 1800.

Meanwhile, Henry had also had been busy with preparations. Now that he had some disposable income and hopes of getting back his old incumbencies, he desired that all traces of the French occupation be removed from his home in Frascati, as well as from the Palace of the Papal Chancellery in Rome. After the long months of stringent economies and money worries, he was in no mood for further economies. He wrote to Monsignor Altobelli, his faithful canon in Frascati, instructing him to refurbish La Rocca. He ordered new beds, including one for himself to replace the bed that had been lost in the flooded river of the Pontine Plain. A Neapolitan silversmith was engaged to make him a new pastoral staff and gilded silver candlesticks for the Cathedral altar to replace the ones stolen by the French. He sent instructions for repairs to be carried out in the Chancellery Palace, which had suffered extensive damage, and ordered new stables, storerooms and kitchens and a large-scale restoration of the prestigious *piano nobile,* where he had his private apartments. He also ordered five new carriages to replace the ones requisitioned by enemy officers, as well as twelve horses and a couple of mules.

Henry left Venice with his servant Moretto soon after the departure of Pius VII. To Gigi's relief, he decided that sea voyages were not for him and they would travel overland, stopping off at Siena for a few days on route. His spirits had revived and his general health had also improved now that his face was finally turned towards home. Only his swollen and infected leg gave him trouble and Moretto continued to dress it carefully every day as he had observed the Arab doctor do.

They entered by the Flaminia Gate a week before the Pope, on the twenty-fifth of June. As they crossed the vast piazza and entered the street of the Corso, they were met by thousands of cheering citizens, who had got word of his imminent arrival. They hailed him as the 'Good Lord Chancellor' and the 'Protector of the Poor'. Ladies leaning out of their windows waved silken handkerchiefs and threw down flowers. He had to stop innumerable times to give his blessing.

When he finally reached the Chancellery Palace, he found his household assembled in the courtyard to greet him. Many of them were weeping with emotion. They jostled each other to come forward and kiss his hand. He would have preferred to leave immediately for Frascati, but his servants had prepared a feast to celebrate his return, with banners waving and musicians playing in the forecourt, and he felt obliged to spend some time with them. He toured the *piano nobile*, where the restoration work he had ordered was in progress. Everything, he noted, was to his satisfaction and he gave a generous tip to the overseer and the workmen, who cheered him loudly from their perches on the scaffolding. It was late afternoon before he was finally able to set off for Frascati.

The paving stones of the Appian Way glowed gold in the setting sun as they left Rome and headed towards the Alban hills. Henry breathed in the air of the pines that lined the road. On either side stretched stubble fields and grazing land. In the distance, on his right, the long line of arches of the Roman aqueducts straddled the horizon. With each mile, Henry felt the years drop off him. He turned to Moretto and saw that the Boy was crying with emotion.

When they reached the foot of the Tusculum Hills, they met Annibale, Garani and a guard of honour lined up waiting for him, along with a crowd of jubilant parishioners.

"We've been waiting here for your arrival since dawn, sire," Annibale said, bowing low. "Your people here sent carters on ahead to spy out the road from Rome and tell them the minute they caught sight of your carriage. Giacinto is preparing a great banquet for the whole town to celebrate your return."

A band came marching down the road to meet him, headed by MacLaren, magnificently attired in his plaid and blowing into his pipes as hard as he was able. He was doing his best to drown out the flutes and drums, which were playing an entirely different tune. As they paraded into the town, all the church bells began to peal, adding to the clamour. The windows and balconies along his route were draped with silken tapestries and coloured rugs woven with Henry's coat-of-arms and images of the Virgin and Child. Night had fallen but the streets were illuminated as brightly as at mid-day.

Henry's head was reeling by the time they passed the Cathedral Square, which was packed with his parishioners shouting, "*Cardinale degli Organi*! Our Cardinal of the Organs! He's come back! He is back with us!"

Angelo Cesarini was waiting at the top of the steps of La Rocca. He had prepared a speech of welcome, but in his excitement it dropped out of his hands as he rushed to embrace his old friend. His face was hot and shining like an apple with emotion.

"Are you all safely home from Messina?" Henry enquired.

"Look around you!" was all that Cesarini could say. The Family, in fact, was grouped at the bottom of the steps.

"All are safe!" Cesarini confirmed in a voice choked with feeling.

Eugenio Ridolfi, his valet, was standing on one side, beaming bashfully. He had a small boy with him, who was holding his hand. The Cardinal beckoned him to come nearer. The child was shy and tried to hide but Ridolfi pulled him firmly forward and, blushing deeply, he said, "This is my son, sire, born while we were in Sicily, but growing up strong and well just the same. He's been baptised but…" He blushed even redder, turning to a fresh-faced girl who stood just behind him, her eyes downcast. "We preferred to wait so that we could have your blessing on our union. I hope we did right?"

Henry looked at the girl. She kept her eyes modestly down. Her arms were crossed over her swelling abdomen. He could not find it in him to reproach them.

"I think you have already delayed too long, Eugenio," he said. He tried to make his voice stern but the smile on his lips betrayed his true feelings. He laid his hand on the child's head. "However, you shall have your wish. A wedding in our Cathedral of San Pietro and I personally will make an honest man of you and your lady will become a true wife in the eyes of God."

His secretary, Giovanni Landò came down the palace steps, carrying Henry's little dog in his arms. The animal began to yelp with joy when it saw Henry. Squirming out of Landò's grasp, it ran straight to the Cardinal, barking and whining with excitement. Henry could not bend, but he motioned to Moretto to pick the dog up and put it in his arms.

"My old friend King Charles!" he exclaimed, holding it up high while it wriggled and tried to lick his face. "What has happened to you? You have become too fat. You are so heavy I can hardly hold you!"

He cast a reproachful look at his secretary who looked abashed.

"You haven't given him enough exercise!" he said.

Landò spread his arms. "He didn't want to go out. He was pining for you. He just sat around under your chair waiting for your return – as, indeed, all of us were! We counted the days of your absence – exactly two years, four months and twenty-two days."

"Always precise, my dear Landò," remarked Henry with a chuckle. "I can assure you that it lasted longer than that! It lasted at least two hundred years!"

A procession of canons and vergers arrived from the Cathedral and knelt at his feet.

"Your Grace," ventured Canon Altobelli. "We have retained the faithless canon who tried to stir up a revolt against you. As soon as the French left, we kept him locked in the crypt awaiting your return, so that you could deal with him yourself."

A trembling Arini was thrust forward. He was dressed in penitent's sackcloth, with bare feet and a chain round his ankle. He threw himself face down on the road at Henry's feet.

"Forgive me!" he cried. "Your Majesty, forgive me! I was mad, I lost my head. I was carried away by those false doctrines of the French republicans. I have had time to see my error. I repent and will do any penance you decide to inflict upon me."

Henry looked down at the desperate upturned face. Arini had not been an outstanding servant and he had hardly noticed him among the other canons when he was officiating at the Cathedral. Now he saw that he was quite a young man, pasty faced and unnaturally thin. He suspected that he had suffered ill treatment at the hands of some of the lesser clergy and choristers during his imprisonment.

Knowing Stuart's tendency towards leniency, Cesarini frowned. "Do not trust him, Henry," he whispered in his ear. "He's a slippery fish. He changes direction quicker than the weathercock! He is not trustworthy."

At that moment, however, Henry was too happy to be back home to be able to hold a grudge. He thought that Arini's betrayal seemed a small thing compared with the great upheavals in the world around them. He had come too close to so many greater dangers, sufferings and hatreds during his exile.

He therefore said that he would forgive Arini, but he would keep him for a period under observation. If he was then convinced that his repentance was sincere, he would have him transferred to another diocese. Otherwise, he would be sent away with no recommendation to beg his bread in the world.

With that, he turned away abruptly, while the prisoner was attempting to kiss the hem of his robe, and with Moretto's help climbed the steps up to La Rocca.

Don Angelo leaned towards Landò and muttered in his ear, "Just like him! He's too forgiving. Do you remember how he pardoned these two sodomites living together here in Frascati like husband and wife? The law said they should have been imprisoned for life, locked away from decent people!"

"Yes, I remember. Must be about twenty years ago. I had just entered his service and I was quite shocked. But I remember he had me pen a letter to the Holy Father saying one of them was married and the young wife would be left destitute, without a husband. The other one was just a boy – not even *emancipato.* In the end they got off very lightly."

"Well, I'll make sure Arini doesn't get off lightly. I'll put Annibale on his heels! He'll give him a bit of the lesson he deserves. Our lord need know nothing about it. The man won't dare to complain after what he got up to!"

"The best thing would be if he disappears completely," Cesarini re-joined very quietly, after a moment's thought. "I'll drop a hint to Annibale to help him on his way. He won't stir up any more rebellions!"

Meanwhile, Henry had entered La Rocca. The servants who had remained had tried to make his homecoming as welcoming as possible. They had brought back many of the pieces of furniture, the paintings and sculptures which they had kept hidden during the French occupation. There had not been much structural damage and the wall decorations by the Polish artist, Taddeo Kuntz, whom the Cardinal had befriended, still adorned the rooms.

He strolled through the *piano nobile* reception hall, where the pavement had collapsed years ago, admiring the rows of medallions on the walls with the portraits of the fifty-five bishops of Frascati who had preceded him. The spaces for himself and his successors that he had ordered the artist to leave blank, were still there, awaiting the inevitable passage of time. The next room, decorated with landscapes and grotesques, was his favourite. He had wanted it to be light and festive, with pastel colours and scenes from Nature and Kuntz, as ordered, had applied a delicate hand. His private chapel, too, was intact. His parishioners had brought back the altarpiece with the painting of the Virtues and the Boat of St Peter that he specially treasured, as it had been gifted to his father by Pope Clement XII, who had supported the Stuart cause.

Although it was already late and the townspeople were still feasting noisily, seated around the long tables set out in the square and along the surrounding streets, he insisted on walking to his library. To his great joy, he found it intact. Landò explained, beaming with satisfaction, that the servants had artfully concealed the entrance by putting up a barn door and covering it with piles of hay. The trick had worked. The French soldiers had been deceived and they had concentrated on raiding La Rocca in the hope of finding treasure.

Next, he turned into the seminary. Fortunately, it had not been badly damaged. He strolled around the empty rooms and dormitories, smiling. Soon he would open it again. Soon the corridors and lecture rooms would ring once more with young student voices.

Lost Kingdoms

The time to bring students back, however, was still not ripe because Bonaparte showed no signs of abandoning his dreams of conquest. He declared war against the troublesome Kingdom of Naples, which was still in a state of chaos after the Bourbon restoration. Early in 1801, Napoleon's brother-in-law, Joachim Murat, defeated the Neapolitan army and Ferdinand was forced to sign the Treaty of Florence, where he had to submit to all Napoleon's demands. Napoleon insisted on an amnesty for all the surviving republican sympathizers who were still in prison or in exile and the return of their property. The King of Naples also had to hand over a large collection of works of art and antiquities from the buried cities of Pompeii and Herculaneum, destined to enrich museums in Paris.

Ferdinand had to agree to bear the costs of French garrisons billeted at Brindisi, Otranto and Pescara to block British shipping from entering or leaving the Adriatic ports of his kingdom. This was part of Napoleon's plan to turn southern Italy into a base for his campaign against British trade in the Mediterranean.

Soon afterwards, Henry received a hysterical letter from Maria Carolina, filled with bitterness against her husband for agreeing to terms she found totally unacceptable:

"A shameful, ignominious peace! Iniquitous treaty! My heart bleeds. I think of it a thousand times a day and I cannot stop weep-

ing," she poured out her desperation. *"My forty-four years of marriage have been forty-four years of martyrdom. But it has all been in vain. The people hate me. I live in fear. I have no friends, apart from Lord Acton, but the Corsican tyrant has ordered me to send him away. I have lost my dear Emma, who has returned to England with her husband and Lord Nelson. I am alone. Should I return to Vienna and live on the charity of my son-in-law? What, dear brother, do you advise me to do?"*

After some hesitation, Henry wrote back with what words of comfort he could find. He said he could not give her advice. His own grandfather, James II and VII, had been forced to flee from his country and live the rest of his life as an exile. His son, Henry's father, had seen his two Stuart aunts reign in his place. He had been a melancholy man, with his heart constantly set towards his lost realm, unable to accept the fact that he, the rightful king, was unable to fulfil the role assigned to him by divine right. He hoped that she would be able to find more peace.

Meanwhile, he desired nothing more than to be able to ignore the momentous upheavals that were taking place in the world outside his peaceful and pleasant diocese. He settled down to enjoy the pleasures of his former life. Although he could count on the pension he had been granted by the British crown, as well as the recovery of some of the revenues from his ecclesiastic estates, his income was quite considerably reduced compared with the past. Nonetheless, he lived like a prince and entertained lavishly. His hospitality, in fact, was proverbial and no one was ever turned away from his door.

By now, he had become something of a legend, regularly receiving visits from British aristocrats on their Grand Tour. As was his habit, he would eat sparingly out of plain pottery plates, while his guests were served with the very best silverware and porcelain. Once the meals were over and the dishes had been cleared away, he enjoyed showing off his little dog King Charles. He would set it on the table and command it to roll over or stand on its hind legs, which it still managed to do, despite its fat little belly, and he would reward it with titbits fed from his own fingers.

During his second summer back in Frascati, Consalvi rode up from the Vatican to tell him that the King of Sardinia, Charles Emmanuel IV of the House of Savoy, was in Rome and intended to come to visit him. Charles Emmanuel descended from Henrietta, the youngest daughter of Charles I of Great Britain and was acknowledged as the last Stuart heir of the blood.

Consalvi was breathing heavily. He had another, more important communication to deliver and he made an effort to control the excitement in his voice.

"I am telling you this in the strictest confidence, Your Majesty, so remember to act accordingly and show yourself surprised," Consalvi urged in flustered tones, forgetting his usual courtier's composure. "But His Holiness Pope Pius is planning to accompany him. He wishes to give you this great honour as a sign of his particular regard."

It was known that Pope Chiaramonti seldom strayed from Rome and then only on very special occasions. Unlike some previous popes, he shunned public gatherings and entertainment. It was totally out of character for him to pay a mere social call so Henry guessed that there must be some other reason for him to come on a personal visit.

Although it was supposed to be an impromptu call, Henry sent out instructions to the palace staff to ensure a proper reception for his cousin, the King of Sardinia, without mentioning the Pope's name. However, he could not contain his impatience and anxiety as the expected hour of the visit approached. He hobbled out onto the road on Moretto's arm, so he was outside waiting when the cavalcade of coaches came driving up the hill.

Pius VII did not seem perturbed that the Cardinal had received advance notice of his alleged surprise visit. He was aware that his every move was observed and reported and he would have been more surprised if he had dropped in on a Cardinal Stuart unprepared. The announcement of a 'secret visit' was simply a coded message that the formalities were to be kept to the minimum. He greeted Henry with genuine warmth and insisted he come into the carriage with him to be conveyed the last half mile to La Rocca.

That afternoon, after a lavish luncheon in the course of which the Pope had complimented Giacinto the cook, reducing him to a dazed state of beatitude, Henry and his guests retired to his private study, where they would not be disturbed.

Henry had been disconcerted to see that his cousin was dressed in deep mourning, but he had been careful to say nothing until they were alone. Now, in the privacy of the Cardinal's room, Charles Emmanuel, his voice choking and his eyes full of tears, confided that his dear wife, Marie Clotilde, had just died. They had been happily married for thirty years and he said he could not continue to reign without her support.

"I have decided to renounce my throne and abdicate in favour of my brother," he said.

Henry was startled. He had never heard of a king who voluntarily gave up his throne. He leaned forward and placed his hand in sympathy on his cousin's trembling shoulder.

"I have already confided in our Holy Father," Charles Emmanuel whispered. "He has approved my decision to take holy orders. I shall be" – and here he gave a small wry smile – "a priest-king. I have come to see you, to ask your permission to enter a religious community in your diocese."

Henry was taken aback, but he quickly recovered and moved to embrace his cousin warmly.

"Nothing would make me happier," he said. "I shall once more have a brother."

Afterwards, when he recounted events to Consalvi, he remarked ironically, "Two Pretenders in the one place. That will save the English spies a great deal of running around!"

The following year, Henry's old friend, Cardinal Gianfranco Albani died. Henry succeeded him as Dean of the Sacred College and was appointed to take his place as Bishop of the prestigious see of Ostia and Velletri. Cardinal Doria Pamphilj, who had followed Pope Pius VI into exile as far as Genoa, became the new Bishop of Frascati. Henry, however, was reluctant to leave his home. He had been Bishop of Frascati for over forty-two years and had come to know all his parishioners intimately. He had watched children grow up and form new families. He had administered, comforted and assisted three generations. He felt he was too old to change. He asked to be allowed to continue to live in Frascati at his home La Rocca. Doria raised no objections. He preferred to stay around the papal court in Rome and limit as much as possible his duty visits to Frascati.

Henry, however, had to honour the official appointment he had been given. On the twentieth of November, 1803, he entered Velletri in state to take formal possession of his new see. His reception was, if anything, even more lavish than the one organised in Frascati for his welcome home. He entered the city in procession, passing under a triumphant arch erected in his honour. The city fathers had been determined to outdo the Frascati parishioners. The streets were decorated with flowers and hangings embroidered with his personal coat-of-arms. The mayor had gone to great pains to find what he believed was a suitable greeting for the royal personage. Kneeling in the road to consign the keys of the city, he addressed Henry as 'the sole surviving son and heir of the unconquered and immortal James III, King of Great Britain, of Scotland and Jerusalem and valiant defender of the Catholic faith'.

The religious solemnities and the festive banquet were followed by a mock tournament in the main square. At nightfall, the streets were lit up with lanterns painted with his royal insignia. As the festivities drew to an end, an elaborate firework display, erected on a ninety-foot frame surmounted by the figure of an angel playing a harp, shot rockets of light and showers of coloured stars into the night sky.

Napoleon the Emperor

Cardinal Consalvi arrived at Frascati early one morning. He was visibly agitated and asked to speak to Henry in private. Henry had not quite finished dressing, but he immediately dismissed Eugenio and Moretto and invited Consalvi into his bedroom.

"I don't know how to tell you this, sire," said a breathless Consalvi, kneeling down at Henry's feet out of old habit, although his promotion to the cardinalate after the conclave had elevated him to equal rank. "Napoleon has announced that he wishes to become an Emperor, like the Caesars or Constantine the Great. He plans to have a ceremony that will eclipse all other princes. He has said publicly that he will shortly cross the English Channel and conquer the British Isles and then he will be master of the entire world."

"The man has lost his head!" stuttered Don Angelo, emerging from the window alcove, where he had been sitting reading. "He's become drunk with grandeur! He does not even have one drop of royal blood in his veins. How can he believe he can stand beside anointed kings?"

Ercole Consalvi hung his head. "I have not told you the worst part of the news, my lords. He demands that our Holy Father go to France to crown him. He believes he can deceive the people into accepting his impossible claims if they are sanctioned by the Pope in person."

Cesarini was rendered speechless. He was overcome by a fit of coughing and withdrew into a corner of the room.

Henry felt the familiar twitching in his nose and he fought to control the hot bile that rose up in his throat.

"What about his grand revolutionary principles?" he said. "Equality, brotherhood and liberty? These were the ideals that took him to power. That was why the people of France followed him so devotedly. They will never accept this. They murdered their rightful kings. They will not accept an imposter like him on the sacred throne of St Louis."

Consalvi's mouth twisted in an expression of disgust. "It would seem that he has forgotten all these fine dogmas – especially equality. The Dictator no longer believes in equality. In fact, he sees himself as another Charlemagne. I have been told that he has had an imperial catechism drawn up establishing that his reign will be sanctified by God. Pardon me, Your Majesty, but he has adapted the holy principle of Divine Right to fit himself."

Henry crossed his arms over his chest. He felt feverish. The doctrine of the Divine Right of kings had been instilled in him from birth; that the sacred blood that ran in the Stuart veins made them answerable only to God and to no other authority. He had always believed that the consecration of an anointed sovereign constituted a great responsibility, which he had often felt thankful that he had not been called on to fulfil. According to the dogma of Divine Right, kings were the fathers of the nation, chosen by God and acting under the direction of Heaven to preserve the wellbeing of their peoples. His childhood upbringing had been directed towards this ideal. He had been taught that his ancestors had defended this belief even at the risk of their lives. It had cost his great-grandfather Charles I his head, and his grandfather and father their thrones.

To him, it seemed impossible that this upstart, a commoner, with no claims to justify his absurd and abominable aspirations, dared to defy the laws of God and step into the shoes of a hereditary royal. If Napoleon succeeded in his intent, it would overturn the whole concept of society as the Cardinal knew it. The established order would be swept away: if beggars could be kings, kings could become beggars. He swayed on his feet, dizzy at the great void he saw opening up before him – a world in chaos, where the strongest would trample the weakest in an undisciplined scramble for positions and power that would become the prize of anyone who was able to grab them.

Consalvi, unaware of the conflict running through the Cardinal's head, went on to explain that he had been contacted by Napoleon's uncle, Cardinal Joseph Fesch, the Archbishop of Lyons, and asked to persuade Pius VII to agree to the Dictator's request.

"Chiaramonti will never agree!" Henry said.

Henry was mistaken. Pius VII, after much hesitation, did agree to officiate at Napoleon's coronation. He hoped, through his cooperation, to finally obtain the concessions for the Church he had been demanding without success ever since he had signed the Concordat in 1801. However, his decision was bitterly criticised, not only by the clergy but also by the citizens of Rome, who covered Pasquino, the Talking Statue, with caustic lampoons.

A group of prelates, including Henry's friend, Cardinal Stefano Borgia and Giuseppe Doria Pamphilj, who had taken his place as Bishop of Frascati, reluctantly assented to accompany Pius VII to Paris. Henry excused himself, pleading ill health.

This was not a ploy. A few weeks previously, he had taken seriously ill, to the point that his Family had feared for his life. To the surprise of the attendants at La Rocca, one of the visitors who came to see him was the Countess Louise of Stolberg, Prince Charles Edward's widow. Weeping copious tears, she said she had rushed posthaste from Florence to be at her dear brother-in-law's bedside. Cesarini would not allow her to go into Henry's bedroom. He said that no visitors were allowed. Louise pleaded in vain. Don Angelo knew that his suffering friend would not want to see her, but he was moved by her elaborate show of grief and sat talking to her for some time.

Moretto, who was hovering near the door of the sickroom in case the doctors called him, observed the scene and described it later to Annibale and Giacinto, when they were gathered in the kitchen later that evening, playing cards:

"He was completely taken in at first, the old fool of a priest! In the end, she got round to admitting what she really wanted. She was worried that her allowance would be stopped if our master died. You know, he's been paying it out for years – even when he was virtually destitute – to honour his brother's memory."

"Is she still with the poet?" Giacinto asked, one eye fixed on a kitchen boy who was plucking a chicken at the other end of the table.

"No, Alfieri died last year, but I've heard that she already has a replacement. An artist, they say, young enough to be her son."

"Well, she used to be a beauty. I can remember when they called her the Queen of Hearts!"

"Not now, they won't. She's become fat and old. She wears a blonde wig and powders and rouges herself to seem younger," said Maclaren, who had just come in to join them. "Her tongue is as forked as ever. I've heard her speak badly about our dear lord!"

Annibale nodded. "She's nothing but a dressed-up slut. I knew one of her maids when I was in Siena and the girl thought she would amuse me by showing me a letter her mistress was writing to her friend, Countess Mocenni. She called the Lord Cardinal an 'incubus', whatever that may mean, but it certainly wasn't praise! She said he was 'very dull' and 'he bored everyone he met'.

They all sat up, full of indignation to hear the good Cardinal so brazenly insulted by his brother's widow. That the information came from a private letter neither troubled nor surprised them. All domestics kept their ears and eyes open and had their sources of information about their master and mistress's secret lives. There was very little in the households of the rich that the servants did not know about, although they served at table with faces as fixed as puppets and always made a show of ignorance.

"Well, her poor opinion of her benefactor has never prevented her taking advantage of his generosity!" commented Moretto angrily. He remembered how cleverly she had deceived the Cardinal regarding her affair with the Italian poet Vittorio Alfieri, and how shocked and troubled the Cardinal had been when he had found out the truth. It had been a sad blow to his pride. She had, however, managed to convince him that she was an innocent victim of slander. Henry, who had often suffered from the malicious insinuations about himself and his family put about by Hanoverian spies, chose to believe her, despite all the evidence to the contrary. Closing his eyes and ears to further gossip, he had continued over the years to pay her an allowance, out of respect for his dead brother.

The Coronation, December 2nd, 1804

The Pope and his party left Rome on the second of November, a month before the date fixed for the ceremony in Notre Dame Cathedral. His train included forty high-ranking prelates and aristocrats. Almost all of them were elderly and had various health problems. The journey was slow because winter had set in and they often had to stop and take shelter for days on end.

Napoleon was impatient and constantly nagged them to hurry up. The trek over the Alpine pass in icy winds and snow took its toll. Many fell ill and Cardinal Borgia, who had a weak heart, died when they finally reached Fesch's see at Lyons. The funeral preparations took some time, and during the company's enforced stay, Fesch used all his powers of persuasion to convince Pius VII of his nephew's benevolent intentions regarding the future of the Church. Chiaramonti was sceptical, but he played along, counting on the fact that that his co-operation would win him the concessions that his heart was set on.

On the twenty-fourth of November, they reached the outskirts of Paris, where Napoleon met them at Fontainebleau. The coronation was due to take place in eight days' time. Incredibly, it had taken less than ten years for an obscure army officer named Napoleone Buonaparte and his Creole wife to graduate to the ranks of Emperor and Empress, ruling over a large part of continental Europe.

The couple had been married in the town hall of the II arrondissement, Rue d'Antin, Paris, on the ninth March, 1796, where he cancelled out his Corsican origins by registering himself, not by his true Italian name of Buonaparte, but as the more French-sounding Bonaparte. His widowed bride, *citoyen* Rose Beauharnais, whose husband had died on the guillotine, also changed her name to the more distinguished Josephine. Both had lied about their ages. She declared she was twenty-eight, although she was actually thirty-three. Buonaparte said he was also twenty-eight, though he was really two years younger.

Napoleon and Josephine had therefore only contracted a civil marriage. This was a major obstacle from the Pope's point of view, as the Church did not consider a civil union valid. As far as Pius VII was concerned, Josephine was a concubine, not a wife. He said that if he officiated at the coronation it would appear that he was condoning a sin against the Church of God and the sacred sacraments.

His objections fell on fertile ground because Josephine was also keen to have a religious ceremony. She suspected that Napoleon was toying with the idea of replacing her and she knew it would be easy for him to dissolve their present union. The Revolution had sanctioned divorce and if their marriage was declared void, that would leave him free to marry a new wife, one who would give him more prestige, such as a European princess, and a Catholic to appease the Church.

Josephine therefore wanted their marriage to be recognised by the Church at all costs, and she added her tears to the Pope's arguments. Napoleon was furious. With a weeping wife on one hand and a stubborn old Pope on the other who was refusing to go on with the coronation he had set his heart on, he did not know how to break the impasse.

In the end a compromise was reached. Instead of an actual wedding ceremony, a religious benediction of their union would be held at the Tuileries Palace on the eve of the coronation. This would be conducted by Cardinal Fesch, without the presence of witnesses. Josephine was not satisfied but Napoleon's rage was reaching boiling point and she realised she would not obtain any further concessions. So in the end, she settled for a certificate of proof that the ceremony had taken place. Pius VII was not happy either with this solution, but Fesch reassured him that his compliance would bring him Napoleon's grateful and, he hinted, tangible recognition.

Several sticky problems of protocol also had to be solved. Napoleon considered it was essential to avoid any act that would suggest he was receiving his power from the Pope, so a new coronation formula had to be invented. It was decided that the Pope would not crown the sovereign but simply consecrate him. Pius VII agreed but he refused to endorse the constitutional oath that the Emperor intended to pronounce as he feared this could be interpreted as a renunciation of the Church's temporal powers. In the end it was agreed that the Emperor would swear the oath after the Pope had left the Cathedral.

Henry and his servants got a full description of the coronation ceremony in Notre-Dame later from Cardinal Doria Pamphilj, who showed a little too much enthusiasm for Henry's liking. He told them about the magnificence of the robes worn by the Emperor and Empress – their ermine mantles were so heavy, he said, that both of them could only advance down the aisle with the greatest difficulty. Josephine's train was carried by her sisters-in-law, who, it was said, dragged it out of spite, almost pulling her off-balance. Napoleon had flashed them a furious look to bring them back into line. He described Napoleon's golden myrtle leaf circlet and his crown, decorated with diamonds, amethysts, pearls and eight enormous emeralds.

"There were three hundred musicians and a four-hundred voice choir," he recounted in glowing tones. "When the Emperor advanced towards the altar, the choir broke into Paisiello's 'Mass' and his '*Te Deum*'. What a magnificent sound! It swelled up to the very vault! I would not have been surprised if the roof had lifted off."

Henry became impatient listening to all these trivial details. "Is it true that he crowned himself?" he broke in brusquely.

"Oh yes, indeed. He crowned himself and the Empress as well, but it was arranged with the Holy Father. It was not a slight as so many are now saying. The Holy Father simply anointed them both with the chrism and blessed the enthronement. He left the Cathedral before the oath."

"Well, you seem to have enjoyed it anyway!" Henry commented with a touch of sarcasm in his voice.

Doria flushed. He replied quickly, on the defensive, "Indeed, it was as fine a spectacle as anyone could imagine and our Holy Father condoned it with his presence. So who can object? We expect great things – the reconciliation of the Church with the Republic. Surely this goal is sufficient justification?"

Unfortunately, the Pope did not obtain the advantages for the Church that he had hoped to gain by collaborating with Napoleon's dreams of grandeur. Napoleon continued to refuse to comply with most of the Pope's requests. Pius VII had asked to be recognised as head of the Church in France. He wanted monastic communities re-established, Sunday brought back as the day of rest and worship as well as divorce abolished. He also demanded the return of all confiscated Church property.

Napoleon had no intention of giving in to any of these requests. He did agree to re-introduce the traditional Gregorian calendar and suppress the new republican calendar, which had never been popular in any case. But since saints' days would replace revolutionary martyrs' days, he put himself among the saints by introducing a Feast Day of St Napoleon, allegedly in honour of a similarly named Egyptian martyr. It was to be celebrated each year on August fifteenth, which coincidentally was Napoleon's own birthday.

Pius VII left Paris the following spring, a bitter and defeated man.

Some months later, Henry received a letter with the Queen of Naples' seal. It had obviously been tampered with, but this no longer surprised or troubled him. Bonaparte's agents were everywhere and almost all messages were intercepted.

"My Lord Cardinal, Dear Brother," she wrote, *"you will be surprised, no doubt, to receive this missive from me but I take this liberty to write to you in the name of our old friendship forged in happier days in Naples and Caserta."*

Henry frowned. He noted that her hand had become less decisive. Her writing, which was previously so precise, scrambled untidily over a page pockmarked with impatient inkblots.

"When we received the news of the French Dictator's intention to crown himself Emperor we at first did not believe he would dare so much – to go against the laws of man and God. But then my disbelieving ears heard of the coronation of the Corsican and his whore in Paris and that the Holy Father not only consented to this outrage but was actually present and allowed himself to be humiliated by having the crown lifted from his hands by that jumped-up peasant, that imposter, that upstart, that Corsican dog, who thought fit to crown himself and his concubine!

"The news has now reached us that he has had himself crowned once more, in Milan Cathedral as the King of Italy. He placed on his own head the Iron Crown of the Holy Roman Empire, which is by right the crown of my son-in-law, Francis II. I would like to know what my daughter thinks about that, but she does not correspond with me. Her husband has set her against me.

"We have also heard that this low-born upstart has begun to appoint members of his family princes and princesses as if he were God himself. Lord Acton has warned me that he intends to set his brother Joseph on our throne of Naples if we do not do his bidding.

"I cannot tell you how many tears I have shed. My thoughts have turned to you and your suffering – a true king, anointed by God in the true faith, denied his heritage by unbelievers who preferred to set a puppet king, who did not even speak the language of your people, upon your rightful throne.

"I admire the patience and forbearance you have always shown in these circumstances. I wish I could say the same of myself. My rage is so strong I fear the flames of Hell. Send me a word of comfort, I beg you, as you would to any one of your humble sinners, your parishioners. My heart is breaking. I do not know how much longer I have to live..."

Meanwhile, Napoleon continued to reap triumphs. His defeat at the Battle of Trafalgar by the British navy in 1805 forced him to give up his plans to invade Great Britain, but this was only a temporary setback. Only two months later, he scored a decisive victory at Austerlitz, forcing the Austrians and their allies to surrender.

Henry was grieved to hear of the death of Admiral Nelson.

"A valiant commander," he remarked sadly to Cesarini. "I visited him on his ship after his great Victory of the Nile to pay him my respects and congratulate him."

"Yes, a truly great commander," Don Angelo agreed. He sniffed, "A pity he stooped to living in sin. I have been told that he left his lawful wife and has generated a bastard with Lord Hamilton's wife..."

"Listening to gossip again, eh Angelo?" Henry cut him off. "I do wonder where you get your information!"

Cesarini scowled, "You may well mock, Henry. Take care before you cast the first stone! You are not so blameless either – keeping up a correspondence with that harlot, the Queen of Naples!"

Henry's long nose twitched. He drew his head up haughtily. "She is a poor woman, deserted by all and stands to lose her kingdom. I too have informers and they tell me that all her allies, the Austrians, the Russians and the British, are withdrawing from Naples. This is the latest letter that she wrote me. Read it for yourself and judge her situation!"

He took the letter out of his desk and handed it over. Don Angelo took it reluctantly between two fingers, as if it were in some way contaminated.

"I have been forced, for the good of my country and family," he read aloud. *"To humble myself and write a begging letter to the Corsican tyrant, addressing him as His Imperial Royal Majesty – a title to which, as you know, he has no right, but his vanity is such that he insists upon it – telling him that I now renounce being his enemy and I appeal to his generosity and count on it. He has not troubled to reply. He has made up his mind to remove the Bourbons from the throne of Naples."*

Napoleon, in fact, had decided to replace Ferdinand with his own brother Joseph, as part of a grand plan to transform his family into kings and viceroys who would rule, under his control, his conquered European kingdoms. Before he gave the order to invade Naples, however, he made what he considered a conciliatory gesture. He asked Maria Carolina to give one of her daughters in marriage to his stepson Eugène de Beauharnais. To his surprise, she categorically refused

In January 1806, his army crossed the frontier into the Kingdom of Naples. Ferdinand did not wait for them to arrive. He sailed off in all haste to his other kingdom of Sicily, which was under the control of the British navy, leaving his son Francesco in charge. His aristocratic friends in Palermo gave him an enthusiastic welcome and carried him off merrily to the theatre. The following day, he went fishing.

Maria Carolina was left alone. She tried to stir up some resistance against the imminent French invasion. She organised a solemn procession in honour of San Gennaro with paid supporters mingling in the crowds shouting: "Long live the King! Death to the French!" But most of the bystanders simply stood watching in grim silence. No one had forgotten the terrible days of the restoration when so many Jacobin supporters had been executed without trial.

When the fortress of Capua, less than 20 miles from Naples, surrendered without a fight, the Queen realised there was no hope.

The end had come for the Bourbon monarchy. A few days after her husband, she too left for Sicily with her son Francesco. Once more, they ran into bad weather. Buffeted by contrary winds, their ship was blocked in Naples harbour for five days before they were able to set sail for Sicily and safety.

The long war dragged on, with treaties and alliances made and broken. Napoleon tightened his grip on his vassal states, while the sister republics were transformed into monarchies, ruled by members of his family. His relationship with the Pope continued to deteriorate. Chiaramonti had declared the Papal States neutral but this interfered with Napoleon's plans to control the whole of southern Italy and the Mediterranean.

When Britain, Russia, Sweden, Prussia and Saxony formed the Fourth Coalition against France just after he had managed finally to defeat Austria, Napoleon began to put additional pressure on the Pope, asserting that the neutral states effectively offered 'a wide-open door for Italy's enemies'. He ordered the Pope to expel all the citizens of the coalition nations as well as anyone connected with the Kingdom of Sardinia, which was another thorn in his flesh. "All my enemies must become yours as well," he told Pius VII.

The Pope's reaction was to excommunicate him. In reprisal, Bonaparte invaded and gained control of all the lands of the Church.

The future looked black but Henry continued to travel up and down to Rome to attend to his duties at the Chancellery Palace. His last public appearance was at the Feast of St Peter and St Paul in 1805 when he headed the procession up the long aisle of the basilica to the foot of the papal throne. But the long ceremony exhausted him and he asked to be allowed to retire definitely to Frascati.

As Henry entered his eighty-second year, he no longer kept up with politics, preferring to spend his time in restful pursuits, like listening to music and watching his young seminarians chatting and playing ball games together during breaks between lessons. He still entertained as lavishly as before, although he was now kept on a strict diet by his doctors. Visitors continued to be entertained by little King Charles' tricks performed on the dining table.

The Death of the Last Stuart King

July 13th, 1807
Letter addressed to Cavalier Heinrich Huber, Vienna.

"Dear friend,
My dear lord, dearer to me than a father and to whom I have dedicated my life, breathed his last this morning of the 13th day of July in the Year of Our Lord 1807.
He had reached the venerable age of eighty-three and had been the Bishop at Frascati for 46 years. He had been ill with a chill for two weeks, his fever never abated and he grew weaker day by day. It took him more than fifteen days to die, growing weaker and weaker hour by hour. It is customary to say that death is peaceful but I find this is seldom the case. His every breath became a great effort, drawn up from the depths of his being. When he knew that he could no longer rise from his bed, he had an altar erected in his room and Monsignor Cesarini came to say mass every morning. During his last illness, I never left his side, holding to his lips what food and drink he was able to swallow and helping his doctors administer to him. When he no longer had the strength to raise himself on his pillows I supported him, holding up his head to try to give him some relief.
I watched in anguish the struggle of the soul to leave the body. Why should this be so hard if the soul desires – as his most ardently did – to be reunited with God the Father and his blessed Son? And yet it clings with such desperate determination to the flesh – a wasted shell capable only of giving pain and suffering.
I sat with him these long days and nights counting every laboured breath, expecting each to be his last, the final release from his sufferings. His pulse was weak, but continued to beat like a clock that marks the slow passage of existence.
Some days before the end he asked me to carry him to the window that overlooks the Campagna Romana with its meadows and vineyards stretching far towards the city of Rome. In the far distance we could see the great dome of St Peter's, ablaze in the gold of the

setting sun. When I raised him in my arms, he seemed as brittle as a bird. I could carry him as easily as a child. He gazed out of the window for a long time while the sun sank and stained the sky with streaks of bloody red.

One night he awoke and called me: 'Gigi, dear friend,' he said: 'I am thankful my brother did not live to see this new order – this is a world ruled by a low-born tyrant who has succeeded in conquering a whole continent, bringing war when before there was peace. My brother offered his life to the cause of regaining our rightful throne. He went to battle to retake what was his, appointed to our House by God. That was how it should have been, but he did not succeed. There was a flaw in the scheme of things and I can no longer see any sense in anything around me. The world has been turned inside out like an old coat re-made. The old values are quite gone and I cannot perceive that they have been replaced with anything better. I fear that you and I, my dear Moretto, are outside the plans of God, our Father. We have become actors in a play that no one comes to see. We perform before an empty theatre. Our role is finished'.

That was the last conversation I had with him. It troubled me that he was not more serene. But this was not my business, but that of his confessor who must release the immortal soul from the burden of its doubts. He received Extreme Unction and the Last Rites from the hand of his Eminence Cardinal Doria Pamphilj, who was also his friend.

In the end, his death was peaceful. He fell into a very deep sleep and woke no more.

And then the house prepared to honour the dead. Monsignor Cesarini, Cardinal Consalvi and other important members of the clergy and his household surrounded his bed. I was no longer admitted, but must wait outside the door with all the servants.

He did not have the royal funeral due to his ancient House, like his father, the old King James, in the great Basilica of St Peter's, or even that of a prince like his brother Charles, who should have been King. He lay in state, instead, in the Chancellery Palace as a bishop and arch-priest, deacon of the Holy Roman Church. I walked beside his black draped coach on his last journey. When he was conveyed from Frascati to Rome, he was accompanied by a troop of cavalry and such a vast number of coaches that they could not be counted.

His catafalque, with its heavy purple velvet drapes, was surrounded with hatchments bearing his coat-of-arms and illuminated by many candles on silver candelabras. The Swiss Guards stood in attendance. He was laid out in his bishop's robes with his mitre on his head. His crozier was laid at his side and his red hat at his feet. It was I, however, who personally placed at the foot of the catafalque the shield with his royal coat of arms, bearing the symbols of his four lost realms – the Leopards of England, the Lion Rampant of Scotland, the Harp of Ireland and the Lilies of France. I said this had been his express instructions on the point of death. That was untrue. He was too modest to ask for any such thing, but I desired him to have this last honour.

Fortunately, no one objected, although thousands filed past his open coffin to pay their respects during the three days he lay in state.

His funeral was held in Sant'Andrea della Valle, which is the Church of St Andrew, the patron saint of Scotland. The Holy Father was present along with the members of the Sacred College and many dignitaries, as well as a great crowd of humble people crowding the roads and squares outside. He has been entombed beside his father in the crypt of St Peter's and I am told that soon the remains of his brother Prince Charles Edward will be brought from Frascati to join them.

A few days after the funeral, Monsignor Cesarini summoned all the servants to the Great Hall. There he told them that the Cardinal had left provision in his will for them all and that as soon as the legal necessities were dealt with, they would be issued with their share. Moretto was not surprised, because the Cardinal had confided his intentions to him, but a great deal of excitement and speculation circulated among the other members of the Family.

Giacinto the cook said, "At last I can buy a piece of land and be my own master. There's a girl I've had my eye on for years – I watched her grow up. Her father has a nice little farm just over the hill Marino way – a vineyard and grazing land – a good living. The girl is willing – she is fond of my pies – says no one makes them like me – but her father would never give his consent. Now I can buy him out, the old skinflint! It will be a great satisfaction to see his face, when I put a bag of gold in front of the notary!"

Eugenio too was full of dreams. His children were growing up. His boy, he said, showed great promise as an artist and he would be able to apprentice him to one of the important workshops in the city. "I'll be able to marry my daughter well," he said, "now that she'll have a good dowry. She's comely and she'll have a queue of suitors. I'll be able to choose the best match for her… maybe into the nobility – a country knight around these parts."

MacLaren toyed with the idea of returning to the country of his birth, but he decided that he had been away too long and had become a stranger. Instead, he decided to open a hostelry in Frascati with Annibale. They talked over their plans night after night, arguing over which were the best wines of the area, and sampling them to put them to the test.

Many of the sixty-five servants in the Family had grown old in Henry's service and dreamt of nothing else but retiring and enjoying an old age of leisure.

Several weeks went by while the Cardinal's servants waited with bated breath, knowing that legal procedures and lawyers were always slow. Monsignor Cesarini's secretary confided to Moretto in a whisper that His Grace had left many bequests that had to be respected before their claims could be met. He disclosed that the usurpers of Hanover had been named and that Cesarini had sent them two very valuable jewels – the diamond Cross of St Andrew that had belonged to the Stuart King Charles I, as well as the sapphire ring that had been part of the ancient regalia of Scotland. Moretto thought that it was typical of his master to repay his debt of gratitude to the English king who had helped him in his moment of distress while he was in Venice. However, he was disconcerted to hear that his master had also left gifts for Prince Charles Edward's widow – the adulterous and undeserving Countess of Albany, who had always treated the Cardinal with scorn.

As the months passed, the servants became more and more restless. They urged Moretto to seek information on their behalf, since he had a certain familiarity with Monsignor Cesarini due to his continuous presence at the side of his lord. But he could not get a straight answer. Cesarini became increasingly evasive and secretive. He was always too busy to see him. Finally, he sent his secretary to advise them that the matter was very complicated. The Cardinal had always lived like a royal prince and he had left many debts. He had not understood that his income had been eroded by the taxes and expropriations introduced by the Napoleonic regime, which had cost him the loss of many of his ecclesiastic preferments in Flanders, Naples and France.

At the present time, Cesarini explained, the remainder of His Majesty's estate was tied up in Mexico where there was a current state of unrest and it was therefore impossible to effectuate any type of financial transaction. He assured the servants, however, that the new Bishop of Frascati, Cardinal Giuseppe Doria Pamphilj, had taken the matter to heart and had appealed to our master's old benefactor, the English lord Sir John Hippisley, to help him find a solution. There was nothing for it but to wait patiently.

As the winter passed, the servants became more and more uneasy and discontented. Some of them had contracted debts, offering the heritage they had been promised as surety. Others were virtually penniless because Cardinal Pamphilj preferred to stay in Rome and rarely came to La Rocca and, when he did, he brought his own retainers to serve him. Food and fuel became scarce as money to pay the suppliers ran out.

Moretto wrote a last letter to his friend Heinrich:

"Dear Friend,

I received your letter and I congratulate you on your marriage. A widow with her own means and still young and comely enough is indeed a fine catch. I wish you all happiness. My own story will take a different turning.

A few days ago, I was summoned urgently by Monsignor Cesarini's personal servant, in a great state of agitation. His master, he said, had died suddenly in the night. His heart had betrayed him. Nothing had been resolved regarding our situation. We had lost our last friend who could intercede on our behalf.

Our late master's affairs have been taken over by Cardinal Consalvi. He has told us that there is no chance in the near future of our inheritance arriving. I take this to mean that it will not arrive ever. He took a few of our Family into his employ but I knew he had never loved me and I could expect little from him.

I have lived too long in the shadow of the Church to know another life and I have decided to do what my lord always advised me to do. I have requested to join the Benedictines in Subiaco and I shall spend what is left of my time in their rocky fortress high over the Valley of the River Aniene.

This will therefore be the last correspondence I shall exchange with you, old friend. At this point, I close my book of life and bid you my last farewell."

Post Script

On the 5th July, 1809, Pope Chiaramonti was arrested by the French and imprisoned in Savona for three years before being transferred to Fontainebleau. This was the culmination of the power struggle between Napoleon and the Church and a re-enactment of the misadventures of his predecessor and namesake, Pius VI.

Subjected to all kinds of pressure and threats, the Pope eventually agreed to the terms of a new Concordat with the French, in which he abdicated his temporal powers. Even then he was not allowed to return to Rome. His territories were only restored to him after Bonaparte's final defeat in 1815. Although he had every reason to hold a grudge against Napoleon, Pius VII was the only head of state who begged the British to show the Emperor mercy. The Pope also offered refuge in Rome to Napoleon's mother, who lived for the rest of her life in a palace on the corner of Piazza Venezia.

Pius VII survived his ordeal and died in 1823 at the age of 83.

Maria Carolina, the Queen of Naples, died in exile in Vienna in 1814, consumed by bitterness and rancour. Many of the tales told about her were simply evil gossip, invented by Count Giuseppe Gorani, a notorious scandal writer and author of *'Secret and Critical Memoires of the Courts of Italy and Particularly of Naples'*, published in Paris in 1793. The book was full of erotic anecdotes involving the Queen. Maria Carolina was furious and deeply offended but she was unable to bring any action against Gorani, who had taken refuge in Geneva. There is no evidence, either of an amorous liaison with Acton, or a lesbian relationship with Emma Hamilton, although the Queen's preference for her two favourites aroused a great deal of jealousy and malicious talk within court circles.

Less than three months after his wife's death, King Ferdinand married his mistress, Lucia Migliaccio, the Duchess of Floridiana. He was restored to his throne in 1816 and settled down to enjoy the rest of his life in peace and comfort. He died in 1825.

The papier-mâché crown used in the coronation of Pius VII survived and was used on various occasions by other Popes, who preferred the imitation version because it was much lighter and easier to wear. In the 20th century, Pope Benedict XV had all the jewels removed and replaced with glass, to help pay for the care of the wounded in World War 1.

After the Allied Landing in Anzio during World War II, Frascati was badly bombed and many churches and monuments were destroyed, including the Herboracum Seminary, which was razed to the ground. By a miracle, the adjacent library only suffered minor damage and the Cardinal's collection of books was intact. Twelve monks from the nearby Camaldolese monastery were called to help remove the collection and transfer it to safety in the Vatican. Clambering over piles of rubble, the monks formed a human chain to pass out the 12,000 volumes and illuminated manuscripts and load them onto the one available truck, which made the trip to and from Vatican City for nine days. The books are now incorporated into the Vatican Library collection.

The three uncrowned Stuart kings lie together in the Vatican crypt in a travertine sarcophagus surmounted by a bronze crown set on a cushion. The inscription on the front says: "To James III – son of James II, King of Great Britain – to Charles Edward – and to Henry, Dean of the Cardinal Fathers – sons of James III – the last of the Royal House of Stuart."

The same inscription can be seen on the Stuart funeral monument in the left aisle of St Peter's, sculpted by Canova. The monument was commissioned by Angelo Cesarini and financed mostly by Pope Pius VII, with a small contribution from the British Prince Regent, the future George IV, who had visited the Cardinal in his home at Frascati. On the opposite side of the aisle is the monument to Maria Clementina Sobieska, James III's wife, where she is described as 'Queen of Great Britain, France and Ireland'. Maria Clementina's heart was interred in the Church of the Holy Apostles, next to the Stuart residence Palazzo Muti.

The next legitimate heir to the Stuart claim was Charles Emmanuel IV of the House of Savoy, which, half a century after Henry's death, was to become the ruling royal house of Italy. However, some researchers claim that there are direct, illegitimate descendants. Letters from Charles Edward's daughter Charlotte to her mother, discovered in the mid-20th century, revealed a secret relationship between her and Ferdinand Maximilien de Rohan, the Archbishop of Bordeaux, which resulted in the birth of three children, Maria Victoire, Charlotte Maximilienne and Charles Edward

Stuart, who were known by the surname of Roehenstart – a combination of Rohan and Stuart. Maria Victoire, at least, is known to have married and had children. For further information:

Henrietta Taylor: "Prince Charlie's Daughter: Being the Life and Letters of Charlotte of Albany." Batchwork Press, London 1950.

Peter Pinninsky: "The Stuart's Last Secret: The Missing Heirs of Bonnie Prince Charlie." Tuckwell Press, 2002

Main Sources

Acton Harold: "I Borboni di Napoli", Editore Giunti 1997

Astarita Tommaso: "Between Salt Water and Holy Water – a history of Southern Italy", W.W. Norton & Company 2005

Bindelli Pietro: "Enrico Stuart Cardinale Duca di York", Associazione Tuscolana "Amici di Frascati" 1982.

Buonocore Marco & Cappelli Giovanna: "La Biblioteca del Cardinale", Gangemini Editore, 2008

Chessell C.I.: "Britain's Ionian Consul: Spiridion Foresti and Intelligence Collection (1793-1805)", ChessellMMHNPaper.doc, www.um.edu.mt/

Coletti Alessandro: "La Regina di Napoli, la vita appassionata di Maria Carolina", Agostini 1986

Consiglio Giuseppe: "La Revoluzione Napolitana del 1799", Rusconi 1999

Cryan Mary Jane: "Travels to Tuscany", Etruria Editions, Davide Ghaleb Editore, Vetralla (VT) 2004

Del Nero: "Storie della Valle Latina", Parco Regionale dei Castelli Romani, 2008

Del Puglia Raffaella: "La Regina di Napoli". Editoriale Viscontea, Pavia 1989

Diocesi Suburbicaria Tuscolana: "Palazzo Vescovile, Storia e Arte Catechistica", 2012

Ewald Alex. Charles: "The Young Pretender", Chatto & Windus, London 1875.

De Ferrari Giovanni Battista & Mariano Vasi: "Viaggio da Roma a Napoli", 1826

Esdaile Charles: "Napoleon's War", Viking 2008

Fothergill Brian: "The Cardinal King", Faber & Faber Ltd. 2010

Fugier André: "Napoleone e L'Italia" (Vol. 1 & 2), Editore J.B. Janin, Paris, translation, introduction & updating by Prof. Raffaele Ciampini 1970

Grande Gregorio: "In Carrozza con il Cardinale Duca, Enrico Stuart, i suoi luoghi, il suo tempo", Edizione Controluce, 2013

Guerri Giordano Bruno: "Povera Santa, Povero Assassino", Bompiani, 1985

Kelly Bernard W: "Life of Henry Benedict Stuart, Cardinal Duke of York; With a Notice of Rome in His Time", R.T. Washbourne, London 1899

Lefevre Renato: "Storia e Storie dell'Antichissima Ariccia", Comune di Ariccia 1996

Lo Jacono Vittorio & Zanda Carmen: "I Borboni in Sicilia, Palermo, Ficuzzo e Dintorni", Ed. l'Epos, 2011

McFerran Noel: "The Jacobite Heritage", www.jacobite.ca

McLaren Morag: "Bonnie Prince Charlie", Rupert Hart-Davis Ltd., London 1972

Quilici Lorenzo: "La Via Appia Antica Monti Aurunci", Regione Lazio 2010

Raggi Oreste: "I Colli Albani e Tusculani", Unione Tipografico-Editrice Torinese, Roma, 1879

Rullent Marina: "Taddeo Kunze al Palazzo Vescovile di Frascati", 2013

Sacchi Martino: "Le Grandi Vittorie della Royal Navy", Ledizioni 2013

Shield Alice & Lang Andrew: "Henry Stuart: Cardinal of York and His Times", Longmans, Green & Co., London, 1908

Spinosa Antonio: "Napoleone il Flagello D'Italia", Mondadori 2010

Toffanello Giuseppe: "Frascati Civitas Tusculana", Edizioni Tuscolo Frascati 1966

Vaughan Herbert Millingchamp: "The Last of the Royal Stuarts, Henry Stuart, Cardinal Duke of York", E.P Dutton Co. 1906

References

Diary of Henry Benedict Stuart, Cardinal, Duke of York, kept by don Giovanni Landò, years 1798–1802; British Library, London, Manuscript collections

Stuart Papers at Windsor Castle: letters of Christmas greetings from Maria Carolina, Queen of Naples

The Catholic Encyclopedia: Henry Benedict Maria Clement Stuart

"I Papi e Gli Antipapi, La Storia della Chiesa", Strumenti TEA

Fondazione Parchi di Palermo: Storia della Palazzina Cinese, www.parcodellafavorita.it

"Palazzo Vescovile, Storia e Arte Catechistica", Diocesi Suburbicaria Tuscolana, 2012

"Turkish Historical Review 3 (2012) 168–195", Kahraman Sakul,

Department of History, Istanbul Sehir Universities, Istanbul

Websites consulted:
jacobite.ca/gazetteer
individual.utoronto.ca/jacobites
royalstuartsociety.com
cathopedia, l'enciclopedia cattolica: Conclave da 1799–1800
"Sede Vacante 1799-1800", www.csun.edu/

Author's Note

I live in Italy, only a few miles away from the town of Frascati, so I have had every opportunity to consult Italian documents and biographies of Cardinal Henry, Duke of York while I was gathering material for this book. From these, I have been able to build up a picture of Henry's character.

The English spies who circulated in the exiled Stuart court and continued, even after the death of the Young Pretender, Charles Edward, to forward reports on the Cardinal, had every reason to discredit him. They described him as 'simple', 'bigoted' and 'foolish' – a strange depiction of a man who was plainly highly cultured, benevolent, hospitable and tolerant.

Many of the anecdotes I have introduced into the book are documented by local writers. He did adopt the stray dog he found at St Peter's and dubbed 'a King Charles dog'. He did visit the abandoned squatter community at La Molara and funded rehousing, schools and a church for the inhabitants. He did allow his coachman to race the carriage of the Princess of Rezzonico on the way to a reception and he was known affectionately to his parishioners as 'the Cardinal of the Organs'.

It became obvious that he had a fine sense of humour, as well as an excellent command of English. I was particularly struck by an incident reported in several sources. During the final phase of his life, when he was returned with every honour to his Frascati diocese, he became something of a tourist attraction, visited by numerous Grand Tour travellers. One was a certain Mr Joseph Forsyth, an antiquarian, who was touring Italy in 1802–3. On being introduced, Cardinal Henry remarked that he had heard of second sight in Scotland, but never 'foresight' in England. Mr Forsyth apparently did not see the joke and reported disparagingly on his experience as a guest of honour at the Cardinal's dinner table, remarking that 'his host said little, and in that little, nothing of interest'. [1]

---

[1] From "The Life of Henry Benedict Stuart, Cardinal Duke of York: With a Notice of Rome in his Time" by Bernard William Kelly, 1899